STUDIES IN FINANCIAL OPTIMIZATION AND RISK MANAGEMENT

COMPUTATIONAL TECHNIQUES FOR BANKING AND RISK MANAGEMENT

STUDIES IN FINANCIAL OPTIMIZATION AND RISK MANAGEMENT

CONSTANTIN ZOPOUNIDIS - SERIES EDITOR –

TECHNICAL UNIVERSITY OF CRETE, CHANIA, GREECE

Computational Techniques in Economics and Finance
Constantin Zopounidis (Editor)
2011. ISBN: 978-1-61324-558-3

Financial Services: Efficiency and Risk Management
Meryem Duygun Fethi, Chrysovalantis Gaganis, Fotios Pasiouras and Constantin Zopounidis (Editors)
2012. ISBN: 978-1-62100-560-5

Computational Optimization in Economics and Finance Research Compendium
Constantin Zopounidis (Editor)
2012. ISBN: 978-1-62081-928-9

New Trends in Bank Efficiency
Kyriaki Kosmidou and Constantin Zopounidis (Editors)
2013. ISBN: 978-1-62618-824-2

Computational Techniques in Modeling and Simulation
Victor Krasnoproshin, Anna M. Gil Lafuente and Constantin Zopounidis (Editors)
2013. ISBN: 978-1-62808-017-9

Computational Techniques for Banking and Risk Management
C. Zopounidis and M. Doumpos (Editors)
2013. ISBN: 978-1-62618-522-7

STUDIES IN FINANCIAL OPTIMIZATION AND RISK MANAGEMENT

COMPUTATIONAL TECHNIQUES FOR BANKING AND RISK MANAGEMENT

C. ZOPOUNIDIS
AND
M. DOUMPOS
EDITORS

nova publishers
New York

For permission to use material from this book please contact us:
Telephone 631-231-7269; Fax 631-231-8175
Web Site: http://www.novapublishers.com

NOTICE TO THE READER

Library of Congress Cataloging-in-Publication Data

Computational techniques for banking and risk management / editor, Constantin Zopounidis.
pages cm
Includes bibliographical references and index.
ISBN 978-1-62618-522-7 (hardcover: alk. paper) 1. Bank management--Mathematical models. 2. Banks and banking--Mathematical models. 3. Financial risk--Mathematical models. 4. Decision making--Mathematical models. I. Zopounidis, Constantin.
HG1615.C645 2013
332.1068'1--dc23

2013011837

Published by Nova Science Publishers, Inc. †New York

CONTENTS

PREFACE

The last decades have been strongly characterized by vertiginous technological, social and economic changes. Those changes have in part positively affected our lives; however they also led to an increasing uncertainty and instability at every field of human activity. In addition, the interdependence and the interrelationship among various fields and especially between the global financial markets have created a fragile environment, which requires delicate handling and attentive movements. Thus the complexity of the systems considered in every field, nowadays, more than ever, needs the skillful manipulation of the known methodologies and techniques for the best management.

Research and development give emphasis on the computational optimization as an essential, critical component. At every field of human activity optimization is more than important. Everybody tries to optimize, minimize or maximize the cost, profit, efficiency, output. In the area of economics and finance, simple and more complex tools have been created towards this direction. Different methodologies and analytical techniques have been developed to analyze a vast number of problems such as risk management, asset pricing, portfolio construction, forecasting, interest rate modeling, capital measurement, efficiency estimation, investment evaluation, business failure, etc.

This volume aims to highlight some of the aforementioned aspects, referring to methodologies and applications to computational economics and finance, and it is consisted of papers published in the third volume of the Journal of Computational Optimization in Economics and Finance.

The contents of this volume are varying, covering a wide range of topics, such as credit risk simulation, capital measurement methods, bank efficiency, cash withdrawals forecasting, service quality evaluation, among others.

Closing this preface, we would like to express our sincerely thanks to all the authors that decided to submit their valuable work at the Journal of Computational Optimization in Economics and Finance.

In: Computational Techniques for Banking and Risk Management ISBN: 978-1-62618-522-7
Editors: C. Zopounidis and M. Doumpos

Chapter 1

A CONTROL SYSTEMS APPROACH FOR CREDIT RISK SIMULATION AND CONTROL OF A LOAN PORTFOLIO

J. Leventides**, S. Stavraki and Ch. Pandis

Department of Economics, University of Athens,
Athens, Greece
Control Eng. Centre, City University,
Northampton Square, London, UK

ABSTRACT

In this paper, we study the problem of measurement and control of credit risk in a loan portfolio. We develop a control systems methodology in order to examine the dynamic behavior of a loan portfolio by modeling it as a dynamical system which in turn is used for the definition of an appropriate Optimal Control problem. In fact, we develop two discrete dynamical systems, which describe the process and the evolution of the loan portfolio by following two different approaches. In the first approach we model the evolution of the loan portfolio based on the repayment stati and, we examine the stability and the step response of the system, as well as, by simulating the system, we compute basic indices of the loan portfolio for every time period.

Secondly we enhance the above mentioned approach by using a refined set of variables (representing pools of loans) reflecting the variety of risk categories in the loan portfolio. The inputs of the system are the new loans for each risk category whereas the outputs are the various quality parameters of the loan portfolio such as bad loans ratio, profitability vs. risk etc. This approach may lead to portfolio planning and budgeting either through simulation of the above dynamic model or via determination of an open or closed loop policy using some optimality criterion.

Keywords: Dynamical Systems, Control Systems, Optimal Control, Credit Risk, portfolio theory

---

* Corresponding author: Email ylevent@econ.uoa.gr.

INTRODUCTION

In the early 2000s, the measurement and the prediction of credit risk has become one of the most important risk management challenges. Since the institutions are taking on an increasing amount of credit risk and the credit exposure has multiplied, the need for more sophisticated risk management techniques for credit risk has also increased. Even if more traditional credit processes can manage credit risk, the risk managers are increasingly seeking to quantify and integrate the overall credit risk assessment capturing the exposure to market, rating changes and default changes. A better understanding and further research on credit portfolio behavior will help portfolio managers to better identify not only potential risks and opportunities for diversification, but also the expected credit losses and the uncertainty of loss. With a credit risk-modeling framework based on a quantitative portfolio, we can more systematically address credit risk more rationally and we can predict the uncertainty in the forward value of the portfolio at the specific risk horizon.

In this paper, we study the problem of measurement and control of credit risk in a loan portfolio. We develop a methodology in order to examine the dynamic behavior of a loan portfolio by calculating the amount of new loans for each month. We construct two discrete dynamical systems, which describe the process and the evolution of the loan portfolio by two different approaches. But first we present some of the methodologies that already exist and are uses by financial institutions for the assessment of their portfolio.

The problem of optimizing the expected return of a portfolio against risk constraints is a well established topic within portfolio theory (B. Scherer 2004, S.Zenios 1993). The application of the classical portfolio methods to a loan portfolio is not possible for reasons such as a) a loan cannot be marked to market, b) the loss distributions do not follow normality and c) the credit quality (rating) of a loan is not static.

A common approach to deal with credit risk of a portfolio is the actuarial approach, where the portfolio is separated into pools of similar risk characteristics (Servigny et al 2004). Although the behavior of a single loan in the pool cannot be predicted the pool as a whole behaves in a statistical manner that can be modeled. Both the models we consider fall into this category of models. In fact, we separate the loans into pools according to various risk criteria and we model the transition of loans from the one pool to the others as a discrete dynamical system. The transition equations can be studied either independently, to simulate, predict and understand the evolution of the loan portfolio (1st approach), or to be incorporated as constraints to an optimization problem (2nd approach).

As far as the optimization problem is concerned this is a return (risk adjusted interest income) optimization problem with risk constraints. These constraints are in terms of some forms of credit var as defined by the well known credit risk models such as JPMorgan – credit metrics (Crouhy et al, 2000).

Gabriela del Angel et al. (1998) have developed a stochastic valuation model in order to value a commercial and industrial loan portfolio related to the Mexican bank loan resolution process. Using a Monte Carlo simulation, random trajectories are derived in order to find the probabilities of the estimated transition matrix. In the model, there are three different groups of bidders illustrating the differences between them regarding to valuation criteria and 4 transient subsets and one absorbing state regarding to the restructuring process. Simulating the model, the authors get the probability distributions of the present value of each loan, from which they can compute the probability distribution of the net present value of the portfolio.

Using different approach, Sobehart and Keenan (2004) use hypothetical transition matrices for portfolio loss simulations that preserve the basic relationships observed in the historical transition a default rates obtained by the rating agencies. The matrices can also be obtained considering the macroeconomic factors, the dynamics of credit cycles and generally the economic activity. For each macroeconomic scenario, random ratings migration patterns should be simulated using the structural models and the distribution of unexplained errors.

Araten et al. (2004) examine the bank's internal ratings of borrowers drawing upon six years of internal ratings data from JPMorganChase's exposures to perform a ratings migration analysis. From ratings migration analysis, they obtain an estimation of transition probabilities for obligor credit risk ratings, with emphasis on estimation of empirical default probabilities. The analysis of a bank's rating and default rates are obtained from annual historical data. The number of parents in each rating category is determined at each year-end and then the transition to other ratings categories are measured. The withdrawn ratings (WRs) are important in ratings migration analysis given data and systems issues.

Kosmidou et al. (2001, 2002), and references there in, study the techniques of asset and liability management under the fluctuations of the characteristics of financial markets. Specifically, they developed a methodology, which is based on the multiobjective linear programming method, in order to examine the financial situation of the institution, as well as to predict the behavior of portfolio under risk conditions. The authors are concerned into their model the liquidity risk, the interest rate risk as well as the capital adequacy as constraints. In fact they developed a dynamical system in order to study the asset liability management subject to risk constraints. In the authors' work we use a methodology based on dynamical system including the credit risk as a constraint.

We, on the other hand, study the dynamic approach of the problem in order to measure and control the credit risk of the loan portfolio. We examine the dynamic behavior of a loan portfolio at a risk horizon by constructing dynamic and control system equations. The basic model is a dynamic system with input and output variables. The variables of the model are balances of pools of loans of similar risk characteristics. With such a model, we can simulate the behavior of loan portfolio and compute the provisions and other important indices such as profit, bad credit and losses and the relation of these indices to input variables like the risk distribution of the new loans of every month.

Secondly, we may be able to obtain an optimal control policy such as profitability is maximized using well established tools of optimal control theory.

More specifically, we construct two dynamical systems, which describe the process and the evolution of the loan portfolio. By implementing and simulating the dynamical model, we can predict the balances of loans in various repayment stati including past due loans and bad debts in a monthly basis. This way, we predict and control the losses and the percentage of risk premium in the portfolio value. Predicting the losses and the allowance for doubtful accounts for every month and year, we adopt a suitable policy about the management of loan portfolio. Also, according to the authors' results from the dynamical model, we may propose an appropriate credit and collection policy in order to change the predicted behavior of the loans portfolio, to one which is more preferable.

To summarize, the main scope of the first model is to simulate the way the due loans evolve, in order to find out how certain policies can affect behavior of the credit portfolio in the various repayment stati and the value of the indices used by the financial institutions. Thus a manager can use this model as a decision supporting tool for choosing the scenario that will result at indices with the most preferred values from a list of scenarios. The second model is again a linear time invariant discrete dynamical system which relates the input variables (new loans) with the state variables (loans in various risk categories) and output variables (loan loss provisions, profitability) and other important indices. Both input and state variables are classified into categories based on credit quality as proposed by JP Morgan. By controlling the amount of new loans in each risk category every month (credit policy) we control the evolution, the risk and the profitability of the loan portfolio.

The control problem defined in this setting has as objective to optimize a profit or a utility function subject to the equations of the dynamical system and an inequality constraint defining capital adequacy. The dynamical system is expressed by the transition matrix of its states and in this way is related to the Markov process type of models. The capital constraint is based on the Basel II formulas which in turn are produced by a one factor type of model. Whereas the input optimal policy is which is calculated to maximize the objective function is the monthly risk distribution of new loans. This problem may be solved by tools of optimal control theory and in this paper it is proved to be equivalent to a linear programming problem. The solution is determined by a Sharp type of ratio relating risk to return. If the loan categories are sorted by this ratio in decreasing order the solution can be given by first utilizing that loan category with the highest ratio then moving on to the second highest and so on until the capital charges of the portfolio reaches the minimum capital levels set for this institution.

To sum up, the first model of the present work which refers to the evolution of the various repayment stati of the loan portfolio is more convenient for simulations, bad debt and provision calculations, as well as to modifying the collection policies, whereas the second type of model is more convenient to shaping the credit policy and optimizing the return to risk relation. Both models are time invariant i.e. the model parameters are fixed for the time horizon considered, and therefore their applicability is short to medium term. For longer term horizons a time varying and probably nonlinear model is more suitable and this is a topic for further investigation.

Study of the Model Based on the Loan Classification by Repayment Status

We construct a linear time invariant discrete system in state space form, where the state variables are the amount of current loans X, the amount of past due loans Y and the amount of bad credit loans K. The input of the system (control variable) is the amount of new loans U and the coefficients a, b, c, p_1, p_2, p_3 are the parameters of the system. The coefficients of the system reflect the credit quality (a), the repayment of due loans (b, c, p_2), the recoveries of bad credit (p_3) and the percentage of repayment of current loans (p_1). The construction of the dynamical model is based on the historical data. In the method of system identification, we use monthly data for the variables X, Y, K and U and then we solve an error minimization problem with respect to the parameters of the system. Subsequently, using the system identification results, we examine the stability and the step response of the system and, by simulating the system; we compute basic indices of the loan portfolio for every time period. We have to mention here that in reality this dynamical system is not absolutely linear and time invariant as it is assumed in this paper, but the system parameters may be time varying and may have finite capacity properties. These additional characteristics signify the change in the credit quality in time, and the finite capacity of bank units such as the collections unit. Incorporating all these features into the model we may obtain a much more realistic view of the evolution of the portfolio and investigate its behavior. Simulating the model, we can compute and predict the bad credit, the losses rates and the risk premium and finally we calculate the sensitivity of the variables and the indices of portfolio in terms of the changes of the parameters of the system.

Model Description

In order to develop a method of predicting the loan portfolio behaviour, we need to develop a model describing this loss process. We have divided our loan portfolio into four categories:

1) New loans at time n: u_n
2) Current loans at time n: X_n
3) Past Due loans at time n: Y_n
4) Bad credit loans at time n: K_n

Where the subscript n represents the time period, for our model the n represents the month. Each amount of money in the portfolio belongs to one of these four categories and in the next month is either staying in the same category or moves to another or it becomes "paid" as the following diagram shows:

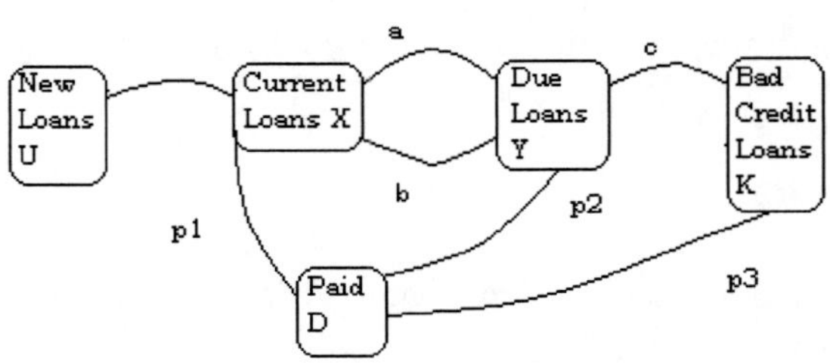

where:

a is the factor that describes the proportion of the current accounts loans that becomes past due loans,

b is the factor that describes the proportion of due loans that becomes current,

c is the factor that describes the proportion of due loans that becomes bad credit, p_1 is the factor represents the proportion of current loans that is repaid, similarly p_2 is the factor that represents the proportion of due loans that is repaid and finally p_3 is the factor that describes the proportion of bad credit loans that is repaid eventually. The set D represent the paid set from all categories of loans. In order to simulate the behaviour of a loan portfolio, we need to construct a dynamical system consisted of linear equations.

$$x_{n+1} = (1 - a - p_1) \cdot x_n + b \cdot y_n + u_n$$
$$y_{n+1} = a \cdot x_n + (1 - b - c - p_2) \cdot y_n$$
$$k_{n+1} = c \cdot y_n + (1 - p_3) \cdot k_n$$
$$D_{n+1} = D_n + p_1 \cdot X_n + p_2 \cdot Y_n + p_3 \cdot K_n$$

with $0 \le a, b, c, p_1, p_2, p_3$ and $b+c+p_2 \le 1$, $a+p_1 \le 1$, $p_3 \le 1$.

The first equation describes the amount of current accounts in the next time period connected with the previous state of loan portfolio.

This means that the factor 1-a-p_1 is the percentage of current accounts in the previous step, which remain current and the "b" is the percentage of past due loans which becomes current in the next step.

The second equation describes the accounts that become or remain the due loans and, finally the last equation describes the loans that become or remain bad credit loans at next time period.

The factor (a) reflects the credit quality and (b), (c) reflect the collection quality. Using the above classification, the equations describing the portfolio evolution as a discrete dynamical system in matrix form are:

$$\begin{pmatrix} x \\ y \\ k \end{pmatrix}_{n+1} = \begin{bmatrix} 1-a-p_1 & b & 0 \\ a & 1-b-c-p_2 & 0 \\ 0 & c & 1-p_3 \end{bmatrix} \cdot \begin{bmatrix} x \\ y \\ k \end{bmatrix}_n + \begin{bmatrix} 1 \\ 0 \\ 0 \end{bmatrix} \cdot u_n \tag{2.1}$$

$$D_{n+1} = D_n + p_1 \cdot X_n + p_2 \cdot Y_n + p_3 \cdot K_n$$

The matrix reflects the probability that measures the likelihood that amount in a particular category will move to another category during the applicable period of time.

Model Identification

To identify the model using historical data, we have to calculate the parameters a, b, c, p_1, p_2, p_3 via a process of error minimization [1].

First, we denote the equations of dynamical system in terms of the parameters to be identified as follows:

$$\begin{aligned} x_{n+1} - x_n - u_n &= (-x_n) \cdot a + y_n \cdot b + 0 \cdot c + (-x_n) \cdot p_1 + 0 \cdot p_2 + 0 \cdot p_3 \\ y_{n+1} - y_n &= x_n \cdot a + (-y_n) \cdot b + (-y_n) \cdot c + 0 \cdot p_1 + (-y_n) \cdot p_2 + 0 \cdot p_3 \\ k_{n+1} - k_n &= 0 \cdot a + 0 \cdot b + y_n \cdot c + 0 \cdot p_1 + 0 \cdot p_2 + (-k_n) \cdot p_3 \end{aligned}$$

The equations can be written in vector form from n=1 to n as:

$$\Delta X = [-X \quad Y \quad -X] \cdot \begin{bmatrix} a \\ b \\ p_1 \end{bmatrix}$$

$$\Delta Y = [X \quad -Y \quad -Y \quad -Y] \cdot \begin{bmatrix} a \\ b \\ c \\ p_2 \end{bmatrix}$$

$$\Delta K = [Y \quad -K] \cdot \begin{bmatrix} c \\ p_3 \end{bmatrix}$$

or collectively in matrix form as:

$$d = F \cdot r$$

where

$$d = \begin{bmatrix} \Delta X \\ \Delta Y \\ \Delta K \end{bmatrix} \quad F = \begin{bmatrix} -X & Y & 0 & -X & 0 & 0 \\ X & -Y & -Y & 0 & -Y & 0 \\ 0 & 0 & Y & 0 & 0 & -K \end{bmatrix} \quad r = \begin{bmatrix} a \\ b \\ c \\ p_1 \\ p_2 \\ p_3 \end{bmatrix}$$

And

$$\Delta X = \{x_{k+1} - x_k - u_k\}_{k=0}^{n}$$
$$\Delta Y = \{y_{k+1} - y_k\}_{k=0}^{n}$$
$$\Delta K = \{k_{k+1} - k_k\}_{k=0}^{n}$$

$$X = \{x_k\}_{k=0}^{n}$$
$$Y = \{y_k\}_{k=0}^{n}$$
$$K = \{k_k\}_{k=0}^{n}$$

subject to the constraints

$$0 \le a, b, c, p_1, p_2, p_3 \;,\; b + c + p_2 \le 1 \;,\; a + p_1 < 1 \;,\; p_3 < 1 \qquad (2.2)$$

We may find r by solving the unconstrained minimization problem $\min\|d\text{-}Fr\|_2$ the solution is given as $r=F^{-1}d$ where F^{-1} is the generalized inverse of F with the risk that r may not satisfy the inequality constraints. To solve the complete problem, we may consider the L_1optimisation problem

$$\min \sum_i | d_i - F_i r |$$

subject to the inequality constraint (2.2).

Where d_i is the i-th entry of d and F_i is the i-th row of matrix F. This problem may be transformed into a linear programming problem by setting $|d_i - F_i r| < \varepsilon_i$ and minimizing the $\Sigma\varepsilon_i$. In this setting the complete the linear programming problem is written as follows:

Minimize $\Sigma\varepsilon_i$
r
subject to

$$\begin{bmatrix} b \\ -b \end{bmatrix} \leq \begin{bmatrix} A & I \\ -A & I \end{bmatrix} \cdot \begin{bmatrix} r \\ \varepsilon \end{bmatrix}$$
$$-1 < -a - p_1$$
$$-1 < -b - c - p_2$$
$$-1 < -p_3$$
$$0 < a, b, c, p_1, p_2, p_3, \varepsilon_i$$

where$\varepsilon = [\varepsilon_i]_i$

The model validation is done through back testing i.e. running the model on historical values and comparing the results; as a matter of fact if the model is run on the construction data the L1 error will be the value of the objective function of the optimisation. *We have to mention at this point that the model assumes constant values of the system parameters and that the variables u, x, y, k have static structure.* To capture the change in credit structure, we should re solve the optimisation problem on every time window that the credit structure remains constant and then consider a piecewise constant in parameters linear dynamical system. After identifying the system parameters we may simulate the future value of the four categories of the loan portfolio and predict the indices and factors that determine loan loss, provisions and risk premium.

System Stability and Steady State Values

The study of stability of the system described by equations (2.1) is very important for the understanding of the nature of the system. If the system is stable then its response to a constant inflow of new loans acquires a steady state i.e. the variables X, Y, K will tend to constant values. The stability of the system depends on the eigenvalues of the system matrix for the model:

$$A = \begin{bmatrix} 1-a-p_1 & b & 0 \\ a & 1-b-c-p_2 & 0 \\ 0 & c & 1-p_3 \end{bmatrix} \tag{2.3}$$

Calculating the characteristic polynomial of A it can be found that:

$$|A-\lambda I| = \begin{vmatrix} 1-a-p_1-\lambda & b & 0 \\ a & 1-b-c-p_2-\lambda & 0 \\ 0 & c & 1-p_3-\lambda \end{vmatrix} =$$

$$(1-p_3-\lambda)\begin{vmatrix} 1-a-p_1-\lambda & b \\ a & 1-b-c-p_2-\lambda \end{vmatrix} = (1-p_3-\lambda)p(\lambda)$$

where p(λ) is given by

$$\left|\lambda^2 + (a+p_1-2+b+c+p_2)\lambda + (1-b-c-p_2-a+ac+ap_2-p_1+p_1b+p_1c+p_1p_2)\right|$$

In order to have stability the roots of the characteristic polynomial (the eigenvalues) must satisfy the formula $|\lambda|<1$. One of the three roots is the number $1-p_3$ which is obviously less than unity. The other two roots are the roots of the polynomial p(λ) which are the eigenvalues of the matrix

$$B = \begin{bmatrix} \theta_1 & b \\ a & \theta_2 \end{bmatrix} \tag{2.4}$$

where

$$\left.\begin{aligned} \theta_1 &= 1-a-p_1 \\ \theta_2 &= 1-b-c-p_2 \end{aligned}\right\}$$

The following theorem states that the eigenvalues of this matrix not only fulfill stability but also satisfy some further properties.

Theorem (2.1) Let B be the matrix given by (2.4) and λ_1 and λ_2 be its eigenvalues. Then if the parameters of the matrix satisfy (2.1), the following hold true:

a) $\lambda_1, \lambda_2 \in R$
b) $1>\lambda_1 \geq \max(\theta_1, \theta_2) > \min(\theta_1, \theta_2) \geq \lambda_2 \geq 0$
c) $\lambda_1 = \max(\theta_1, \theta_2)$ and $\lambda_2 = \min(\theta_1, \theta_2)$ if and only if $ab=0$
d) If $\lambda_1=1$ then $\lambda_2=\theta_1+\theta_2-1$
e) $\lambda_2=0$ if and only if $\theta_1\theta_2-ab=0$

Proof

The characteristic polynomial is:

$$\lambda^2-(\theta_1+\theta_2)\lambda+\theta_1\theta_2-ab$$

Its roots are:

$$\lambda_{1,2}=\frac{\theta_1+\theta_2\pm\sqrt{(\theta_1+\theta_2)^2-4(\theta_1\theta_2-ab)}}{2}=\frac{\theta_1+\theta_2\pm\sqrt{(\theta_1-\theta_2)^2+4ab}}{2}$$

The discriminant satisfies $(\theta_1-\theta_2)^2+4ab>0$ because $(\theta_1\text{-}\theta_2)^2>0$ and $ab>0$. Hence $\lambda_{1,2}\in R$

Due to the fact that ab>0 the discriminant can be written as:

$\sqrt{(\theta_1-\theta_2)^2+4ab}=|\theta_1-\theta_2|+2\varepsilon$ with $\varepsilon>0$

Hence the roots can be written as:

$$\lambda_1=\frac{\theta_1+\theta_2+|\theta_1-\theta_2|}{2}+\varepsilon=\max(\theta_1,\theta_2)+\varepsilon$$

$$\lambda_2=\frac{\theta_1+\theta_2-|\theta_1-\theta_2|}{2}-\varepsilon=\min(\theta_1,\theta_2)\text{-}\varepsilon$$

Hence $\lambda_1>\max(\theta_1,\theta_2)$ and $\lambda_2<\min(\theta_1,\theta_2)$

For the first part of the inequality, there is:

$$\lambda_1=\frac{\theta_1+\theta_2+\sqrt{(\theta_1-\theta_2)^2+4ab}}{2}<1\Leftrightarrow\sqrt{(\theta_1-\theta_2)^2+4ab}<2-\theta_1-\theta_2\Leftrightarrow$$

$$\theta_1^2+\theta_2^2-2\theta_1\theta_2+4ab<4-4\theta_1-4\theta_2+\theta_1^2+\theta_2^2+2\theta_1\theta_2\Leftrightarrow$$

$$-2\theta_1\theta_2+4ab<4-4\theta_1-4\theta_2+2\theta_1\theta_2\Leftrightarrow 4ab<4-4\theta_1-4\theta_2+4\theta_1\theta_2\Leftrightarrow$$

$$ab<1-\theta_1-\theta_2+\theta_1\theta_2\Leftrightarrow ab<(1-\theta_1)(1-\theta_2) \tag{1}$$

It is:

$$\left.\begin{matrix}\theta_1=1-a\text{-}p_1\\ \theta_2=1-b-c\text{-}p_2\end{matrix}\right\}\rightarrow\left.\begin{matrix}\theta_1+a=1\text{-}p_1\\ \theta_2+b=1-c\text{-}p_2\end{matrix}\right\}\xrightarrow{1>p_1,p_2,c>0}\left.\begin{matrix}\theta_1+a<1\\ \theta_2+b<1\end{matrix}\right\}\rightarrow\left.\begin{matrix}a<1\text{-}\theta_1\\ b<1\text{-}\theta_2\end{matrix}\right\}\rightarrow$$

$$ab < (1-\theta_1)(1-\theta_2) \tag{2}$$

Hence from (1) and (2), $\lambda_1 < 1$

For the last part of the inequality, it is:

$$\lambda_2 = \frac{\theta_1 + \theta_2 - \sqrt{(\theta_1 - \theta_2)^2 + 4ab}}{2} > 0 \Leftrightarrow \sqrt{(\theta_1 - \theta_2)^2 + 4ab} < \theta_1 + \theta_2 \Leftrightarrow$$

$$\theta_1^2 + \theta_2^2 - 2\theta_1\theta_2 + 4ab < \theta_1^2 + \theta_2^2 + 2\theta_1\theta_2 \Leftrightarrow 4ab < 4\theta_1\theta_2 \Leftrightarrow ab < \theta_1\theta_2$$

which it is true since

$$\theta_1\theta_2 = (a + p_1 - 1)(b + c + p_2 - 1) = (a - \varepsilon_1)(b - \varepsilon_2) > ab$$

It is:

$$\left.\begin{matrix} \lambda_1 = \max(\theta_1, \theta_2) \\ \lambda_2 = \min(\theta_1, \theta_2) \end{matrix}\right\} \leftrightarrow \left.\begin{matrix} \dfrac{\theta_1 + \theta_2 + \sqrt{(\theta_1 - \theta_2)^2 + 4ab}}{2} = \dfrac{\theta_1 + \theta_2 + |\theta_1 - \theta_2|}{2} \\ \dfrac{\theta_1 + \theta_2 - \sqrt{(\theta_1 - \theta_2)^2 + 4ab}}{2} = \dfrac{\theta_1 + \theta_2 - |\theta_1 - \theta_2|}{2} \end{matrix}\right\} \leftrightarrow$$

$$\left.\begin{matrix} \theta_1 + \theta_2 + \sqrt{(\theta_1 - \theta_2)^2 + 4ab} = \theta_1 + \theta_2 + |\theta_1 - \theta_2| \\ \theta_1 + \theta_2 - \sqrt{(\theta_1 - \theta_2)^2 + 4ab} = \theta_1 + \theta_2 - |\theta_1 - \theta_2| \end{matrix}\right\} \leftrightarrow \left.\begin{matrix} \sqrt{(\theta_1 - \theta_2)^2 + 4ab} = |\theta_1 - \theta_2| \\ \sqrt{(\theta_1 - \theta_2)^2 + 4ab} = |\theta_1 - \theta_2| \end{matrix}\right\} \leftrightarrow$$

$$\sqrt{(\theta_1 - \theta_2)^2 + 4ab} = |\theta_1 - \theta_2| \leftrightarrow (\theta_1 - \theta_2)^2 + 4ab = |\theta_1 - \theta_2|^2 \leftrightarrow ab = 0$$

It is valid that: $\lambda_1 + \lambda_2 = \theta_1 + \theta_2 \xrightarrow{\lambda_1 = 1} \lambda_2 = \theta_1 + \theta_2 - 1$

It is valid that:

$$\lambda_1 \cdot \lambda_2 = \theta_1\theta_2 - ab \xrightarrow{\lambda_2 = 0} 0 = \theta_1\theta_2 - ab$$

Theorem(2.1) proves that the structural inequalities (2.1) imply stability. Furthermore the eigenvalues are real and the system does not possess sinusoidal behavior. This fundamental property of the system implies that it achieves steady state value under a step input. This steady state response for a constant (step) input $u_n = u$ is given below:

$$\underline{x} = A\underline{x} + b \Leftrightarrow (I-A)\underline{x} = b \Leftrightarrow \underline{x} = (I-A)^{-1}b \tag{2.5}$$

Hence:

$$\begin{bmatrix} x \\ y \\ k \end{bmatrix} = \left(I - \begin{bmatrix} 1-a-p_1 & b & 0 \\ a & 1-b-c-p_2 & 0 \\ 0 & c & 1-p_3 \end{bmatrix} \right)^{-1} \begin{bmatrix} 1 \\ 0 \\ 0 \end{bmatrix} u =$$

$$\begin{bmatrix} \dfrac{b\cdot p_3 + c\cdot p_3 + p_2\cdot p_3}{a\cdot c\cdot p_3 + b\cdot p_1\cdot p_3 + c\cdot p_1\cdot p_3 + a\cdot p_2\cdot p_3 + p_1\cdot p_2\cdot p_3} \\ \dfrac{a\cdot p_3}{a\cdot c\cdot p_3 + b\cdot p_1\cdot p_3 + c\cdot p_1\cdot p_3 + a\cdot p_2\cdot p_3 + p_1\cdot p_2\cdot p_3} \\ \dfrac{a\cdot c}{a\cdot c\cdot p_3 + b\cdot p_1\cdot p_3 + c\cdot p_1\cdot p_3 + a\cdot p_2\cdot p_3 + p_1\cdot p_2\cdot p_3} \end{bmatrix} u$$

The steady state ratio of bad credit loans to the sum of the performing loans is given by:

$$k\% = \frac{k}{x+y} = \frac{a\cdot c}{(b+c+p_2+a)p_3} \tag{2.6}$$

Therefore

The ratio does not depend on the input u and the proportion p_1.

To investigate the effect of the factor a and c to the bad loans ratio $k\%$, we should calculate the corresponding partial derivatives of $k\%$ with respect to a and c. Specifically, we have

$$\frac{\partial k\%}{\partial \alpha} = \frac{c\cdot(b+c+p_2+a)\cdot p_3 - p_3\cdot a\cdot c}{[(b+c+p_2+a)\cdot p_3]^2} = \frac{c\cdot(b+c+p_2)\cdot p_3}{[(b+c+p_2+a)\cdot p_3]^2} > 0$$

$$\frac{\partial k\%}{\partial c} = \frac{a\cdot(b+c+p_2+a)\cdot p_3 - p_3\cdot a\cdot c}{[(b+c+p_2+a)\cdot p_3]^2} = \frac{a\cdot(b+c+p_2)\cdot p_3}{[(b+c+p_2+a)\cdot p_3]^2} > 0$$

We observe that both are positive, which means that the larger the a and c are (the a and c are the proportions of the "leakage" to the past due and the bad credit loans) the worse the ratio is.

The larger the proportions b, p_2, p_3 the smaller this ratio is.

Based on the above stability results we may be able to calculate basic indicators of credit risk such as PD. The Probability of Default is the proportion of performing loans that becoming bad credit loans in one year period. This indicator it is directly related to the parameters of the dynamical system and can be calculated as follows.

The new bad credit loans for each month i are given by cy_{i-1} . Hence the new bad credit loans through the whole year are given by:

$$cy_0 + cy_1 + cy_2 + \ldots + cy_{11} = c(y_0 + y_1 + y_2 + \ldots + y_{11}) =$$

$$c\left([0,1]I\begin{bmatrix}x_0\\y_0\end{bmatrix}+[0,1]B\begin{bmatrix}x_0\\y_0\end{bmatrix}+\ldots+[0,1]B^{11}\begin{bmatrix}x_0\\y_0\end{bmatrix}\right)=c[0,1](1+B+\ldots+B^{11})\begin{bmatrix}x_0\\y_0\end{bmatrix}=$$

$$c[0,1](I-B)^{-1}(I-B^{12})\begin{bmatrix}x_0\\y_0\end{bmatrix}$$

Because the system is stable it is valid that the eigenvalues are smaller than 1. Hence it is safe to presume that $B^{12}\approx 0$

Then PD is given by

$$PD\approx\frac{c[0,1](I-B)^{-1}\begin{bmatrix}x_0\\y_0\end{bmatrix}}{x_0+y_0}=c[0,1](I-B)^{-1}\begin{bmatrix}x_0\%\\y_0\%\end{bmatrix} \tag{2.7}$$

where $x_0\%=\dfrac{x_0}{x_0+y_0}$, $y_0\%=\dfrac{y_0}{x_0+y_0}$ and $B=\begin{bmatrix}1-a-p_1 & b\\ a & 1-b-c-p_2\end{bmatrix}$

$$(I-B)=\begin{bmatrix}a+p_1 & -b\\ -a & b+c+p_2\end{bmatrix} \text{ and } (I-B)^{-1}=\frac{1}{|I-B|}\cdot\begin{bmatrix}b+c+p_2 & b\\ a & a+p_1\end{bmatrix}$$

Therefore,

$$PD=c[0,1](I-B)^{-1}\begin{bmatrix}x_0\%\\y_0\%\end{bmatrix}=c\cdot\frac{a+p_1\cdot y_0\%}{a\cdot c+a\cdot p_2+p_1\cdot c+p_1\cdot(b+p_2)}$$

We observe that:

PD depends positively on $y_0\%$

To investigate the relation between PD and a, c, we calculate the corresponding partial derivatives

$$\frac{\partial PD}{\partial a}=\frac{c\cdot[(a\cdot c+a\cdot p_2+p_1\cdot b+p_1\cdot(c+p_2))]-(a+p_1\cdot y_0\%)\cdot(c+p_2)}{(a\cdot c+a\cdot p_2+p_1\cdot c+p_1\cdot(b+p_2))^2}\Leftrightarrow$$

$$\frac{\partial PD}{\partial a}=\frac{c\cdot[p_1\cdot b+p_1\cdot(c+p_2)\cdot(1-y_0\%)]}{(a\cdot c+a\cdot p_2+p_1\cdot c+p_1\cdot(b+p_2))^2}\Leftrightarrow$$

$$\frac{\partial PD}{\partial a}=\frac{c\cdot[p_1\cdot b+p_1\cdot(c+p_2)\cdot(x_0\%)]}{(a\cdot c+a\cdot p_2+p_1\cdot c+p_1\cdot(b+p_2))^2}>0$$

and $$\frac{\partial PD}{\partial c} = \frac{(a + p_1 \cdot y_0 \%) \cdot (a \cdot p_2 + p_1 \cdot (b + p_2))}{(a \cdot c + a \cdot p_2 + p_1 \cdot c + p_1 \cdot (b + p_2))^2} > 0$$

PD gets worse as factors a and c increase.

Simulation Results

This study can be used to address the questions

- What are the provisions for the bad credit for the following year
- What is the credit risk pricing for the following year
- What are the credit risk pricing and the provisions when the portfolio reaches steady state?
- How the parameters a, b, c affect risk and how much they should change to improve the current state of the portfolio.

To this end, first, using a time series of monthly bank data we identified a portfolio model by solving the L1 optimisation problem described previously. The identified parameters of the model are

a:	4, 52%
b:	46, 00%
c:	0, 32%
p(1)	0, 95%
p(2)	0, 19%
p(3)	0, 43%

The system is stable with eigenvalues (0.9957, 0.9905, 0.5303) and steady state response X=104, 7u , Y=1, 02u and K=0, 76u which in turn give rise to a yearly PD equalling to 0, 71%. Using the identified parameters we simulated the behaviour of the loan portfolio, assuming u_n=10, predicting balances for the following year as described at the following graph

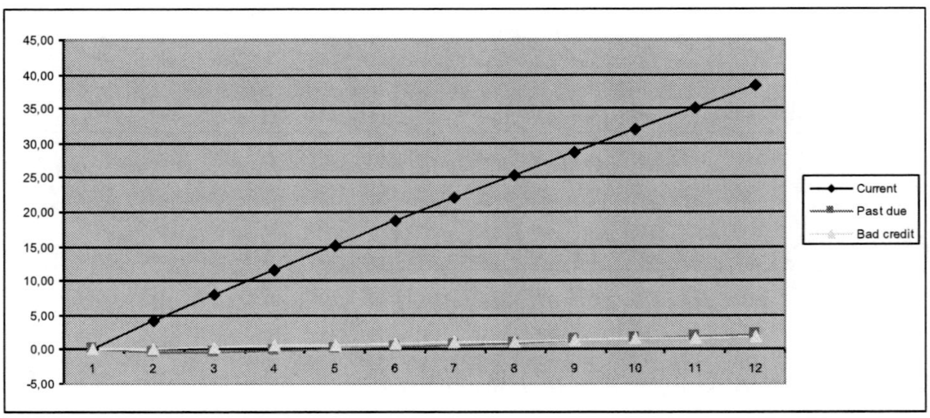

Evolution of the loan portfolio in the year (increase in balances)

We have calculated that the bad credit for the year will increase by 1, 9 giving maximum additional provisions of the same amount for this year. The maximum figure for the risk premium, P, is 0, 271% for the year and its elasticities relative to the model parameters a, b, c are given by the following table

aDP/PDa	0, 93
bDP/PDb	-0, 9
cDP/PDc	1, 1

In order to examine how the capacity of the collections department influences the amount of bad credit of the portfolio, we have studied the behavior of the bad credit loans in terms of the capacity parameters k_c and y_c of the collections.

We have to check the proportional change of the bad credit loans in the specific time period, 1 year, using simulation i.e how the factor $\frac{\Delta k}{k_0} = \frac{k_1 - k_0}{k_0}$ changes as a function of y_c and k_c.

We have calculated the factor using different values of the variables k_c and y_c. The lower prices of k_c and y_c, the higher this increase is. The results of this simulation are:

- The highest value of yearly increases of bad credit is 150% and this happened when k_c, y_c=0
- For every acceptable level a% we construct a contour line which divides the parameter space (y_c, k_c) into an acceptable and non acceptable subspace, as it is shown in the following graph.

According to our bank data, the shape of the contour line is strongly related to the y_c. The factor k_c affects the contour line only in terms of its lower values. This means that in order to examine the factor $\frac{\Delta k}{k_0}$, we have basically to change the value of y_c. Graphically, this can be shown in the following diagram:

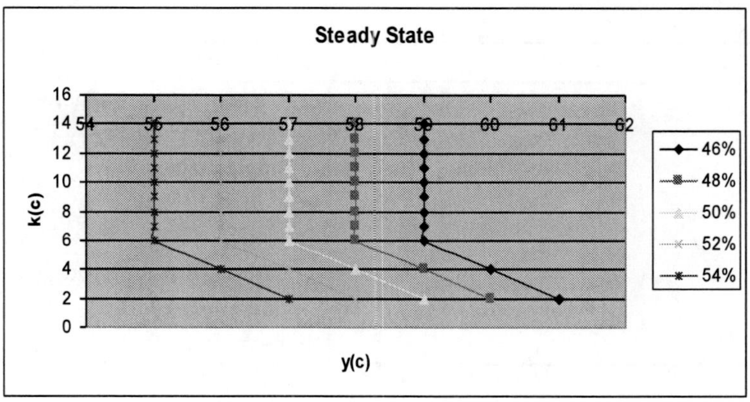

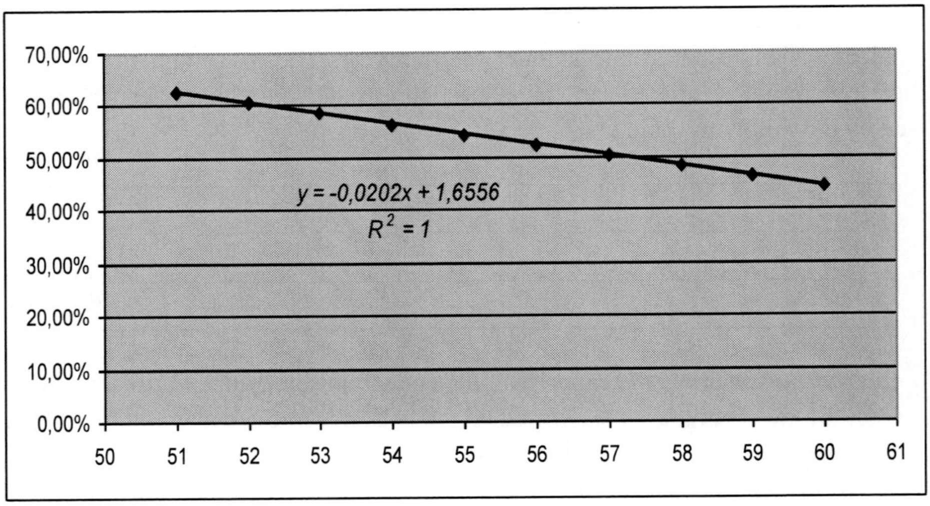

The line can be described at the equation $a\% = -0.0202y_c + 1.6556$ with R^2=1 and $50<y_c<61$. This means that increase by 10 units of y_c implies decrease in bad credit by 20%.

Study of the Model Based on the Loan Classification by Rating

Next, we describe the process of dynamical system approached by an optimal control problem that we have developed in order to estimate important factors and indices of the loan portfolio such as profit, loan loss provisions and risk premium rates. Initially, we have categorized the loans into 7 categories based on credit quality as proposed by JPMorgan. We have distinguished the loans into 2 basic sets related to repayment status. So, we have defined as U the amount of new loans, and as X the amount of current loans. This implies that the loans of the two different sets, (U, X), have been categorized into 7-subcategories related to credit quality. So, each set U, X is consisted of 7-categories, which denote the risk exposure, i.e. n=AAA highest credit quality. The seven categories are illustrated to the following table derived from the rating agencies.

Rating	Credit quality
AAA	Extremely strong capacity
AA	Very strong capacity
A	Strong capacity
BBB	Adequate capacity
BB	Inadequate capacity
B	Greater vulnerability to default
CCC	Vulnerable to default
D	In payment default

So, we have classified the 2 sets of loans (U, X) into 7 categories that reflect the risk exposure and credit quality. By controlling the amount of new loans, we can calculate the maximum profit as well as the expectancy rates according to which amounts of each category move to another. The procedure will be described by a dynamical system of linear equations.

First, we have defined the state variables of the system as the amount of current loans X^n for each category of credit quality and the amount of default loans D, as well as the input of the system (control variable) as the amount of new loans U^n. The parameters of the system are the elements of the transition matrix and the coefficients *r*. Each element of the system reflect the probability of migrating from the current credit quality state to any possible credit quality state at the given risk horizon. Moreover, the coefficient *r* reflects the returns of paid loans from each category. The following table shows the return connected to each credit quality category.

Rating	Credit quality	Forward zero curves yields
AAA	Extremely strong capacity	r_{AAA}
AA	Very strong capacity	r_{AA}
A	Strong capacity	r_{A}
BBB	Adequate capacity	r_{BBB}
BB	Inadequate capacity	r_{BB}
B	Greater vulnerability to default	r_{B}
CCC	Vulnerable to default	r_{ccc}
D	In payment default	

Having the model of a system, it is often very important for analysis, simulation and prediction. Simulating the model, we can find and predict the new loans, the bad credit and risk premium indices by maximizing the profit. Moreover, we can calculate the sensitivity of the indices of portfolio in terms of the changes of the parameters of the system.

Model Description

In order to develop a method of predicting the loan portfolio behavior, we need to develop a model describing the process. We have divided our loan portfolio into 2 sets of loans:

- New loans at time t: u_t^n
- Current loans at time t: x_t^n
- Default loans at time t: D_t

Where the subscript t represents the time period; for our model the t represents the month, and the superscript n represents the credit quality. The variable u^{AAA} represents the amount of new loans in AAA rating category. The variable x^{AAA} represents the amount of current loans in AAA rating category. The set "Default" reflects the loans that become default at the specific time t. Initially, each amount of loan in the portfolio is classified to be either on set U or on set X and then each amount of loan may belong to one of these 7 categories and in the next month is either staying in the same credit quality category or moves to another or it becomes "default" as the following diagram shows:

Schematically:

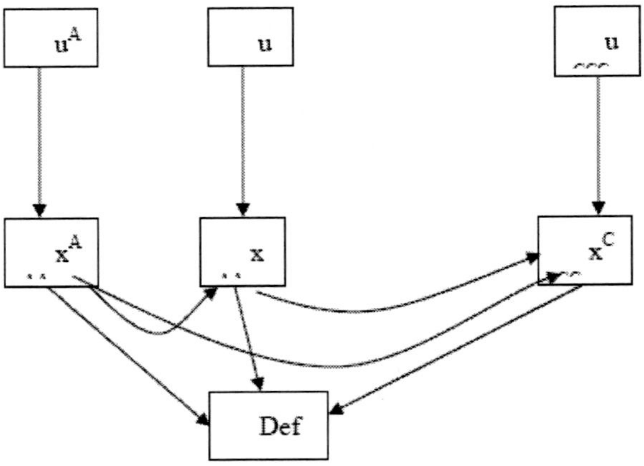

Next, in order to simulate and study the behavior of a loan portfolio, we need to construct a dynamical system consisted of linear equations described the process. The following equations describe the process of the system and they reflect the dynamical behavior of the loan portfolio through the time horizon. The coefficients α_{11}, α_{12}, ...α_{77} are the parameters of the system and they represent the probabilities for a loan to migrate to any possible credit quality state. Finally, the coefficients *d*, included in the default equation, represent the percentage of loans from each rating category that become default in the next time period.

$$x_{t+1}^{AAA} = a_{11} \cdot x_t^{AAA} + a_{12} \cdot x_t^{AA} + a_{13} \cdot x_t^{A} + a_{14} \cdot x_t^{BBB} + a_{15} \cdot x_t^{BB} + a_{16} \cdot x_t^{B} + a_{17} \cdot x_t^{CCC} + u^{AAA}$$

$$x_{t+1}^{AA} = a_{21} \cdot x_t^{AAA} + a_{22} \cdot x_t^{AA} + a_{23} \cdot x_t^{A} + a_{24} \cdot x_t^{BBB} + a_{25} \cdot x_t^{BB} + a_{26} \cdot x_t^{B} + a_{27} \cdot x_t^{CCC} + u^{AA}$$

$$x_{t+1}^{A} = a_{31} \cdot x_t^{AAA} + a_{32} \cdot x_t^{AA} + a_{33} \cdot x_t^{A} + a_{34} \cdot x_t^{BBB} + a_{35} \cdot x_t^{BB} + a_{36} \cdot x_t^{B} + a_{37} \cdot x_t^{CCC} + u^{A}$$

$$x_{t+1}^{BBB} = a_{41} \cdot x_t^{AAA} + a_{42} \cdot x_t^{AA} + a_{43} \cdot x_t^{A} + a_{44} \cdot x_t^{BBB} + a_{45} \cdot x_t^{BB} + a_{46} \cdot x_t^{B} + a_{47} \cdot x_t^{CCC} + u^{BBB}$$

$$x_{t+1}^{BB} = a_{51} \cdot x_t^{AAA} + a_{52} \cdot x_t^{AA} + a_{53} \cdot x_t^{A} + a_{54} \cdot x_t^{BBB} + a_{55} \cdot x_t^{BB} + a_{56} \cdot x_t^{B} + a_{57} \cdot x_t^{CCC} + u^{BB}$$

$$x_{t+1}^{B} = a_{61} \cdot x_t^{AAA} + a_{62} \cdot x_t^{AA} + a_{63} \cdot x_t^{A} + a_{64} \cdot x_t^{BBB} + a_{65} \cdot x_t^{BB} + a_{66} \cdot x_t^{B} + a_{67} \cdot x_t^{CCC} + u^{B}$$

$$x_{t+1}^{CCC} = a_{71} \cdot x_t^{AAA} + a_{72} \cdot x_t^{AA} + a_{73} \cdot x_t^{A} + a_{74} \cdot x_t^{BBB} + a_{75} \cdot x_t^{BB} + a_{76} \cdot x_t^{B} + a_{77} \cdot x_t^{CCC} + u^{CCC}$$

$$D_{t+1} = D_t + d_A \cdot x_t^A + d_{BBB} \cdot x_t^{BBB} + d_{BB} \cdot x_t^{BB} + d_B \cdot x_t^B + d_{CCC} \cdot x_t^{CCC}$$

$$\Pr_{t+1} = \Pr_{t+1} + r_{AAA} \cdot x_t^{AAA} + r_{AA} \cdot x_t^{AA} + r_A \cdot x_t^A + r_{BBB} \cdot x_t^{BBB} + r_{BB} \cdot x_t^{BB} + r_B \cdot x_t^B + r_{CCC} \cdot x_t^{CCC}$$

The first 7 equations describe the amount of loans for each category in the next time period connected with the previous state of loan portfolio. This means that the factor α_{11} is the percentage of AAA rating loans in the previous step, which remain in the same category. The equation D_{t+1} describes the amount of loans that is default and the last equation describes the profit in the next time period connected with the previous state of loans portfolio. The parameter *r* represents the return of a current loan related to its credit quality category.

Model Identification

In order to identify the dynamic system, we use the transition matrix published by SandP and Moody's. The transition matrix published by rating agencies has been calculated by observing the historical pattern of rating change and default. The following table illustrates the 1-year transition matrix, i.e the probabilities per rating category to migrate to any other possible rating category in one year.

One year transition matrix

Rating at year-end	AAA	AA	A	BBB	BB	B	CCC
AAA	90.81%	0.70%	0.09%	0.02%	0.03%	0.00%	0.22%
AA	8.33%	90.65%	2.27%	0.33%	0.14%	0.11%	0.00%
A	0.68%	7.79%	91.05%	5.95%	0.67%	0.24%	0.22%
BBB	0.06%	0.64%	5.52%	86.93%	7.73%	0.43%	1.30%
BB	0.12%	0.06%	0.74%	5.30%	80.53%	6.48%	2.38%
B	0.00%	0.14%	0.26%	1.17%	8.84%	83.46%	11.24%
CCC	0.00%	0.02%	0.01%	0.12%	1.00%	4.07%	64.86%
Default	0.00%	0.00%	0.06%	0.18%	1.06%	5.20%	19.79%

The last row of the above matrix indicates the probabilities of each rating (column) to become default in the end of the year. Now, considering the classification mentioned in the previous part, we set the equations describing the portfolio evolution as a discrete dynamical system in matrix form:

$$\begin{bmatrix} x^{AAA} \\ x^{AA} \\ x^{A} \\ x^{BBB} \\ x^{BB} \\ x^{B} \\ x^{CCC} \end{bmatrix}_{t+1} = \begin{bmatrix} a_{11} & a_{12} & a_{13} & a_{14} & a_{15} & a_{16} & a_{17} \\ a_{21} & a_{22} & a_{23} & a_{24} & a_{25} & a_{26} & a_{27} \\ a_{31} & a_{32} & a_{33} & a_{34} & a_{35} & a_{36} & a_{37} \\ a_{41} & a_{42} & a_{43} & a_{44} & a_{45} & a_{46} & a_{47} \\ a_{51} & a_{52} & a_{53} & a_{54} & a_{55} & a_{56} & a_{57} \\ a_{61} & a_{62} & a_{63} & a_{64} & a_{65} & a_{66} & a_{67} \\ a_{71} & a_{72} & a_{73} & a_{74} & a_{75} & a_{76} & a_{77} \end{bmatrix} \cdot \begin{bmatrix} x^{AAA} \\ x^{AA} \\ x^{A} \\ x^{BBB} \\ x^{BB} \\ x^{B} \\ x^{CCC} \end{bmatrix}_{t} + \begin{bmatrix} u^{AAA} \\ u^{AA} \\ u^{A} \\ u^{BBB} \\ u^{BB} \\ u^{B} \\ u^{CCC} \end{bmatrix}_{t}$$

or in vector form,

$$\underline{X}_{t+1} = A \cdot \underline{X}_t + \underline{U}_t$$

Including the default rates equation the above matrix formula becomes:

$$\begin{bmatrix} x_{AAA} \\ x_{AA} \\ x_{A} \\ x_{BBB} \\ x_{BB} \\ x_{B} \\ x_{CCC} \\ D \end{bmatrix}_{t+1} = \begin{bmatrix} a_{11} & a_{12} & a_{13} & a_{14} & a_{15} & a_{16} & a_{17} & 0 \\ a_{21} & a_{22} & a_{23} & a_{24} & a_{25} & a_{26} & a_{27} & 0 \\ a_{31} & a_{32} & a_{33} & a_{34} & a_{35} & a_{36} & a_{37} & 0 \\ a_{41} & a_{42} & a_{43} & a_{44} & a_{45} & a_{46} & a_{47} & 0 \\ a_{51} & a_{52} & a_{53} & a_{54} & a_{55} & a_{56} & a_{57} & 0 \\ a_{61} & a_{62} & a_{63} & a_{64} & a_{65} & a_{66} & a_{67} & 0 \\ a_{71} & a_{72} & a_{73} & a_{74} & a_{75} & a_{76} & a_{77} & 0 \\ d_{81} & d_{82} & d_{83} & d_{84} & d_{85} & d_{86} & d_{87} & 1 \end{bmatrix} \cdot \begin{bmatrix} x_{AAA} \\ x_{AA} \\ x_{A} \\ x_{BBB} \\ x_{BB} \\ x_{B} \\ x_{CCC} \\ D \end{bmatrix}_{t} + \begin{bmatrix} u_{AAA} \\ u_{AA} \\ u_{A} \\ u_{BBB} \\ u_{BB} \\ u_{B} \\ u_{CCC} \\ 0 \end{bmatrix}_{t}$$

So, default equation in vector form is:

$$\begin{bmatrix} \underline{X} \\ d \end{bmatrix}_{t+1} = \begin{bmatrix} A & \underline{0} \\ \underline{d} & 1 \end{bmatrix} \cdot \begin{bmatrix} \underline{X} \\ d \end{bmatrix}_{t} + \begin{bmatrix} \underline{u} \\ 0 \end{bmatrix}_{t}$$

where $\underline{X}_{t+1}$ denotes the vector of current loans for each rating category in the next time period, $\underline{X}_t$ denotes the vector of current loans for each rating in current time period, d denotes the amount of defaulted loans and finally the $\underline{U}_t$ denotes the vector that contains the amount of new loans from each rating at the current time period.

The transition matrix A reflects the probability that measures the likelihood that amount in a particular category will move to another category during the applicable period of time. We have calculated the transition matrix per month since we examine the dynamic behaviour of loan portfolio per month. For the calculation of the matrix, we find the eigenvalues of the initial matrix A following the relations:

$$A = S\Lambda S^{-1} \Rightarrow A^{1/12} = S\Lambda^{1/12} S^{-1}$$

Following the same methodology, we find the transition matrix per month related to default rates. From the above equations and the matrix properties, we derive the following relation:

$$d_{year} = d_{month} \cdot (I - A_{month})^{-1} \cdot (I - A_{year}) \Rightarrow d_{month} = d_{year} \cdot (I - A_{year}) \cdot (I - A_{month})^{-1}$$

So, calculating the default rates per month the one-month transition matrix becomes:

One-month TRANSITION MATRIX							
Rating at month-end	AAA	AA	A	BBB	BB	B	CCC
AAA	98.97%	0.36%	0.11%	0.00%	0.00%	0.00%	0.00%
AA	0.54%	98.96%	0.00%	0.24%	0.37%	0.25%	0.15%
A	0.27%	0.00%	99.14%	0.58%	0.45%	0.29%	0.13%
BBB	0.00%	0.24%	0.58%	99.10%	0.00%	0.00%	0.00%
BB	0.00%	0.15%	0.21%	0.00%	98.69%	0.00%	0.00%
B	0.00%	0.10%	0.15%	0.00%	0.00%	98.18%	0.00%
CCC	0.14%	0.10%	0.22%	0.00%	0.00%	0.00%	96.32%
Default	0.00%	0.00%	0.00%	0.00%	0.00%	0.00%	0.23%

The coefficient r reflects the returns of paid loans from each category. For the return of paid loans, we use the spread yields for each rating category published by JPMorgan.

Rating	Credit quality	1- year Yields
AAA	Extremely strong capacity	3.6
AA	Very strong capacity	3.65
A	Strong capacity	3.72
BBB	Adequate capacity	4.1
BB	Inadequate capacity	5.55
B	Greater vulnerability to default	6.05
CCC	Vulnerable to default	15.05

The above variables of the system may define the basic ingredients the for risk and return of the loan portfolio, which may be used for the shaping of the optimal control policy that optimize return while keeping risk within acceptable limits.

Definition and Solution of the Open Loop Optimal Control Problem

In order to study the behavior of loan portfolio and to predict the appropriate credit policy, we construct an optimal control problem. An optimal control problem can be approached either with the open loop method or with the closed loop method. For the open loop optimal policy, we need to define the control variables (inputs), the objective function (profit, risk adjusted interest income), and the relation between the two (dynamical system). For the purposes of this study, we define as inputs, the new loans granted by the bank for the various risk categories.

As time evolves, new loans get into the system and loans change category, by improving or worsening their quality, or even becoming default. Because it is practically impossible to monitor this system continuously, we choose certain points of time (month), where we calculate the system variables. In other words time becomes discrete. With this approach, we may find the amount of loans in each category each period. We simply compute the amount of the loans on each period recursively from the previous period.

The dynamic model as already said is described in vector form by the next equation:

The dynamic model as already said is described in vector form by the next equation:

$$\underline{X}_{t+1} = A \cdot \underline{X}_t + \underline{U}_{t+1} \tag{3.1}$$

whereU_t are the input loans at period t.

There is also another category of loans that become default. The balances of defaulted loans $\underline{D}_t$ follow the following dynamic equation:

$$\underline{D}_{t+1} = \underline{d} \cdot \underline{X}_t + \underline{D}_t \tag{3.2}$$

where $\underline{d}$ are the percentages of the loans from each category that become default.

As it is clear, the two sets of equations (3.1-3.2) form a linear time invariant dynamic system and can be dealt by the relevant theory of dynamical systems.

From (3.1), using induction it can be derived that:

$$\underline{X}_{t+1} = A^{t+1} \cdot \underline{X}_0 + A^t \cdot \underline{U}_1 + \cdots + A \cdot \underline{U}_t + \underline{U}_{t+1} \tag{3.3}$$

where X_0 is the initial condition (the amount of loans in each category at the beginning) hence known, A^i is the matrix power of the system matrix and U_t are the input variables of the system (new loans) in each time period. So the values of the current loans in each category for every time period can be easily calculated from the inputs of the system.

From (3.2), using induction it can be derived that:

$$\underline{D}_{12} = \underline{d} \cdot (\underline{X}_{11} + \underline{X}_{10} + \cdots + \underline{X}_0) + D_0 \tag{3.4}$$

where D_0, are the initial default loans which are known. Using (3.3) with (3.4), we may derive:

$$\begin{aligned} \underline{D}_{12} &= \underline{d} \cdot ((A^{11} \cdot \underline{X}_0 + A^{10} \cdot \underline{U}_1 + \cdots + A \cdot \underline{U}_{10} + \underline{U}_{11}) + (A^{10} \cdot \underline{X}_0 + A^9 \cdot \underline{U}_1 + \cdots + A \cdot \underline{U}_9 + \underline{U}_{10}) + \\ &\cdots + (A^2 \cdot \underline{X}_0 + A^1 \cdot \underline{U}_1 + \underline{U}_2) + (A \cdot \underline{X}_0 + \underline{U}_1)) + X_0 + D_0 \Rightarrow \\ \underline{D}_{12} &= \underline{d} \cdot ((A^{11} + A^{10} + \cdots + A + I)\underline{X}_0 + (A^{10} + A^9 + \cdots + A + I)\underline{U}_1 + \cdots + (A + I) \cdot \underline{U}_{10} \cdot + \underline{U}_{11} \end{aligned}$$

Or equivalently:

$$\underline{D}_{12} = \underline{d} \cdot (\Omega_{11} \cdot \underline{X}_0 + \Omega_{10} \cdot \underline{U}_1 + \cdots + \Omega_1 \cdot \underline{U}_{10} + \underline{U}_{11}) \tag{3.5}$$

with $\Omega_n = \sum_{k=0}^{n} A^k$.

The profit of the loans portfolio is considered as the output of the system, since it is almost always the most important factor, for the financial institutions. The profit (risk adjusted interest income) directly relates with the income gained by the performing loans (interest rate) of each loan category and the expense spent by the defaulted loans (loan loss provisions). Saying that the yield for each loan category i is r_i and the loss from the default loans is L, where L is the percentage of the default loans that cannot be retrieved, the profit (risk adjusted interest income) can be found from the next formula:

$$P_t = E_t - L\, D_t \tag{3.6}$$

The aggregate earnings for each period are calculated from the next formula:

$$\underline{E}_{t+1} = E^t + r_{AAA} x_t^{AAA} + r_{AA} x_t^{AA} + r_A x_t^A + r_{BBB} x_t^{BBB} + r_{BB} x_t^{BB} + r_B x_t^B + r_{CCC} x_t^{CCC} \tag{3.7}$$

or else in vector form:

$$\underline{E}_{t+1} = E^t + \underline{r} \cdot \underline{X}_t \tag{3.8}$$

where $\underline{r} = \left[r_{AAA}, r_{AA}, ..r_{CCC}\right]$ and $\underline{x}_t = \left[x_t^{AAA}, x_t^{AA}, ..x_t^{CCC}\right]$

From this, using induction and the fact that $E_0 = 0$, it can be derived that:

$$\underline{E}_{t+1} = \underline{r} \cdot \left(\underline{X}_0 + \underline{X}_1 + \cdots + \underline{X}_{11}\right) \tag{3.9}$$

Using formula (9) with (3) it can be derived that:

$$\begin{aligned} &\underline{E}_{12} = \underline{r} \cdot (\left(A^{11} \cdot \underline{X}_0 + A^{10} \cdot \underline{U}_1 + \cdots + A \cdot \underline{U}_{10} + \underline{U}_{11}\right) + \left(A^{10} \cdot \underline{X}_0 + A^9 \cdot \underline{U}_1 + \cdots + A \cdot \underline{U}_9 + \underline{U}_{10}\right) + \\ &\cdots + \left(A^2 \cdot \underline{X}_0 + A^1 \cdot \underline{U}_1 + \underline{U}_{21}\right) + \left(A \cdot \underline{X}_0 + \underline{U}_1\right) + \underline{X}_0) \Rightarrow \\ &\underline{E}_{12} = \underline{r} \cdot (\left(A^{11} + A^{10} + \cdots + A + I\right)\underline{X}_0 + \left(A^{10} + A^{9} + \cdots + A + I\right)\underline{U}_1 + \cdots + (A + I) \cdot \underline{U}_{10} \cdot + \underline{U}_{11} \end{aligned} \tag{3.10}$$

or equivalently:

$$\underline{E}_{12} = \underline{r} \cdot \left(\Omega_{11} \cdot \underline{X}_0 + \Omega_{10} \cdot \underline{U}_1 + \cdots + \Omega_1 \cdot \underline{U}_{10} + \underline{U}_{11}\right) \tag{3.11}$$

Using at formula (6) the formulas (5) and (11) we have:

$$\begin{aligned} &\underline{P}_{12} = \underline{r} \cdot \left(\Omega_{11} \cdot \underline{X}_0 + \Omega_{10} \cdot \underline{U}_1 + \cdots + \Omega_1 \cdot \underline{U}_{10} + \underline{U}_{11}\right) \\ &- L \cdot \underline{d} \cdot \left(\Omega_{11} \cdot \underline{X}_0 + \Omega_{10} \cdot \underline{U}_1 + \cdots + \Omega_1 \cdot \underline{U}_{10} + \underline{U}_{11}\right) \end{aligned} \tag{3.12}$$

The previous formula can be better written as:

$$\underline{P}_{12} = \left(\underline{r} - L \cdot \underline{d}\right) \cdot \left(\Omega_{11} \cdot \underline{X}_0 + \Omega_{10} \cdot \underline{U}_1 + \cdots + \Omega_1 \cdot \underline{U}_{10} + \underline{U}_{11}\right) \tag{3.13}$$

As it can be seen from this equation the profit (risk adjusted interest income) of one period is affected by the inputs of the previous periods, hence we can say that the system has a kind of "inertia" since the results from improved input will appear in the future periods after the change of the input.

The goal is to maximize the profit by altering the input variables accordingly. The time period where the profit must be maximized is 12 months. As it is clear from the previous equation, the first part $\Omega_{11} \cdot \underline{X}_0$ is constant independent what the U_0, U_1, …, U_t values are, so it doesn't affect the maximization point. Thus for simplicity they can be ignored, and the objective function becomes:

$$\max\left(\underline{r} - L \cdot \underline{d}\right) \cdot \left(\Omega_{10} \cdot \underline{U}_1 + \Omega_9 \cdot \underline{U}_2 + \cdots + \Omega_1 \cdot \underline{U}_{10} + \Omega_0 \cdot \underline{U}_{11}\right) \tag{3.14}$$

The constraints of the problem said are:

$$0 \le \underline{U}_i \le \underline{U}_i^{\max} \tag{3.15}$$

where $\underline{U}_i^{\max}$ is the maximum amount of new loans for each category that can be processed by the bank.

Finally there is an important additional constraint (capital adequacy) that relates the credit risk taken by the institution to the capital help by it. This is given by

$$\frac{capital}{RWA} \geq 8\%$$

The RWA (risk weight assets) for the final month are given by

$$RWA = c_{AAA} \cdot x_{11}^{AAA} + c_{AA} \cdot x_{11}^{AA} + c_{A} \cdot x_{11}^{A!} + c_{BBB} \cdot x_{11}^{BBB} + c_{BB} \cdot x_{11}^{BB} + c_{B} \cdot x_{11}^{B} + c_{CCC} \cdot x_{11}^{CCC}$$

where c_i represents the risk weights per loan category (they are numbers related to the risk of its loan category). This gives rise to the following inequality constraint:

$$c_{AAA} \cdot x_{11}^{AAA} + c_{AA} \cdot x_{11}^{AA} + c_{A} \cdot x_{11}^{A!} + c_{BBB} \cdot x_{11}^{BBB} + c_{BB} \cdot x_{11}^{BB} + c_{B} \cdot x_{11}^{B} + c_{CCC} \cdot x_{11}^{CCC} \leq b = \frac{capital}{8\%}$$

or in vector form

$$\underline{C} \cdot \underline{X}_{11} \leq b \tag{3.16}$$

where $\underline{C} = (c_{AAA}, c_{AA}, .. c_{CCC})$. Using (3.3) with (3.16) it derives that:

$$\underline{C} \cdot \left(A^{11} \cdot \underline{X}_0 + A^{10} \cdot \underline{U}_1 + \cdots + A \cdot \underline{U}_{10} + \underline{U}_{11}\right) \leq b \tag{3.17}$$

The optimization problem is of the Linear Programming type with objective function (3.14) and constraints (3.15) and (3.17). It can be also rewritten as:

$$\max\{(\underline{r} - L\underline{d}) \cdot [I, \Omega_1, \Omega_2, .. \Omega_{10}] \cdot \begin{bmatrix} \underline{U}_{11} \\ \underline{U}_{10} \\ \cdots \\ \underline{U}_1 \end{bmatrix}\} \tag{3.18}$$

Subject to

$$0 \leq \underline{U}_i \leq \underline{U}_i^{\max} \; i=1, \ldots 11 \tag{3.19}$$

and

$$\underline{C}\begin{bmatrix} I & A & \cdots & A^{10} \end{bmatrix} \cdot \begin{bmatrix} \underline{U}_{11} \\ \underline{U}_{10} \\ \cdots\cdot \\ \underline{U}_{1} \end{bmatrix} \leq b - \underline{C} \cdot A^{11} \underline{X}_0 \tag{3.20}$$

In inequality (3.20), b is the maximum allowable amount of Risk Weighted Assets of the financial institution.. When a financial institution issues a loan, it undertakes a certain amount of risk. If this risk is added to the already existing risk, it cannot be greater than the financial institution's risk capacity "b", which in turn depends on the size of its capital. $\underline{C} \cdot A^{11} \cdot \underline{X}_0$ represents the already undertaken risk of the issued loans, before the beginning of the period. Hence the capacity of the financial institution to undertake (new) risk finally is $b - \underline{C} \cdot A^{11} \cdot \underline{X}_0$. This must be greater or equal than the risk the financial institute undertakes from the new loans as it is described in (3.20).

To solve the above linear programming problem it is worth noting that all coefficients of the problem are positive. Indeed matrix "A" represents transition probabilities so its elements are all positive. So do the elements of Ω, which is derived from powers and summations of matrix A as well as the identity matrix. The gain vector $(\underline{r} - L \cdot \underline{d})$ represents the risk adjusted interest income which has to be positive for all loan categories. If there is a category that its corresponding gain is negative it has to be excluded from the analysis.

In order to calculate the solution that satisfies (3.18), (3.19), (3.20) we set:

$$[c_n^k] = \underline{C}\begin{bmatrix} I & A & \cdots & A^{10} \end{bmatrix},\ [\omega_n^k] = (\underline{r} - L\underline{d}) \cdot [I, \Omega_1, \Omega_2, ..\Omega_{10}] \tag{3.21a}$$

$$y^k{}_n = c^k{}_n u^k{}_n,\ b' = b - \underline{C} \cdot A^{11} \cdot \underline{X}_0 \tag{3.21b}$$

and substitute it at equation (3.20):

$$\sum y_n^k \leq b' \tag{3.22}$$

Solving (3.21b) to $u^k{}_n$:

$$u_n^k = \frac{y_n^k}{c_n^k} \tag{3.23}$$

We substitute (3.23) to (3.18) and we have:

$$\max\left(\sum \omega_n^k \frac{y_n^k}{c_n^y} \right) \tag{3.24}$$

or equivalently

$$\max\left(\sum a_n^k \cdot y_n^k\right) \tag{3.25}$$

with $\alpha_n^k = \dfrac{\omega_n^k}{c_n^k}$

We substitute also (3.23) to (3.19) and we have:

$$0 \le \frac{y_n^k}{c_n^k} \le \bar{u}_n^k \Rightarrow 0 \le y_n^k \le c_n^k \cdot \bar{u}_n^k \Rightarrow 0 \le y_n^k \le \bar{y}_n^k \qquad (3.26)`$$

Therefore the linear programming problem becomes

$$\text{Maximize } \left(\sum a_n^k \cdot y_n^k\right) \tag{3.27a}$$

Subject to

$$\sum y_n^k \le b' \tag{3.27b}$$

$$0 \le y_n^k \le \bar{y}_n^k \tag{3.27c}$$

In order to maximize (3.27a) we see that the greater the coefficient a_n^k of y_n^k the more the objective function increases. Therefore if we put the coefficients a_n^k into descending order and we take the y_n^k corresponding to the largest coefficient equal to the maximum allowable value $\bar{y}_n^k$. If (3.27b) holds true we take the y_n^k corresponding second largest coefficient equal the maximum allowable value for this variable. We repeat this process until (3.27b) becomes invalid. At this point we set the value of the last variable y_n^k equal to the difference between b' and the sum of the values of all the previous variables. Finally all the remaining variables take "0" values. All the above are summarized to the next algorithm.

Sort $y_n^k, \bar{y}_n^k$ according to the size of a_n^k in descending order ie. $y_{n_1}^{k_1}, y_{n_2}^{k_2}, \ldots, y_{n_m}^{k_m}$ such that $a_{n_1}^{k_1} \ge a_{n_2}^{k_2} \ge \ldots \ge a_{n_m}^{k_m}$

Define $A(i) = \bar{y}_{n_1}^{k_1} + \bar{y}_{n_2}^{k_2} + \ldots + \bar{y}_{n_i}^{k_i}$ and find the integer "i" such that

$$A(i) \le b' < A(i+1)$$

The solution of the optimization problem is given by

$$y_{n_1}^{k_1} = \overline{y}_{n_1}^{k_1}, y_{n_2}^{k_2} = \overline{y}_{n_2}^{k_2}, \ldots, y_{n_i}^{k_i} = \overline{y}_{n_i}^{k_i}, y_{n_{i+1}}^{k_{i+1}} = b' - A(i), y_{n_{i+2}}^{k_{i+2}} = 0, \ldots, y_{n_m}^{k_m} = 0$$

Example. Solve the following optimization problem

Maximize $0.15y_1^1 + 0.2y_1^2 + 0.1y_2^1 + 0.25y_2^2$

Subject to

$$y_1^1 + y_1^2 + y_2^1 + y_2^2 \le 90$$
$$0 \le y_1^1 \le 50$$
$$0 \le y_1^2 \le 30$$
$$0 \le y_2^1 \le 20$$
$$0 \le y_2^2 \le 50$$

To solve this problem we first sort $y_n^k, \overline{y}_n^k$ according to the coefficients of the objective function ie. $y_2^2, y_1^2, y_1^1, y_2^1$ and 50, 30, 50, 20. Secondly we calculate *A(i)*ie*A(1)=50, A(2)=50+30=80, A(3)=80+50=130, A(4)=140+20=150.* Since A(2)=80<90<A(3)=130, the solution is given by:

$$y_1^1 = 50$$
$$y_1^2 = 30$$
$$y_2^1 = 90 - 80 = 10$$
$$y_2^2 = 0$$

Open Loop Solution – Case Study

In an open loop method, the control variables of the dynamic system are the input variables. We set the initial conditions of the system and then we control the input variables using the dynamic system by changing the initial values. Since the control variables are represented by the amount of new loans from each credit category, initially we define the constraints of the inputs, i.e. we set the maximum and minimum value of control variable from each rating category.

Simulating the dynamic model, we study the behavior of loan portfolio and moreover we examine important indices and critical ratios of the portfolio. A significant index of the loan portfolio is the ratio of the return over the probability to default for each rating category.

The dynamic system stresses all the categories of loans in order to get the maximum profit and simultaneously the minimum bad credit ratio. Simulating the dynamic behavior of the loan portfolio, we see what loan categories are stressed by the system and what quantitative results are derived. We conclude that the loan categories with high profit ratio are stressed by the system to the maximum values, while the categories with low profit ratio are stressed to the minimum values. This is happened because the amounts of loans with low profit ratio are non-profit categories, and since we are looking for the maximum value of profit, the dynamic system set then to minimum value.

The following graph illustrates the relation between profit and capital. The main concept is that additional capital causes additional risk that can be taken and therefore additional profit. However, above the certain threshold, it is not possible to increase the profit because we reach the capacity of the bank, since the amount of new loans is bounded.

On the contrary, in this case, if we include cost of capital, the additional capital will cause additional cost that cannot be balanced from additional growth. Thus, after the capacity threshold is reached, additional capital will cause the profit to decline.

Initially, it is observed that as the capital increases, the profit increases as well. However, there is a value of the capital in which the system cannot further improve results. At this point any increase in capital doesn't result greater profit.

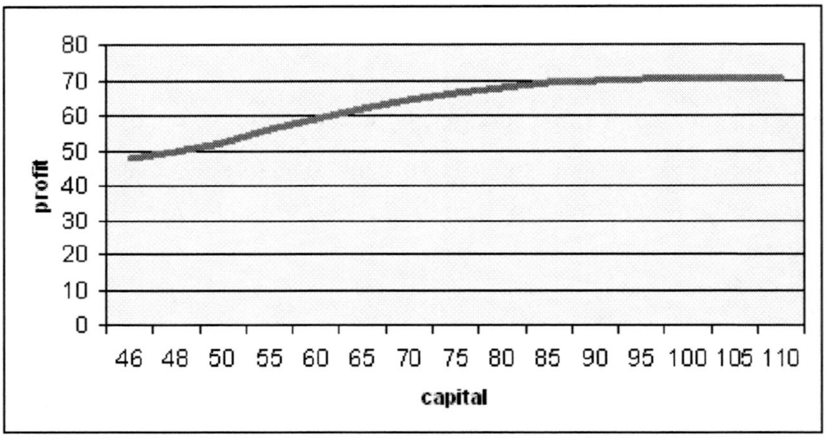

Generally, the dynamic system tends to set the amount of loans in categories with high profit to risk ratio to the maximum values at the beginning of time period. This occurs because the loans in those categories have greater profit ratio than the other categories.

Rating	Profit to risk ratio
AAA	1.47%
AA	1.07%
A	0.78%
BBB	0.61%
BB	0.58%
B	0.46%
CCC	0.78%

Initially where the amount of capital is low, the system set the amount of loans with high profit to risk ratio, i.e. the first two categories, to the maximum values for the first 5-6 months, and moreover, the last category of loans with high low profit to risk ratio to the maximum value but only for 1 month. As the value of capital increases, the grant of loans with high profit to risk ratio, i.e. in that case the first 3 categories, is in the maximum value for a longer time period. Furthermore, the amount of loans belongs to the highest category is set to its maximum value for the next 3-4 months. With even higher value of capital, the amounts of loans, which belong to categories high profit to risk ratio, are set to their maximum values for the entire simulated period. And because of the high capital capacity, the system set the amount of loans with risk and profit ration to the maximum values. Finally, we find that there is a maximum value for profit, which means that any further increase in capital doesn't result higher profit. In that case, the amount of loans with high profit ratio is at its maximum value, and as the simulated time goes, the amount from all categories are set to their maximum values, without affecting the profit.

CONCLUSION

Two methods of representing and budgeting the credit risk of a loan portfolio were presented. Both approaches were based on dynamical systems and control theory methodologies. The management of the bank may examine the results and use them in order to shape its credit and collection policy and determine profitability and provisioning.

Considering the results of the open loop method, an important conclusion derived from the simulation of the dynamical system is the determinant role of capital capacity. In the beginning where the capital is low, the system chooses mainly the loans that belong to the categories with low risk. While when the capital increases, the system sets the amount of loans with higher risk to its maximum value, provided the profit to risk relation is satisfactory.. The important factor that determines the risk exposure of the loan portfolio is the capital. The capital determines the amount of risk that the financial institution can undertake.

One general conclusion is that the models developed here, are generic, and can be used for the study of any loan portfolio. Using the methodology the decision maker can determine the credit policy that maximizes the profit of the loan portfolio and keeps the basic risk indices within acceptable limits.

REFERENCES

Araten, M., M. Jacobs, Jr., P. Varshey, C. R. Pellegrino, 2004, An internal ratings migration study, *The RMA Journal* v.86 no.7, 90-95.

Campbell, T.S and J.K Dietrich, 1983, The determinants of default on insured conventional residential mortgage loans, *Journal of Finance* 38, 1569-1581.

Crouhy, M., D. Galai and R. Mark, 2000, A comparative analysis of current credit risk models, *Journal of Banking and Finance* 24, 59-117.

Cyert, R.M, H.J Davidson and G.L Thompson, 1962, Estimation of the allowance for doubtful accounts by Markov Chains, *Management Science* 8, 287-303.

Del Angel, G.F., J.M. Diez-Canedo and E.P. Gorbea, 1998, A discrete Markov chain model for valuing loan portfolios. The case of Mexican loan sales, *Journal of Banking and Finance* 22, 1457-1480.

Kosmidou, K. and C., Zopounidis, 2001, Bank Asset Liability Management Techniques: An overview, C., Zopounidis, P. M. Pardalos, G. Baourakis (Eds.), Fuzzy Set Systems in Management and Economy, *World Scientific Publishers*, 139-150.

Kosmidou, K. and C., Zopounidis, 2002, Amultiobjective methodology for bank asset liability management, P. Pardalos, V. Tsitsiringos (Eds.), Fiancial Engineering, e-Commerce and Supply Chain, *Kluwer Academic Publishers*, 139-150.

Lando, D., 2004, Credit Risk Modeling, Theory and Applications, Princeton Series in Finance, Princeton University Press.

Lawrence, E.C., L.D Smith and M. Rhoades, 1992, An analysis of default risk in mobile home credit, *Journal of Banking and Finance* 16, 299-312.

Ong, M.K., 2000, Internal credit risk models, Capital Allocation and Performance Measurement, Risk Books, Risk Publications.

Scherer B., 2004, Portfolio Construction and Risk Budgeting, Risk Books.

Servigny, A. D., and O. Renault, 2004, Measuring and Managing Credit Risk, McGraw-Hill Professional.

Sethi S. P. and G.L. Gerald, 2000, Optimal Control Theory, Applications to Management Science and Economics, Springer.

Smith Douglas L. and Lawrence Edward C., 1995, Forecasting losses on a liquidating long-term loan portfolio, *Journal of Banking and Finance* 19, 959-985.

Sobehart, J. and S. Keenan, 2004, Modeling ratings migration for credit risk capital and loss provisioning calculations, *The RMA Journal* v.87 no.2, 74-81.

Soderstrum T. and Stoica P., 1988, System Identification, Prentice Hall, International series in system and Control Engineering.

Zenios, S., 1993, Financial Optimization, Cambridge University Press.

In: Computational Techniques for Banking and Risk Management ISBN: 978-1-62618-522-7
Editors: C. Zopounidis and M. Doumpos

Chapter 2

MONEY LAUNDERING (ML) POLICIES IN THE GREEK BANKING SECTOR AND PERSPECTIVES RELATED TO AN EFFECTIVE CONFRONTATION FRAMEWORK

***Christos Lemonakis*[*, 1], *Michalia Kadianaki*[2], and *Constantin Zopounidis*[3]**

[1]Department of Production Engineering and Management, Technical University of Crete, Chania, Greece

[2]Business Economics, Finance and Banking, Department of Economics, University of Portsmouth, Portland Street, Portsmouth, UK

[3]Department of Production Engineering and Management, Technical University of Crete, Financial Engineering Laboratory, Chania, Greece

ABSTRACT

Purpose - This paper aims to analyze Money Laundering (ML) policies in the Greek Banking Sector. It identifies and scrutinizes the causes that led to the implementation of policies against ML and it analyses the confrontation framework used in Greek banks. The intention of this research is to reveal the weaknesses of the national and global policies against ML and to find out perspectives related to an effective confrontation framework. Thus, there are suggestions of appropriate characteristics in strengthening the national and international financial system against the ML phenomenon.

Originality/value – The paper's value lies in presenting the Greek regulatory framework against ML, providing available data on investigations on the spot and sanctions enforced to Greek banking institutions during the period 2006 to 2007.

Keywords: Greek Banking Sector, Money Laundering, Policies

---

[*] Email: culemon2004@yahoo.gr.

1. INTRODUCTION

According to the daily terminology and experience, Money Laundering (ML) is all that actions and procedures, the practices or omissions that deliberately happen with the purpose of disguising and transforming by any means or methods the identity of the illegally acquired "dirty" money, so that it gets the desired legitimacy, in order to look like it was acquired or that it comes from a legal cause or origin (Tragakis, 1996).

The phenomenon of money laundering hasn't come up the last years, not even the last century. According to Stenimahitis C. (2002), the hiding of legal and illegal wealth has its origin even earlier, having a history of 3.000 years ago. The historian Sterling Seagrave, in his book "Lords of Rim", describes that, even before 1000 B.C., traders in China were hiding their fortune, out of fear that the governments would bag the wealth they had gathered through trading. The techniques Seagrave describes –conversion of money into easily transportable valuable elements, export of cash out of the country, "overvaluation" for emigration of capital - are also used up to a point nowadays as well.

The term "money laundering" seems that comes from the United States during the decade of 1920s (Lilley P., 2003). Gangs of criminals at that time were trying to do the same thing they are trying to do today: to dissociate the product of their criminal actions from the same criminal actions. In order to achieve that, they were setting up businesses that had very high profits in cash, like for example laundries or launderettes or car washers and they were mixing the legal earnings with their illegal earnings. This way, they had a great alibi for the possession of great amounts of cash. According to Tragakis G. E. (1998), "cash" gives the desirable and necessary anonymity in most forms of criminal action, while it is also the most usual mean of exchange in smuggling and in retail drug trafficking, in the "markets" or "pitches" of big and small towns. So, while today the term "money laundering" is metaphorically connected with the cleaning and purification of "dirty money", it seems that its origin has to do with the "washing" and "laundry" businesses of the United States of 1920s.

Nowadays, ML has taken tremendous dimensions. With the evolution of technology, millions of U.S. Dollars can go across the whole planet in less than a second (Lilley P., 2003), while more than two trillion U.S. Dollars are transferred worldwide every day. Organized crime takes the advantages of the rapid development in information technology, globalization, the almost unimpeded money transferring ability, the inexistence of the national boundaries thanks to the modern payment systems and the Internet while it has extended its "activities", not only to drug trafficking – which initially was the main source of income – but to other sectors as well. And as a result, the rapid increase of its income which calls to be legalized somehow.

Cyber Laundering (CL) signifies the transition of ML into the cyberspace via information technologies and the Internet. Moreover, the ongoing evolution of computer systems creates security issues that may make these systems prone to exploitation by launderers (Granville, 2003).

Indicatively, according to Human Development Report of 1999 of the United States (Lilley P., 2003), the income of organized crime sums up to 1.5 trillion U.S.D. annually. On March of 1998, Dow Jones News reported that ML comes between the 2% and the 5% of the World Gross Product. At a national level, it indicatively mentions the following:

- In Great Britain, Bank of England estimated in 1994 that 2.4 billion GBP were laundered every year.
- In Switzerland, the Ministry of Economics confirmed in 1998 that the country was involved in the laundering of 500 billion USD annually.
- In Greece, the former President of Money Laundering Committee, Counter Public Prosecutor Judge of a Court of Appeal Mr P. Nikoloudis (Kalliagopoulou F. and Tsioutsia N., 2001), reported that in 2000 there were attached 4.3 billion drachmas coming from the effort to legalize income from illegal actions while in 1999 there were attached 2.5 billion drachmas (increasing tension). In 2002 there were attached about 23.5 million Euro (about 8 billion drachmas), according to the report of the Institution and Transparency Committee (Ravanos A., 2003). However, in 2006 (FATF/OECD, 2007), the Greek Ministry of Economy and Finance prepared a study consists of four types of illegal activity: illegal prostitution, drug trafficking, and cigarette and alcohol smuggling. In that study, the estimated gross amount earned in 2000 from those four forms of criminal activity is approximately €1.6 billion (1% GDP in 2000).

Although there is a tremendous increasing tension in money laundering year by year, it is noticed that the above mentioned amounts were supposed small compared to the real amount of capital that is laundered.

The most impressing characteristic in the research of ML phenomenon is the inventiveness of criminals. The whole system displays a remarkable dynamic: the moment that the authorities find out an application of "money laundering", the same time, somewhere else by someone else, a new form of action is found out.

The scope of this research is to find the deficient or/and not proper application of the existing anti-money laundering policies in the Greek Banking System. Furthermore, to search for the optimum perspectives of improving the money laundering sources monitoring systems and facilitating the more progressive collaboration amongst the miscellaneous anti-money laundering organizations in local and international level.

The rest of the paper is structured as follows: the Methodology section reviews the existing legislation in national and international level and its implementation from Greek banks. The section Money Laundering Framework gives the definition and in depth characteristics of ML phenomenon (i.e. stages, sources, off-shore companies), along with its implications worldwide. Awareness against money laundering phenomenon section gives important steps towards the realization of the need to take particular measures for dealing with money laundering in national and international level. Application of the policies against money laundering in the Greek Banking Sector section describes the Greek regulatory framework on the prevention and suppression of ML through standing laws and Government Gazettes. Enrollment of the Greek regulatory framework sections presents the framework against ML in a major Greek banking group, that of "Piraeus Bank". Investigations on the spot and sanctions enforced from Bank of Greece section gives relevant data for the Greek banking institutions during the period 2006 to 2007. Conclusion section presents where do we stand against ML in national and international level and in what ways should we be able to improve the confrontation framework.

2. Determination of the Problem of Money Laundering and the International Experience

The legalization of income coming from illegal actions is an integral part of the evolution and transformation of modern societies and it expresses the effort of modern organized crime to "clean up the dirty money" their actions bring in. The level of the amounts of money and the constant character of that procedure, demonstrates the magnitude of the risk the economical systems are facing.

Many kinds of criminals followed money laundering phenomenon that came from various illegal actions, during the history. But we shouldn't ignore the fact that nowadays, the criminality levels have ejected and apart from drug traffickers, there are also many categories of criminals and crimes that face the need to find ways to legalize their incomes.

After the internationalization of economies and the abrogation of controlling of capital transfer, organized crime was tremendously facilitated to find methods for money laundering while on the other hand the efforts for finding and punishing that phenomenon were obstructed.

The realization of the complexity, the extension of the problem and its implications in the social and political stability of nations and in the solvency and security of credit institutions, has led the international community to intervene for the adoption of joint and particular proceedings and policies.

The main of these interventions are the following:

- The "Basel Committee Principles" since December of 1988, with the purpose of the establishment of new templates in the transaction behavior of the banks.[1]
- The "United Nations Agreement" in December 20th, 1988, that enforced the contracting nations to enact criminal penalties in cases of legalization of income from criminal actions. (United Nations, "United Nations Convention Against Illicit Traffic in Narcotic Drugs and Psychotropic Substances, 1988".[2]
- The "Strasbourg Agreement of the member nations of the European Committee" in November 8th, 1990, where the contracting parties have the obligation to introduce in their internal legislation stipulations for the suppression and punishment of "money laundering". [3]
- The decision for the establishment of "Financial Action Task Force" (F.A.T.F.) from the seven biggest industrial countries and the European Community Committee in July 15th, 1989, with the purpose of preventing the legalization of income from illegal actions.[4]
- The Guideline 308/91 of the European Commission, that obligates the member nations to care for the prohibition in their land of the legalization of income from illegal actions.
- The Law 3691/08 that incorporates the Directive 2005/60/EC of the European Parliament and the Council, as well as Commission Directive 2006/70/EC for

[1] Basel Committee-BIS "Money laundering and terrorist financing".
[2] http://www.unodc.org/pdf/convention_1988_en.pdf.
[3] http://eur-lex.europa.eu/LexUriServ/LexUriServ.do?uri=CELEX:52004PC0559(01):EL:HTML.
[4] FATF, "History of the FATF".

Greece. Also, law 3691/2008 is the third Anti-money laundering law passed in Greece, after laws 2331/95 and 3424/05, which had transposed Directives 91/308/EEC and 2001/97/EC, respectively.

3. Methodology

The methodology used in this paper for the approach of ML phenomenon is the presentation of its different aspects according to the current banking experience, since that is the main source not only for the suspicious transactions but also for the policies applied against the problem in Greece as well.

Theory comes from the material gathered from different organizations and banking institutions and especially from Bank of Greece. Existing bibliography and studies on this matter are also taken into account, but the main point of the theory has to do with the policies that are used from banking institutions against ML.

The method used, concerns the quotation of the existing legislation in national and international level and the implementation from the Greek banks, of circulars and enactments of Bank of Greece for the prevention and suppression of ML phenomenon.

Finally, there is an effort for recording the way of action of the different ML nets and the way the numerous organizations against ML cooperate in national and international level for the confrontation of the problem.

4. ML Framework

4.1. Definition of ML

ML is the legalization of income from any criminal action through the financial system. The purpose of most of the criminal actions is to create individual or joint earnings. ML is the procedure used in order to hide the illegal origin of the capital acquired and to change its identity as if it is shown that it was acquired by a legal source (Tragakis G., 1995).

The term "criminal action" by which it is possible to be acquired the ill gotten property that is wanted to be legalized, goes to the punishable acts that are determined by the Laws No 2331/1995 and No 3424/2005 and No 3691/2008 of the Hellenic Republic. Some of the most important are the following:

- Crimes that are anticipated by the law for combating proliferation of narcotic drugs
- Crimes that are anticipated by the law as far as weapons, ammunition etc. is concerned
- The crime of robbery
- The crime of extortion
- The crime of abduction
- The special cases of theft
- The illicit appropriation of articles of particularly high value
- The illicit appropriation involving abuse of confidence

- The fraud resulting in particularly large damage
- The commitment of fraud as an occupation or habitually or under circumstances proving that the perpetrator is particularly risky
- The illicit trading in antiquities
- The theft of ship cargo of particularly high value
- The removal and transplantation of human tissues and organs
- The embezzlement against the government
- The crimes out of ionizing radiation
- The crimes on games of chance and other games

Money launderers, for gain or for the purpose of concealing or disguising the illicit origin of the property or assisting or abetting any person who is involved in criminal activity, purchase, conceal, receive as a pledge, acquire possession or in any way become beneficiaries, convert or transfer to another person any property which has resulted from such activity.

They can also give witness or report to any judiciary or other authorities, intentionally disguise or conceal the true nature, source, disposition, movement or location of the property, knowing that such property is derived from criminal activity. Finally, they can establish or acquire an undertaking or set up an organization for the purpose of committing one of the above mentioned offences. Most of ML actions pass through the banking and financial institutions, leasing companies, factoring companies, venture capital companies and exchanges.

The responsible authority in Greece, that is in charge of supervising and controlling these institutions, is Bank of Greece. But one can also meet ML actions in insurance companies and other financial organizations for which the responsible authority is the Hellenic Capital Market Commission (HCBC).

4.2. The Implications of ML PHenomenon

Countries with increasing and developing financial centers are especially vulnerable in ML phenomenon. Offenders take the advantage of differences between the confrontation methods against ML phenomenon from country to country. That is why they transfer their networks to countries and financial systems with deficient and ineffective countermeasures.

If the phenomenon cannot be kept under control, the social and political cost is and will be very serious. Organized crime can intervene in financial organizations, taking the control of wild sectors of the economy, bribing systematically even functionaries, judicial authorities and political authorities as well. That can result in weakening social building and democratic statutes of modern society.

ML phenomenon, because of its origin from criminal actions, enlarges and supplies corruption in political and banking system. A determined fight against that phenomenon has great importance on the promotion of democracy, the legal system and the human rights (Gilmore C. William, 1999). ML restrictions could be a fatal blow against the organized crime, since the utilization of ill-gotten gains obtained from such actions would tend to get minimized.

4.3. ML Stages

ML takes place especially through the following (Tragakis G., 1990):

- Transactions in cash
- Bank accounts and safe deposit boxes
- Exchanges
- Insurance companies
- Capital markets
- Estate agencies
- Casinos
- Commercial transactions
- Foreign countries called “tax heavens”
- Offshore companies
- Bank executives involved in criminal actions
- Bank credit of loans

Cash money offers anonymity in most forms of criminal actions. That fact gives rise to the need of continuous hiding of the real origin of capital gathered from such actions, the maintenance of controlling of that capital as well as the need for transforming it.

The three stages of “ML” during which numerous transactions take place are the following:

Stage I: The stage of “placement”

The most usual way of legalizing “dirty” money is by depositing the packets of money, usually in small nominal value, in one or more financial institutions or by exchanging that money with objects of high value, like jewels, works of art, etc. This practice consists of the first stage of a complicated system of financial transactions, which is the most crucial and the easiest to be located in “ML” action and for the further surveillance of the whole procedure. The physical transportation of cash and its deposit to a bank consists of the weakest point of the organized crime during the “ML” procedure.

Stage II: The stage of “layering”

Since the income from criminal actions is introduced in the financial system, the second stage of “layering” takes place. In that stage, money launderer makes a series of conversions or movements of amounts in order to send them away from their source. The amounts can be followed through markets and sales of depositing, investing on insurance products or they can be netted through a series of money transfers from account to account in different banks worldwide. That use of scattered bank accounts is being used and is especially spread in countries that do not steadily cooperate against ML phenomenon, like the Caribbean countries, small island countries of the Pacific and Indian Ocean, even also small European countries. The purpose of this stage is the misleading of inspecting authorities, the alteration of checking evidence and the supply of anonymity of the beneficiaries of bank accounts to their advantage.

Stage III: The stage of "integration"

In this stage, the apparent legalization of the ill-gotten wealth is succeeded. Having effectively passed the ill-gotten gains through the first two phases of "ML" procedure and having changed their real identity, they are introduced again in the financial network, under the cloak of the normal business investments, through the investments on real estate, the establishing of new businesses, the purchase of works of art, the donations and charities, the entrance in sections with mass effect like professional athletics, etc.

4.4. ML Sources

A few years ago, outlaws were worrying about how they would appear in front of the counter of the bank carrying whole suitcases full of banknotes, without raising suspicions to the bank emploees. Nowadays things have become even more complicated and of course that doesn't imply the usual and seemingly simple method of "ML" through purchasing real estate. Indicatively, there are some –least- brainwave methods of "ML" that became widely known:

- "ML" through lottery and lottery coupons (Bougatsou A., 2005). In practice, it goes in the following way: some winning lotteries or lottery coupons are bought from the real winning owners (unambiguously against a higher price) and in continue the coupons in question are deposited by their new owners who receive the payment of the earnings and simultaneously a legal certification of the earnings (through which the capital is legalized since they are presented as earnings from lottery or lottery coupons).
- "ML" through casinos (Nikolopoulos G., 2001). It concerns businesses that accept cash and not checks (because of the existence of the risk of bringing bad checks). This way, a supposed player can visit a casino, bringing a large amount of cash, buy chips, play, lose a short portion of his money, stop and ask the staff of the casino in charge to give him the remaining of his initiative capital in the form of a bank check (this way, the initially illegal capital that was brought is legalized).
- "ML" through the Stock Exchange (Kotsis V., 2005). The practice is simple, although the first step is considered the most difficult: the basic thing is the code to be opened and the first buy of shares to be made (usually, companies that increase their stock fund with gratis shares are preferred, with the intention, the final number of shares that will be liquidated, to be higher). In continue, the aspiring "launderer" carries out a large number of transactions, in order to generate problems in a possible investigation of the authorities and to make it difficult for the first transaction to be found. Afterwards, the launderer aims to "break" the capital in many codes, in different securities companies and in continue he proceeds to liquidations: so, this way, he ensures the "origin" of his capitals.
- "ML" through the trade of antiquities and auctions (Antoniou D., 2006). Antiquities – generally originating from smuggled excavations – are usually sold and bought during auctions from the same person, who mysteriously appears as an anonymous collector (as the first contributing member) and as an offshore company (as the second contributing member).

4.5. Off-Shore Companies and ML

The biggest part of "dirty money" gathered from illegal actions is in cash. The main three scenarios, recorded out by pursuing authorities and the officials against "ML" observations, as far as the procedures and the way of action of the "launderers" is concerned, for the physical transportation of the dirty money, are the following:

- The first scenario is the one where the cash stays in the country where it is gathered and people are found, that do not belong to the network, but systematically are occupied with the "laundering" on behalf of money holders and owners. These people are "beyond" any suspicion and they are carefully chosen, taking especially into account their professional activities that from their nature should gather and transfer amounts of cash every day. Of course, those people are informed about this action and they quite often deposit in one or more banks either small amounts or higher amounts of money. That money in a following phase is transferred in other countries' banks, being presented as products of exports or loans.
- The second scenario is the one where the cash is not transferred abroad, nor is "broken" into smaller amounts, but it is deposited in big amounts without its origin being suspicious. This case refers to countries where the banking secrecy exists in its rigorous form and ML business hasn't been penalized.
- Finally, the third scenario is the one where the cash is identically transferred with different methods (by boats, crafts, airplanes, etc.) from the country where it is gathered out of illegal actions to a destination that is usually a tax "heaven". The money is deposited in a bank in that country and that is the way the "laundering" through the international banking system begins.

Although globalization has provided the potential of financial development, on the other hand it has also given tremendous capabilities for the expansion of organized crime without having supranational mechanisms to confront it. The whole issue is a matter of each nation separately. Offshore companies offer a variety of services that are not normally available in other countries. These services include secret bank accounts, establishment of counterfeit companies and foreign trusts. That is why money launderers are easy to exist in those companies. The countries that are attractive to ML have at least one of the following characteristics (Douvis P., 2003):

- Fragile financial infrastructures with private banking systems that are in the first development stages or that are capable to be bought in such a low cost that make them just available with the possession of a small controlling proportion.
- Lack of substantial and special regulation as far as ML is concerned.
- Not well trained and not well equipped personnel of controlling and of banking services, on the tracing and on succeeded prosecution of offences that have to do with ML.

In Greece, according to the law 2238/1994, "Offshore companies are meant the companies that have their headquarters in a foreign country and according to their legislation they are exclusively activated in other countries and they are in favor of an especially favorable tax treatment".

5. Awareness against MLPhenomenon

Whoever studies the many-pleated ML phenomenon in depth comes to the conclusion that there is a huge menace to the financial and social structure of a country. The examples of Italy, Russia and other countries in Central and South America are indicative. According to a statistical study of the I.M.F. on the last decade, it was calculated that amounts of money on the level of 700 billion dollars are legalized through ML, being increased in a pace of 10% annually. One could include in that amounts the "dirty money" that comes from sources that are directly involved with the political corruption, the illegal commissions, the great tax evasion, the illegal export of currency, the properties of the third-world dictators and the wealth that was gathered by the strong leadership of the previous political and financial form of the government of the East Europe, e.t.c. (Tragakis, 1996). During 1980s, especially in the world of banks, it was realized that institutions and rules of behavior with a long time effect and a great tradition, like the bank secrecy, come often in opposition with the social interest and that is the reason they should be newly defined taking into account the modern conditions and views. It was noticed that inactivity includes the risk that banks could be stamped as shelters of criminals and that their interests are identical with the organized crime and that is why they do not show any sensitivity on the fighting against the curse of drugs, the international terrorism and other serious criminal offences.

Another important step towards the realization of the need to take particular measures was the "Manifestation of Principles" that was adopted by the Basel Committee and who officially formulated the main principles on dealing behavior that should be followed by the banks today in the whole world in order to convince everyone that they are not used as asylums for criminals and as ML machines (Tragakis, 1996). For all these reasons, Basel Committee concluded that the responsible authorities on supervision and controlling of the banking system owe to realize that they also have the additional general role to encourage the observanceof the new templates of professional behaviour in the financial institutions. The formulation of the professional ethics has helped enough until today, on the realization of the need to take legal measures against ML in national level and especially in countries where important financial institutions work in.

6. Application of the Policies against ML in the Greek Banking Sector

6.1. The Greek Regulatory Framework against ML

The Greek regulatory framework on the prevention and suppression of ML is being consisted of regulations included in Laws 1990/1991 (Sheet of the Greek Government Gazette A' 193/16.12.1991, articles 1-13), 2655/1998 (Sheet of the Greek Government Gazette A' 264/1.12.1998, articles 1-44) and 3034/2002 (Sheet of the Greek Government Gazette A' 168/19.7.2002, articles 1-28), the Law 2331/1995 (Sheet of the Greek

Government Gazette A' 173/24.8.1995, articles 1-12) which was amended and complemented by the Law 3424/2005 (Sheet of the Greek Government Gazette A' 305/13.12.2005, articles 1-14), and the Law 3691/2008 (Sheet of the Greek Government Gazette A' 166/05.08.2008, articles 1-56), and the relative administration's circulars and instructions of Bank of Greece.

- By the law 1990/1991 the Vienna Agreement of 1988 was confirmed.
- By the law 2655/1998 the Strasbourg Treaty of 1990 was confirmed.
- By the law 3034/2002 the United Nations' International Treaty of 1999, for the suppression of terrorism financing was confirmed.
- The law 2331/1995 embodies in the Greek Law the regulations of the Guideline 308/1991 of the European Community while the Law 3424/2005 embodies in the Greek Law the Guideline 2001/1997 of the European Parliament and the Committee against the use of the financial system for ML.
- By the law 2331/1995, Bank of Greece is assigned as the responsible authority for the implementation of its regulations on the financial institutions, leasing companies, factoring companies, exchanges and intermediate services companies for money transfer. They also determine the crimes included in the term of criminal activity as well as the penalties imposed on the outlaws and it was established, by the article 7 (Law 2331/1995), the constitution of a committee whose task would be gathering, evaluate and investigate the information transferred to them from the financial institutions and the other financial organizations for suspicious transactions for ML.
- By the law 3424/2005 the financial system is more armed against its usage for ML and terrorist financing, the implementation of its regulations is also enforced to other sectors and professions, the term of basic crimes is expanded, the responsibilities of the Committee of the article 7 of the Law 2331/1995 are strengthened, penal punishment is rationalized, the Ministry of National Economy is assigned as the central coordinating authority for the prevention and suppression of ML phenomenon and the obligations of the banks and the other financial organizations and their supervising authorities are marked out.
- By the law 3691/2008, there is reinforcing and improving the legislative framework on the prevention and suppression of ML and terrorist financing. This new law introduces inter alia the Anti-Money Laundering and Anti-Terrorist Financing (AML/CTF) Commission, supervised by the Minister of Economy and Finance with its main task to collect, investigate and evaluate any information forwarded to it by the obligated persons and other public or private bodies, on suspicious or unusual transactions or activities or business, professional or commercial relationships linked to ML, and carries out special on-site inspections, in situations that it considers to be serious, in co-operation with competent authorities or any other public authority.

The new law transposes into legislation the provisions of Directive 2005/60/EC of the European Parliament and of the Council "on the prevention of the use of the financial system for the purpose of ML and terrorist financing" (Official Journal of the European Union L 309/15/25.11.2005) and certain provisions of Directive 2006/70/EC of the European Commission (Official Journal of the European Union L 214/29/4.8.2006) and replaces relevant provisions of Law 2331/1995 (Government Gazette 173 A).

Under this law there is also the decision No 281/5/17.3.2009 of the Banking and Credit Committee of the Bank of Greece which aims at the specialization of the provisions of Law 3691/2008 for credit and financial institutions who are supervised by the Bank of Greece, favoring appropriate typology of unusual and suspicious transactions in relation to the ML.

6.2. Enrollment of the Greek Regulatory Framework against ML: The Case of "Piraeus Bank"

Trying to find out whether the Greek regulatory framework against ML is being implemented in the internal regulation of the Greek banks, though the gathering of relevant information is quite difficult due to restrictions on publishing relevant information for ML issues, the research takes into account elements and characteristics in compliance policy against ML taken from a major Greek commercial Bank, "Piraeus Bank". The material collected comes to the following conclusions:

- First of all the bank has got a great organization as far as controlling, updating and applying the compliance system in the group. They have a General Director of the Corporate Governance who is above the Chief Compliance Officer and the Deputy Director as well. All of them are above two groups: the AML/CTF Group and the Compliance Group. The first group, AML/CTF Group, gives information about the records of the customers when it is needed for an investigation and generally they apply the AML/CTF policy of the bank. The second group, Compliance Group, works on the compliance of the bank with the regulatory framework against ML which is imposed by the responsible authorities of the country and for its implementation from the branches and subsidiaries of the Group.
- The compliance policy of the bank was in conformity with the regulations that are given from the responsible authorities of the country against ML. It follows the procedures in recognizing and identifying their customers; it implements the "risk – based approach" of ML and terrorist financing; they enforce the due diligence process for intermediaries, while it also keeps records and it gives orders as far as tracing, dealing and reporting suspicious transactions. The bank also has enacted a process of internal control and communication, while there is ongoing education and training in its personnel. It follows the essential procedures on electronic fund transfers, and provides the needed information to its regulatory authority (Bank of Greece).
- The bank is trying to enrich the given regulation, analyzing it with many specific details and in some cases it holds stricter framework than the intended one. For example, the bank does not rent safe deposit boxes but to their customers who must be well identified (Piraeus Bank, Group Compliance Department, "Compliance Policy of the Bank of Piraeus Group", 1st edition, May 2008).

However, taking "Piraeus Bank" as a model, it seems that banks in Greece do comply with the regulation framework imposed by the responsible authorities. So a subsequent question poses: If banks do comply with the imposed regulation against ML then why there is an increase in the amounts of money laundered?

A possible answer could be that money launderers are always finding ways to pass over the obstacles the banking system imposes by its regulation. Because of the big competition between banks, all of their employees are obliged to find ways to increase the earnings of their bank. That can result to not completely adhere to the regulation of the same bank against ML.

6.3. Investigations on the Spot and Sanctions Enforced from Bank of Greece

A more effective framework against ML could involve more often and severe investigations on the banks in terms of ML and impose huge fines and tough sanctions depending on the case. Maybe this way competition between banks could be reduced and banks will use more lawful means for their development.

According to the Basel Committee on Banking Supervision, whatever the legal position in different countries, the first and most important safeguard against money-laundering is the integrity of banks' own managements and their vigilant determination to prevent their institutions becoming associated with criminals or being used as a channel for ML (BCBS, 1988).

In Table 1 it's clear that during the period between 2005 and 2006 there was a decrease in the number of investigations on the spot from Bank of Greece while from 2006 to 2007 there was an increase. According to Bank of Greece Governor's Annual Report for 2007, the number of investigations on the spot cannot be considered as the only evidence of supervisory presence of Bank of Greece. Conversations with the authorized executives of the banks and the daily supervision for the progress of the banks are some crucial factors that help Bank of Greece to form an image timely, taking into account the special risk characteristics of each bank, and making sure its compliance with regulations in effect.

Table 1. Number of investigations on the spot from Bank of Greece

	2005	2006	2007
On banking institutions which concern:	240	200	201
Internal control – risk management	56	55	32
ML	152	97	129
Transparency of transactions	32	48	40
On Financing Institutions	20	23	8
Other Controls	136	101	131
General Total	396	324	340
from which:			
On branches out of Attica	152	164	106
On branches and subsidiaries abroad	6	6	13

Source: Bank of Greece, (2008).

In Table 2 it can be seen that from year 2006 to 2007 there is an increase on the amount in Euro from sanctions imposed from Bank of Greece to the banking institutions while fewer banks are found to have relative problems. This shows that more banks comply with the measures against ML and they do enforce them, but the banks that do not enforce them in practice are accused for big irregularities with great sanctions.

Bank of Greece has cut back expansion plans for banks that were found inadequate on their internal control systems. That is a sanction which is proven for its effectiveness. It has also utilized the potential to increase the minimum capital requirements of the banks.

Within 2007, the valuation of Greece from F.A.T.F. on the prevention and suppression of ML and terrorist financing had been completed. F.A.T.F. observations were quoted on their Assessment Report. In that report the relevant weaknesses of the Greek Financial System were marked and methods for the improvement of supervision framework were suggested (Bank of Greece, "Governor's Annual Report for 2007", 2008).

Table 2. Sanctions that were enforced from Bank of Greece, (Amounts in Euro)

Transparency in transactions			
	2006 (14 banks)	2007 (8 banks)	Total 2006–2007 (22 banks)
Interest - free deposits height	34, 373, 200	14, 400, 000	48, 773, 200
Total Cost (1)	859, 330	360, 000	1, 219, 330
Average Cost	42, 603	45, 000	43, 801
Least Cost (2)	3, 000	10, 000	-
Greatest Cost	77, 778	160, 000	-
ML			
	2006 (14 banks)	2007 (12 banks)	Total 2006-2007 (26 banks)
Interest - free deposits height	13, 413, 200	20, 200, 000	33, 613, 200
Total Cost (1)	335, 330	505, 000	840, 330
Average Cost	14, 436	42, 083	28, 260
Least Cost (2)	6, 108	20, 000	-
Greatest Cost	20, 804	75, 000	-
Calculated with the interest rate of the marginal funding (5%). Calculated with a cost of capital of 7%, the total cost of sanctions for the period 2006-2007 on transparency issues comes up to Euro 1, 707, 062, while on ML issues comes up to Euro 1, 176, 462. Under the principle of proportionality, some categories of penalties cannot exceed the limit of the relative category of the Law 2912/2001 as far as interest rates from compound interest is concerned (e.g. on delayed answers to the clients law determines width of penalties from Euro 2, 934.70 to 14, 673.51).			

Source: Bank of Greece, (2008).

Conclusion

The Erosive Influence of Organized Crime to the Society

ML reflects negatively to the capability of the governments to successfully apply measures for the fiscal and monetary policy. So, it is expected when an important part of financial values is controlled by the organized crime that the basic indexes of the financial activity lose their reliability as far as the configuration of a powerful financial policy is concerned.

The factors that lead the syndicates of the organized crime to their investing decisions are substantially different than that of the legal businesses. It is well known that these illegal companies are mainly used for facilitating ML, its recycling and the development of the criminal activity while the main factors that influence these decisions is their fear of leaving evidences of their identity as well as facilitating these transactions (Tragakis G., 1996).

In developed countries, reliability of the applied financial policy is heavily damaged when a part of the financial system is under the influence and control of the organized crime. The capital managed from the organized crime usually has a damaging influence on the social prosperity during a period when the investing decisions of private sector and the level of country's credit ability from international markets are significantly influenced from the length of the penetration and undermining from the organized nets of crime (Tragakis G., 1996). So, whatever advantages obtained by the inflow of suspicious origin capital are minimized or smashed.

However, the biggest threat from ML is located on the way the organized crime uses the huge amounts of capital they acquire for the corruption of the political-social system and the control of the financial activity of a state. It is observed that society and economy are divided as the legal businesses are not in position to compete with the businesses that belong or are controlled by the organized crime, since they do not pay taxes, they get the best jobs, they are not supervised as they should and in addition they use criminal ways in order to destroy the dynamic and competing competitors (Katsios S., 1998).

On the other hand, the real amount of money involved (Castle, A., 1999) may never be quantified, and this number cannot include sources of money from activities that – though criminal by most international standards – are ignored, hidden or even abetted by state actions. Of these activities, the most significant inter alia are public sector corruption, tax evasion and direct and open state involvement in the drug trade and other criminal economic activity.

International Economy and ML

The general progress of international economy has a causal link with ML. The biggest facility for the transfer of the ill gotten gains abroad is a problem not only to the country of origin of capital but to countries of destination of the capital as well. When the capital of organized crime enters in a country with the form of "investments", the immediate result is decomposition of the business environment, uncertainty and interference of many insurmountable obstacles in the development of those economies (Tragakis G., 1996).

Generally, Third-World Nations and countries have a big need for pulling in capital from abroad for the financing of their development programs and they do not have adequate legislation and mechanisms for the prevention and suppression of ML. For this reason and for others, fighting against that anti-social practice is linked with the promotion of financial progress and the abolition of poverty and unemployment.

As the organized crime enters all the time in different sectors of financial activity, as the universality of the financial system is given and the liberalization of the rules of its set-up, supervision and operation, as electronic fund transfer is nourishing nowadays, we are unavoidably led to the facilitation of the organized crime to legalize its ill gotten gains (Katsios S., 1998).

So, it is at least imperative to arm the financial system with any legal mean for the prevention and suppression of the above mentioned criminal activity. Today, more than ever, the function of the international financial system is threatened by the organized crime. Countries that accept the organized crime are mathematically led to financial destruction, undermining of institutions and of course to the establishment of governmental relations with corruption. This way they are immediately transformed into tax heavens dependant from organized crime gangs (Katsios S., 1998).

On the other hand, while the introduction of the risk- based approach has undoubtedly been an interesting regulatory step, the practical side to its implementation is still at a primary state. The concept of risk creates a level of ambiguity that is reflected at the difficulties of auditing any such risk- based approach, related to ML issues, as Demitis D, 2010 also supports.

General Conclusion-the Greek Case

The new law 3691/2008for the prevention and suppression of ML and terrorist financing is considered as more stringent and precise than its earlier ones. The new regulatory intervention in the financial system has a broader purpose than to prevent its use to commit financial crimes, as also Gortsos, C., 2009 describes. There is aimed at combating money laundering and terrorist financing, but also extended to issues like network and branches security, fraud prevention in electronic payments, as well as dealing with imposition of the capital market. With the new framework more occupational sectors are involved in the effort for confronting this phenomenon. For example, lawyers, who did not have the obligation to give information to the responsible authorities about their clients, when they were involved with ML, because of the secrecy of their job, with the new law they will not only have that obligation but they can also be accused for aiding and abetting criminals if they do not do so.

The incorporation in the legislation of Greece of recommendations from one of the most recognized international bodies in ML, the Financial Action Task Force (FATF) is a reality. But also, due to estimations made by the OECD (FATF) the total amount of ML in 2008 in Greece is up to 5 billion Euros, which represents the 2% of GDP of the country. So, there is a lot of work to be done to increasing the effectiveness of the ML framework as implemented by the country's banking institutions, especially during the coming period. A period with financial turbulences due to the debt crises the country goes through, with the intense need for capital adequacy.

The most interesting conclusion is the fact that after so many years since the enforcement in Greece of the basic law against the legalization of income that comes from criminal actions, the authorities that are occupied with this issue have realized the following:

- There are many potential risks because of the acceptance of transactions with "dirty money"
- The damaging consequences in individual as well as in national level of this illegal action
- The provisional profitability of the acceptance and of transactions with "dirty or black money" for the whole national financial system and
- The international consequences from the exposure of such actions, since a very powerful and effective mechanism has been developed in international level for the harsh punishment of the phenomenon.

Another fact is that the effectiveness of the Greek banking system to combat the phenomenon of ML passes through proper and updated staff training in banking institutions. The training is a key factor in keeping the rules and ML procedures on track in a banking system, as Thanou E. and Foundoukidis A. (2008) also describe in their research.

The restrictions of this paper come along with the fact that the results of ML are not demonstrated easily to the public, under the limits of the essential discretion and the protection of the people who mention such transactions. There are also restrictions related to the methods used in order to detect and trace suspicious transactions since the "specialists" in these transactions take good care in order not to be traced and neither revealed their techniques.

REFERENCES

Baldwin F. N. (2004) "The Financing of terror in the age of the internet: willful blindness, greed or a political statement?" *Journal of ML Control, Vol. 8 No 2.*

Committee on Banking Regulations and Supervisory Practices "Banking secrecy and international co-operation in banking supervision", 2nd revision, BS/81/16.

Castle Allan (1999) "Working Paper No. 2: Asia Pacific money laundering flows and trends", International Centre for Criminal Law Reform and Criminal Justice Policy.

Demetis D. (2010) "Technology and Anti-Money Laundering. A Systems Theory and Risk-Based Approach", Edward Elgar Publishing, Inc.

Thanou E. and Foundoukidis A. (2008) "Money laundering: addressing the issue in the context of the Greek banking sector", Hellenic Open University.

Granville, J. (2003) 'Dot. *Con*: the dangers of cyber crime and a call for proactive solutions', *Australian Journal of Politics and History*, 49 (1), 102–9.

Katsios S. (1998) "ML. The international financial system geopolitics: The phenomenon of legalizing income from illegal actions", Athens, Sakkoulas.

Kerwer Dieter (2005) "Rules that many use: standards and global regulation" *Governance*18 (4): 611-632.

Lilley Peter (2003) "Dirty Dealing", 2nd edition, U.K. and U.S.A., Kogan Page.

Piraeus Bank, Group Compliance Department (2008, May) "Compliance Policy of the Bank of Piraeus Group", 1st edition.
Shelagh Heffernan (2005) "Modern Banking", John Wiley and Sons, Ltd.
Stenimahitis C. (2002) "ML", Seminar, Hellenic Bank Association.
Tragakis G. (1995, Quarter B) "The law against ML and the obligations of the banking and financial organizations", Issue 2, HBA Release.
Tragakis G. (1990, 3rd Quarter) "What it is and how ML happens", Issue 29-30, HBA Report.
Tragakis G. E. (1996) "ML", Law Library Publications.
Vlcek William (2008) "Development vs. Terrorism: Money Transfers and EU Financial Regulations in the UK", *Political Studies Association*, BJPIR, Vol. 10, p. 286-302.

Other Relevant References

Abdullah Y. Shedy (2004) "Should gambling be a predicate for ML?", *Journal of ML Control* 7(3):254-260, Emerald Group Publishing Limited.
Antoniou D. (2006) "The "laundry" of the antiquities and the mission in London", Kathimerini.
Asian Development Bank (2003, March) "Manual on Countering ML and the Financing of Terrorism".
Bank of Greece (1997) "Prevention of ML", Administration's Circular No.2.
Bank of Greece (2004) "Codification of Regulation for the Prevention of ML", Administration's Circular No.16.
Bank of Greece (2006) "Prevention and Suppression of ML and Terrorist Financing", Supplement No.4 of the Governor's Order No.2577.
Bank of Greece (2007) *Decision of the Banking and Credit Affairs Committee* No 242/6.
Bank of Greece (2008) *Decision of the Banking and Credit Affairs Committee* No 257/4.
Bank of Greece (2008) "Governor's Annual Report for 2007".
Borsworth – Davies Rowan (2007) "ML – chapter three", *Journal of ML Control*, Vol. 10 N.1, pp. 47-65, Emerald Group Publishing Limited.
BougatsouAristea (2005) "The big "laundry" of the golden coupons", Kathimerini.
Dahm Evelyn, "The Global Illicit Drug Trade – the Role of the Mediterranean Region".
Douvis P. (2003) "Offshore activities", Athens, Self-issue.
Eder Mine and Hozic A. Aida (2003, March 19-23) "Workshop 9 - Mediterranean Merchants: Politics, Economics and Culture of Informal Trade Networks", Mediterranean Programme – 4th Mediterranean Social and Political Research Meeting Financial Services Authority, "ML".
Geiger Hans and Wuensch Oliver (2007) "The fight against ML. An economic analysis of a cost-benefit paradoxon", *Journal of ML Control*, Vol. 10 N.1, pp. 91-105, Emerald Group Publishing Limited.
Johnson Jackie (2008) "Third round FATF mutual evaluations indicate declining compliance", *Journal of ML Control*, Vol. 11 N.1, pp. 47-66, Emerald Group Publishing Limited.
Kalliagopoulou F. and Tsioutsia N. (2001) "Kokkalis situation in the Parliament", Kathimerini.

Kopp P. (2006) "Drugs and Money: Managing the Drug Trade and Crime – Money in Europe.", Addiction 101(6):902.

Kotsis V. (2005) "How was the money laundered in the A.S.E.", Vima.

Levi M. (2001) "ML : private banking becomes less private", Global Corruption Report.

Mitsilegas V. and Gilmore B (2007) "The EU Legislative Framework Against ML and Terrorist Finance: A Critical Analysis in the Light of Evolving Global Standards", International and Comparative Law Quarterly, Cambridge University Press, Vol.56, pp.119-140.

Nikolopoulos G., (2001) ""Dirty" money searches for ... euro-laundery", Vima.

Petrus C. van Duyne (1998) "Money-Laundering: Pavlov's Dog and Beyond", The Howard Journal, Vol.37 No 4, pp. 359-374.

Pickett Spenser K.H. (2001) "Internal Control – A manager's journey", John Wiley and Sons, Inc.

Ping He (2004) "New trends in ML – From the real world to cyberspace", Journal of ML Control (1): 48-55, Emerald Group Publishing Limited.

Ravanos A. (2003) "How do the laundries of "black" money work?", Vima.

Ross Stuart and Michelle Hannan (2007) "ML regulation and risk-based decision-making", *Journal of ML Control*, Vol. 10 N.1, p. 106-115, Emerald Group Publishing Limited.

Sheet of the Greek Government Gazettes A' 193/16.12.1991, 173/24.8.1995, 264/1.12.1998, 168/19.7.2002, 305/13.12.2005 and 3691/5.8.2008.

Simser Jeffrey (2008) "ML and asset cloaking techniques", *Journal of ML Control*, Vol. 11 N.1, p. 15-24, Emerald Group Publishing Limited.

VaithilingamSantha, Nair Mahendhiran (2007) "Factors affecting ML: lesson for developing countries", *Journal of ML Control* 10(3):352-366, Emerald Group Publishing Limited.

Web Laurence (2004) "A survey of ML reporting officers and their attitudes towards ML regulations" *Journal of ML Control* 7(4): 367-375, Emerald Group Publishing Limited.

Web Resources

Layton Julia "How ML Works", http://money.howstuffworks.com/money-laundering.htm.

Caribbean Financial Action Task Force, "CFATF: An overview", http://www.cfatf.org/.

Council of Europe, "About the Council of Europe", http://www.coe.int/T/e/Com/about_coe/.

Eurasian Group on combating ML and financing of terrorism, http://www.eurasiangroup.org/_1_1_1_1, 00.html.

FATF, "History of the FATF", http://www.fatf-gafi.org/document/ 63/0, 3343, en_32250379_ 32236836_34432255.

FATF, "9 Special Recommendations on Terrorist Financing", http://www.fatf-gafi.org/document/9/0, 3343, en_32250379_32236920_ 34032073_1_1_1_1, 00.html.

FATF, "The 40 Recommendations", http://www.fatf-gafi.org/document/ 28/0, 3343, en_ 32250379_32236930_33658140_1_1_1_1, 00.html.

FATF/OECD, 2007, "Report on Observance of Standards and Codes FATF Recommendations for Anti-ML and Combating the Financing of Terrorism", http://www.FATF-GAFI.ORG.

GAFISUD, "About GAFISUD", http://www.gafisud.org/home.htm.

GIABA, "About GIABA", http://www.giaba-westafrica.org/index.php?option=com_contentandtask=viewandid=17andItemid=37.

Gilmore C. William (1999) "Dirty Money: The Evolution of ML Countermeasures", Council of Europe Publishing http://eur-lex.europa.eu/LexUriServ/LexUriServ.do?uri= CELEX: 52004PC0559 (01):EL:HTMLhttp://www.imolin.org/imolin/index.html.

Gortsos C. (2009), "Money Laundering : The Institutional Framework , Practical Application, International Developments", http://62.1.43.74/7Omilies-parousiaseis/UplFiles/omilies /secgen/Gortsos16-11-2009.pdf.

HM Treasury (2007, January 22) "Implementing the Third ML Directive: Draft ML Regulations 2007", http://www.hm-treasury.gov.uk/consultations_and_legislation.

INTERPOL, "About INTERPOL", http://www.interpol.int/public/icpo/default.asp.

Money Laundering International Conference (2002) "Stop ML!"London, http:// www.antimoneylaundering.ukf.net/.

Organization of American States, "The OAS at a Glance", http://www.oas.org/ key_issues/eng/KeyIssue_Detail.asp?kis_sec=20.

The Asia/Pacific Group on ML, "Background", http://www.apgml.org/.

United Nations, "United Nations Convention Against Illicit Traffic in Narcotic Drugs and Psychotropic Substances, 1988", http://www.unodc.org/pdf/convention_1988_en.pdf.

Wikipedia, the free encyclopedia, "Financial Action Task Force on ML", http://en. wikipedia.org/wiki/FATF.

Wikipedia, the free encyclopedia, "ML", http://en.wikipedia.org/wiki/Money_laundering.

Wikipedia, the free encyclopedia, "Organisation for Economic Co-operation and Development", http://en.wikipedia.org/wiki/OECD.

Wikipedia, the free encyclopedia, "United Nations Office on Drugs and Crime", http://en.wikipedia.org/wiki/United_Nations_Office_on_Drugs_and_Crime.

Wikipedia, the free encyclopedia, "Commonwealth Secretariat", http://en.wikipedia.org/wiki/ Commonwealth_Secretariat.

In: Computational Techniques for Banking and Risk Management ISBN: 978-1-62618-522-7
Editors: C. Zopounidis and M. Doumpos

Chapter 3

ON THE NELSON-SIEGEL AND GAMTAUX YIELD CURVE MODELS

Polychronis Manousopoulos** and Michalis Michalopoulos
Bank of Greece, Athens, Greece

ABSTRACT

A yield curve depicts the term structure of interest rates, being an important financial tool for investment and policy decisions. Yield curves are often estimated by parsimonious methods. These are methods that model the curve using a single function of few parameters. In this paper, we examine two of the most popular parsimonious methods, namely the Nelson-Siegel method as well as its extension proposed by Svensson, along with two of their variants which are rather unknown, namely the Gamtaux and Extended Gamtaux methods respectively. The methods have been tested on a sample of daily data consisting of government bonds. The results indicate that (a) the extended versions of the methods perform better than their simple counterparts, and (b) the rather unknown Gamtaux methods achieve comparable performance compared to the Nelson-Siegel methods.

Keywords: Yield curve, term structure of interest rates, parsimonious methods

1. INTRODUCTION

A yield curve depicts the relationship between the interest rates of a class of debt instruments, such as bonds, and their maturity, i.e. it is a yield valued function of maturity. There is a variety of yield curve types depending on the yield indicator used, e.g. forward or spot rates, while they usually refer to a set of debt instruments of similar characteristics, such as rating. Yield curves reflect the market status and prospect thus providing a useful tool for investment and policy decisions. Their estimation is a broad topic in the literature (see e.g.

---

* E-mail: PManousopoulos@bankofgreece.gr.

[1], [3], [4], [5] and the references therein) and a variety of methods has been devised for this purpose.

A main category of yield curve estimation methods includes the so-called parsimonious methods. These are essentially methods that model the curve using a single function of few parameters. Their main advantage is that they provide a simple, compact representation of the term structure, while being flexible enough to capture any reasonable yield curve shape that may arise in practice. In this paper, we examine two of the most popular parsimonious methods, namely the Nelson-Siegel method (see [6]), as well as its extension proposed by Svensson (see [7], [8]), the so-called Extended Neslon-Siegel method. Moreover, we examine two of their variants which are rather unknown, namely the Gamtaux and Extended Gamtaux methods respectively (see [2] and the references therein). Our aim is to compare their performance and to point out their potential differences.

The paper is organized as follows. In Section 2, we briefly review the necessary background on yield curves, while Section 3 contains the presentation of the aforementioned parsimonious methods. Section 4 contains the results of the application of these methods to daily market data. Finally, Section 5 summarizes our conclusions.

2. Yield Curves

Yield curves and their estimation methods is a broad topic. Here, we briefly present some basic concepts that are subsequently necessary; further information can be found, for example, in [1], [3], [4] and [5].

The *price* of a bond is the present value of its future cashflows:

$$p + ai = \sum_{i=1}^{m} \frac{C}{(1+z(t_i))^{t_i}} + \frac{R}{(1+z(t_m))^{t_m}}, \tag{1}$$

where p is the clean bond price, ai the accrued interest, C the periodic coupon payment, R the redemption payment and $z(t)$ the spot interest rate for maturity t. If the *discount function* is defined as

$$\delta(t) = \frac{1}{(1+z(t))^{t}}, \tag{2}$$

then the bond price equation can be rewritten as

$$p + ai = C\sum_{t=1}^{m} \delta(t_i) + R\delta(t_m). \tag{3}$$

Under the assumption of *continuous compounding*, i.e. that the discount function is continuous and the coupon payments are made continuously so that the interest does not accrue, we have

$$p = C \int_{t=0}^{t_m} \delta(t)dt + Rd(t_m) . \tag{4}$$

The *yield to maturity* or *redemption yield* of a bond, is the single interest rate that discounts its future cashflows to its present price

$$p + ai = \sum_{t=1}^{m} \frac{C}{(1+y)^{t_i}} + \frac{R}{(1+y)^{t_m}} . \tag{5}$$

In the case of zero-coupon bond, i.e. a bond with no coupon payments, it's yield to maturity is the spot interest rate for it's maturity, which is thus called *zero-coupon yield*. The discount factor $\delta(t_m)$ is applied to all the periods until maturity t_m, so it can be considered to be an average rate. If the discount factors $\delta(t_i)$ or the corresponding spot rates $z(t_i)$ are known, we can calculate the implied *forward rates*, i.e. the rates applicable to a single period:

$$r_i = \frac{\delta(t_{i-1}) - \delta(t_i)}{\delta(t_i)} . \tag{6}$$

Under the assumption of continuous compounding, we can define a continuous, instantaneous forward rate function:

$$r(t) = \frac{-\delta'(t)}{\delta(t)} \tag{7}$$

The mean forward rate over a specific maturity interval $[m_1, m_2]$ is the average of r(t):

$$f(t) = \frac{1}{m_2 - m_1} \int_{m_1}^{m_2} r(t)dt \tag{8}$$

The spot interest rate for maturity *m* can be formulated as the mean forward rate in the interval $[0, m]$:

$$z(m) = \frac{1}{m} \int_0^m r(t)dt = \frac{1}{m} \int_0^m \frac{-\delta'(t)}{\delta(t)} dt = \frac{-\ln(\delta(m))}{m} \tag{9}$$

given that $\delta(0) = 1$, since the present value of an amount today ($t = 0$) is the amount itself. The last equation implies that

$$\delta(t) = e^{-tz(t)} \tag{10}$$

The term yield curve often refers to the zero-coupon yield curve or the forward rate curve. In this paper we focus on the zero-coupon yield curve, noting that most alternative formulations are essentially equivalent.

3. Parsimonious Methods

The parsimonious methods for yield curve estimation are based on functions of few parameters. The motivation of these methodologies is to provide a simple, compact representation of the term structure, while being flexible enough to describe any reasonable yield curve shape that occurs in practice. Here, we focus on the Nelson-Siegel and Gamtaux methods as well as their extended versions.

3.1. The Nelson-Siegel Method

The parsimonious method proposed by Nelson and Siegel (see [6]) is motivated by the fact that a yield curve is usually monotonic or has a limited number of inflection points (often one or two at most). Under this assumption, the instantaneous forward rate curve is defined as function of maturity *m*

$$r(m) = \beta_0 + \beta_1 e^{-m/\tau_1} + \beta_2 \frac{m}{\tau_1} e^{-m/\tau_1}, \tag{11}$$

while the respective zero-coupon yield curve is

$$z(m) = \frac{1}{m}\int_0^m r(x)dx = \beta_0 + \beta_1 \frac{1-e^{-m/\tau_1}}{m/\tau_1} + \beta_2 \left(\frac{1-e^{-m/\tau_1}}{m/\tau_1} - e^{-m/\tau_1} \right). \tag{12}$$

These equations imply that the yield curve converges to β_0 as maturity increases, while it converges to $\beta_0 + \beta_1$ as maturity decreases to present; the parameters β_2, τ_1 mostly affect the medium part of the curve. The terms corresponding to the parameters of the zero-coupon yield curve of Eq. 12 are depicted in Figure 1.

3.2. The Extended Nelson-Siegel Method

Svensson extended the method of Nelson and Siegel by adding an extra term to the original function, in order to allow additional inflection points in the yield curve (see [7] and [8]). The new version of the function, often called the Extended Nelson-Siegel function, is able to capture a greater variety of yield curve shapes, most notably in the case of a monetary crisis. The instantaneous forward rate curve is defined as

$$r(m) = \beta_0 + \beta_1 e^{-m/\tau_1} + \beta_2 \frac{m}{\tau_1} e^{-m/\tau_1} + \beta_3 \frac{m}{\tau_2} e^{-m/\tau_2}, \tag{13}$$

while the respective zero-coupon yield curve is

$$z(m) = \beta_0 + \beta_1 \frac{1-e^{-m/\tau_1}}{m/\tau_1} + \beta_2 \left(\frac{1-e^{-m/\tau_1}}{m/\tau_1} - e^{-m/\tau_1} \right) + \beta_3 \left(\frac{1-e^{-m/\tau_2}}{m/\tau_2} - e^{-m/\tau_2} \right). \tag{14}$$

The parameters β_0, β_1, β_2, τ_1 have the same interpretation as in the Nelson-Siegel method, while β_3, τ_2 are similar to β_2, τ_1 mostly affecting the medium part of the curve. It is worth mentioning that the β_2 and β_3 terms are correlated when the τ_1, τ_2 parameters coincide; this may cause difficulties during the estimation process (see [5]).

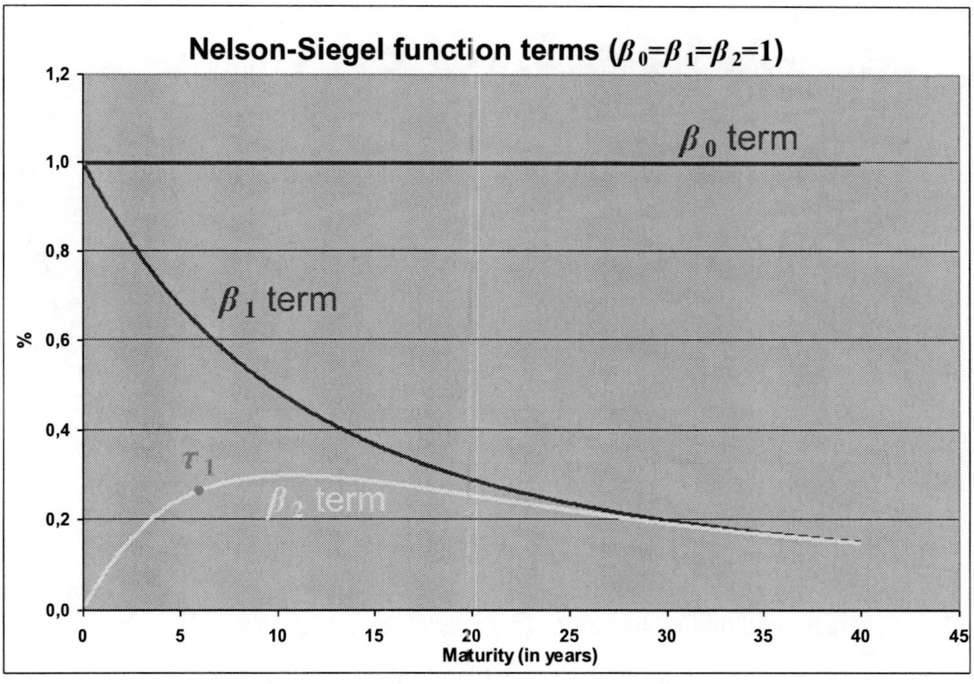

Figure 1. The terms of the Nelson-Siegel zero-coupon yield curve.

3.3. The Gamtaux Method

The Gamtaux method (see [2] and the references therein) is similar to the Nelson-Siegel method, being different in the medium-time term of β_2. Specifically, the zero-coupon yield curve is defined as

$$z(m) = \beta_0 + \beta_1 \frac{1 - e^{-m/\tau_1}}{m/\tau_1} + \beta_2 \left(\frac{\left(1 - e^{-m/\tau_1}\right)^2}{4m/\tau_1} \right). \tag{15}$$

As in the Nelson-Siegel case, the yield curve converges to β_0 as maturity increases, while it converges to $\beta_0 + \beta_1$ as maturity decreases to present; the parameters β_2, τ_1 mostly affect the medium part of the curve. The terms corresponding to the parameters of the zero-coupon yield curve of Eq. 15 are depicted in Figure 2.

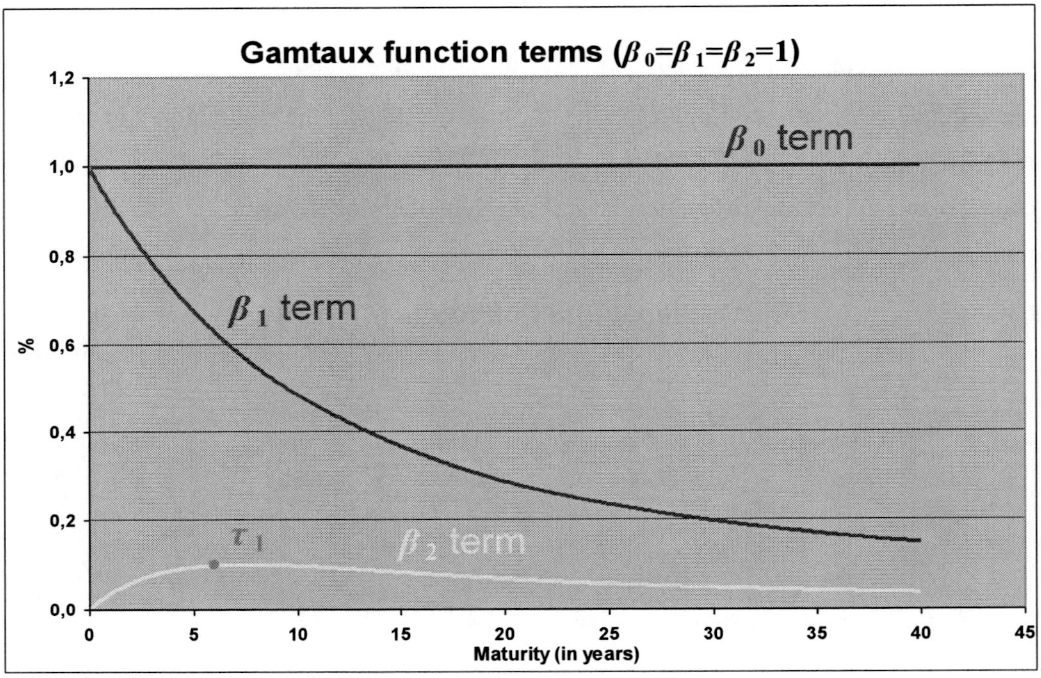

Figure 2. The terms of the Gamtaux zero-coupon yield curve.

3.4. The Extended Gamtaux Method

The Gamtaux method can be similarly extended by adding an extra term to the original function following Svensson's approach (see [2]). In this case, the zero-coupon yield curve is

$$z(m) = \beta_0 + \beta_1 \frac{1 - e^{-m/\tau_1}}{m/\tau_1} + \beta_2 \left(\frac{\left(1 - e^{-m/\tau_1}\right)^2}{4m/\tau_1} \right) + \beta_3 \left(\frac{\left(1 - e^{-m/\tau_2}\right)^2}{4m/\tau_2} \right). \tag{16}$$

The parameters β_0, β_1, β_2, τ_1 have the same interpretation as in the Gamtaux method, while β_3, τ_2 are similar to β_2, τ_1 mostly affecting the medium part of the curve.

3.5. Parameter Estimation

The yield curve estimation problem essentially consists of finding the "optimal" values of the β_i, τ_j parameters so as to minimize an error measure between the observed (i.e. obtained from the market) and fitted (i.e. computed from the yield curve) yields or prices. As shown in Eq. 1, the price of a bond is a function of the zero-coupon yields for the maturities of its (predetermined in time and size) cashflows. In combination with Eq. 12, 14, 15, 16, the fitted price of a bond can be expressed as a function of the β_i, τ_j parameters

$$P_j = P(j, \beta_0, \beta_1, \beta_2, \beta_3, \tau_1, \tau_2), \tag{17}$$

where P_j is the fitted price of the jth bond in the sample and P the function combining the previous equations. Note that the parameters β_3, τ_2 are applicable only in the extended versions of the methods. The fitted yield to maturity of a bond can be similarly expressed as

$$Y_j = Y(j, \beta_0, \beta_1, \beta_2, \beta_3, \tau_1, \tau_2). \tag{18}$$

Denoting by p_i, y_i the market prices and yields respectively, the yield curve estimation results in solving one of the following non-linear optimization problems :

$$\min_{\beta_0,\beta_1,\beta_2,\beta_3,\tau_1,\tau_2} \left[\sum_{j=1}^{N} \left(Y(j, \beta_0, \beta_1, \beta_2, \beta_3, \tau_1, \tau_2) - y_j \right)^2 \right], \tag{19}$$
$$\beta_0 > 0, \quad \beta_0 + \beta_1 > 0, \quad \tau_1 > 0 \quad \tau_2 > 0$$

$$\min_{\beta_0,\beta_1,\beta_2,\beta_3,\tau_1,\tau_2} \left[\sum_{j=1}^{N} \left(P(j, \beta_0, \beta_1, \beta_2, \beta_3, \tau_1, \tau_2) - p_j \right)^2 \right]. \tag{20}$$
$$\beta_0 > 0, \quad \beta_0 + \beta_1 > 0, \quad \tau_1 > 0 \quad \tau_2 > 0$$

The price error may be additionally weighted by each bond's duration. As explained in [5], (a) the solution of these problems is non-trivial and a proper nonlinear optimization algorithm should be used, and (b) the starting values of the parameters may be based on their financial interpretation, e.g.

$$\beta_0 = \frac{1}{M}\sum_{i=1}^{M} y_i, \quad \beta_1 = y_s - \beta_0, \quad \beta_2 = \beta_3 = 0, \quad \tau_1 = \tau_2 = 1 \tag{21}$$

where M refers to the bonds of the longest maturities, usually 2 or 3, and s is the bond of the shortest maturity.

An example of estimation is presented in Figure 3, where the zero-coupon yield curve for the Nelson-Siegel method is depicted, for both the starting and optimal values of the parameters.

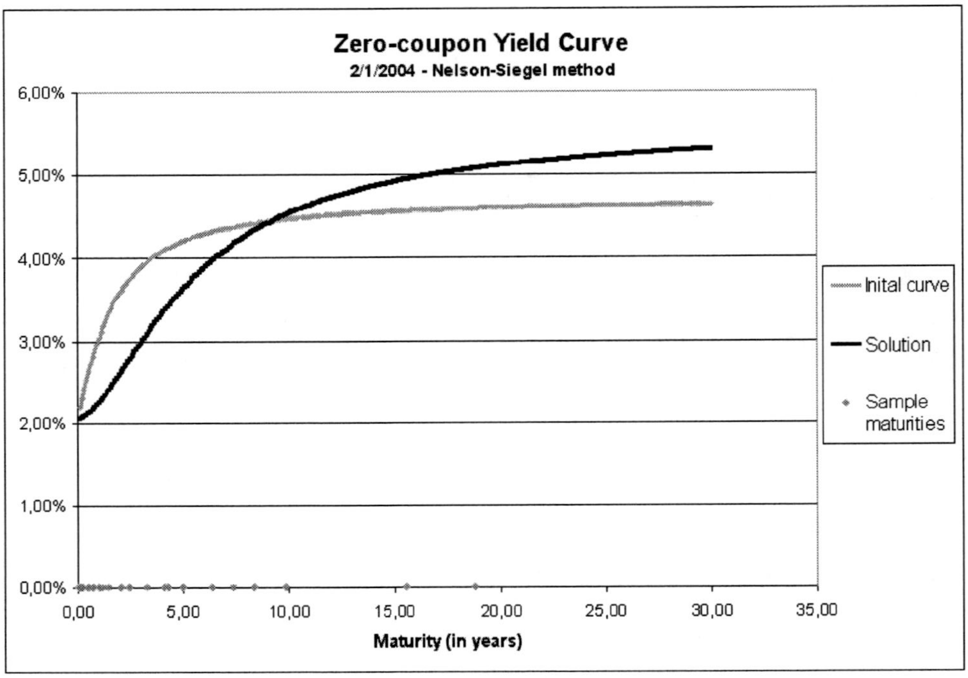

Figure 3. An example of yield curve estimation.

4. RESULTS

We have tested the methods of Section 3 on a sample of Greek government bonds, for the years 2003–2005, a total of 750 market days. The data were obtained from the Greek secondary bond market (HDAT) and the yield curve was estimated on a daily basis, using 20 bonds on average per day. Each daily sample consisted of fixed-coupon government bonds covering the maturity interval between 1 month and 20 years approximately; all bonds were of the same rating and were selected in terms of outstanding amount and volume of transactions, including benchmark bonds. The optimization problem of Eq. 19 was selected, i.e. the minimization of the yield error, using the starting values of Eq. 21.

Table 1 summarizes the daily yield error and variance for each one of the methods. The results of this in-sample test indicate two main conclusions :

- The extended versions of the methods present considerably better performance, as already mentioned in the literature. This is expected since the additional two parameters allow greater accuracy.
- The Gamtaux methods present comparable performance to the Nelson-Siegel methods; indeed they achieve slightly smaller average errors. This implies that, although widely unknown, they provide a noteworthy alternative in practice.

Table 2 summarizes the results of an out-of-sample test using the same bond sample and period. Specifically, for each day we excluded the bond of median maturity and estimated the yield curve using the remaining. Subsequently, we calculated the daily yield error for all bonds and, separately, for the excluded and remaining ones.

Table 1. The absolute yield error and variance for all methods (in-sample test)

Period	*1/1/2003 – 31/12/2005*	
Sample	*20 bonds (average)*	
Method	Absolute error (daily average)	Variance (daily average)
Nelson-Siegel	*0.0181%*	*0.000004%*
Extended Nelson-Siegel	*0.0125%*	*0.000002%*
Gamtaux	*0.0174%*	*0.000004%*
Extended Gamtaux	*0.0121%*	*0.000002%*

Table 2. The absolute yield error (daily average) for all methods and various data subsets (out-of-sample test and in-sample test respective results)

Period	*1/1/2003 – 31/12/2005*		
Sample	*20 bonds (average)*		
OUT-OF-SAMPLE TEST			
Method	All bonds	Excluded bond	Remaining bonds All \ {Excluded}
Nelson-Siegel	*0.0180%*	*0.0195%*	*0.0180%*
Extended Nelson-Siegel	*0.0123%*	*0.0142%*	*0.0122%*
Gamtaux	*0.0173%*	*0.0186%*	*0.0172%*
Extended Gamtaux	*0.0119%*	*0.0136%*	*0.0119%*
IN-SAMPLE TEST			
Method	All bonds	Excluded bond (exclusion referes to the out-of-sample test)	Remaining bonds All \ {Excluded}
Nelson-Siegel	*0.0181%*	*0.0189%*	*0.0181%*
Extended Nelson-Siegel	*0.0125%*	*0.0136%*	*0.0124%*
Gamtaux	*0.0174%*	*0.0180%*	*0.0174%*
Extended Gamtaux	*0.0121%*	*0.0129%*	*0.0121%*

Moreover, we present the daily error from the in-sample test of Table 1 covering the same data subsets. The results of this test indicate that:

- the exclusion of a bond does not notably affect the others. Indeed, the yield error for the whole sample is similar for both the out-of-sample and in-sample tests.

Moreover, in the out-of-sample test the yield error is similar for all bonds and the remaining bonds.

- the yield error for the excluded bond in the out-of-sample test is comparable to the respective error of the in-sample test.

In other words, there is indication of stability and absence of overfitting in the tests. Therefore, we conclude that the results of Tables 1 and 2 provide indeed a reliable comparative picture of the methods.

CONCLUSION

We have examined various parsimonious methods for estimating yield curves. Specifically, we have focused on the Nelson-Siegel, Extended Nelson-Siegel, Gamtaux and Extended Gamtaux methods. These methods have been compared on a sample of daily data consisting of government bonds and covering a three-year period. The results indicate that (a) the extended versions of the methods present considerably better performance than their simple counterparts; this is expected by the existence of the additional parameters and is already mentioned in the literature, and (b) the performance of the Gamtaux methods is comparable to that of the Nelson-Siegel methods. That latter result implies that they offer a noteworthy alternative in practice.

REFERENCES

[1] Anderson N., Breedon F., Deacon M., Derry A. and Murphy G. Estimating and Interpreting the Yield Curve. *John Wiley and Sons: West Sussex*, England; 1996.

[2] Avouyi-Dovi S., Blais T. and Keller S. A Comparison of Different Yield Curve Estimation Methodologies. BNP Global Markets Research, *Working Papers in Financial Economics*, 1997; 3; 1-7.

[3] Choudhry M. Analysing and interpreting the yield curve. *John Wiley and Sons: Singapore;* 2004.

[4] Manousopoulos P. and Michalopoulos M. A comparison of yield curve estimation methods: The Greek case. *Journal of Financial Decision Making* 2005; 1(1); 33-46.

[5] Manousopoulos P. and Michalopoulos M. Comparison of non-linear optimization algorithms for yield curve estimation. *European Journal of Operational Research* 2009; 192(2); 594-602.

[6] Nelson C.R., Siegel A.F.. Parsimonious Modelling of Yield Curves. *The Journal of Business* 1987; 60(4); 473-489.

[7] Svensson L.E.O. Estimating and Interpreting Forward Interest Rates: Sweden 1992-1994; *National bureau of Economic Research Working Paper* WP 4871; 1994.

[8] Svensson L.E.O. Estimating Forward Interest Rates with the Extended Nelson-Siegel Method. *Sveriges Riksbank Quarterly Review* 1995; 3; 13-26.

In: Computational Techniques for Banking and Risk Management ISBN: 978-1-62618-522-7
Editors: C. Zopounidis and M. Doumpos

Chapter 4

MEAN VARIANCE PORTFOLIO SELECTION SUBJECT TO VALUE-AT-RISK CONSTRAINTS APPLIED TO REAL STOCK MARKET DATA

F. Hamza, [1*] ***M. El Kharrim*** [2] ***and M. El hachloufi***

[1]Université Abdelmalek Essaâdi
Département d'Economie et Gestion
Faculté Polydisciplinaire de Tétouan, Tangier, Morocco
[2]CED- Ecole Nationale de Commerce et de Gestion-Tanger
Université Mohamed V Rabat-Agdal
Département de Mathématiques - Faculté des Sciences, Morocco

ABSTRACT

In this paper, an application of portfolio optimization problem based on the interaction between the Value-at-Risk and the Mean-Variance approach is presented. It is illustrated by a numerical computation based on a real data set of stocks prices belonging to the Moroccan Stock Market (2010). We discuss the sensitivity of the optimal feasible portfolios to the chosen loss value and confidence level. For a given loss value and a confidence level, tangent portfolios are determined. All programming and computing tasks were performed under MATLAB environment.

Keywords: Value-at-Risk, Mean-Variance approach, Linear programming, Portfolio optimization, Tangent portfolio

1. INTRODUCTION

Since the publication of JP Morgan's Risk Metrics in 1994 there has been an explosion of research in the areas of value of risk and risk management in general. While the basic

[*] E-mail: fhamza2004@yahoo.fr.

concepts surrounding Value at Risk are founded in the area of market risk measurement they have been extended over the last decade to other areas of risk management [1]. By now, it became a tool for risk management in financial industry (Risk Metrics TM 1995) and part of industrial regulatory mechanisms (Amendment to the Capital Accord to Incorporate Market Risks 1996). Considerable amount of research was dedicated recently to development of methods of risk management based on Value-at-Risk [2]. The interaction between the VaR and the portfolio theory is the subject of a new study that has naturally led to the introduction of VaR as a constraint control in the portfolio optimization models. The main purpose is to provide the investor with a reliable method allowing him to set a maximum loss threshold that can potentially undergo its assets. To achieve this goal, we're led to include an additional constraint set on the VaR in our optimization models.

This study is organized as follows. In section 2, we present a theoretical review of the interaction between the VaR and the Mean-Variance model as it has been previously described in detail in [3] and [4]. In section 3, we summarize the results of our computational study applied to a Moroccan Stock Market data.

2. Theoretical Review of the Interaction between the VaR and the Mean-Variance Model

Value at Risk is a method of assessing risk that uses standard statistical techniques routinely used in other technical fields. Formally, VaR measures the worst expected loss over a given horizon under normal market conditions at a given confidence level [5].

In other words, the VaR of an asset or a portfolio for a given period t and a probability q can be defined as the amount of loss expected so that during the period [0; t], it should not exceed the VaR only with probability (1-q). For instance, a bank might say that the daily VaR of its trading portfolio is 40$ million at the 99% confidence level. In other words, there is only 1%, under normal market conditions, for a loss greater than 40$ million to occur. We express this symbolically as

$$P\left[-\Delta S(t) \leq VaR\right] = \alpha \tag{1}$$

where $\Delta S(t) = S(t)-S(0)$ and S(t) are respectively the values of portfolio at the beginning and the end of the period. After centering and reducing, (1) becomes

$$P\left[\frac{-\Delta S(t) - E(-\Delta S(t))}{\sigma(\Delta S(t))} \leq \frac{VaR_\alpha - E(-\Delta S(t))}{\sigma(\Delta S(t))}\right] = 1-\alpha \tag{2}$$

Let $\tau_\alpha = \dfrac{VaR_\alpha - E(-\Delta S(t))}{\sigma(\Delta S(t))}$ represents the quantile corresponding to the N(0;1) distribution.

Then we have,

$$VaR_\alpha = -E\big(\Delta S(t)\big) + \tau_\alpha \sigma\big(\Delta S(t)\big) \tag{3}$$

Thus, to estimate the VaR, one has to estimate the two portfolio parameters E and σ. Assuming that the value of the portfolio at the horizon T is equal to

$$S(T) = \sum_{i=1}^{n} x_i S_i(T) = \sum_{i=1}^{n} x_i\big[S_i(0) + \Delta S_i(T)\big] \tag{4}$$

We know that according to the market model (CAPM) every return $\tilde{r}_i$ of the asset i (i = 1…n) is linearly related to the return $\tilde{r}_m(T)$ of the market during a period T by

$$\tilde{r}_i(T) = a_i + b_i\big(\tilde{r}_m(T) - r_0\big) + \varepsilon_i(T) \tag{5}$$

It follows that the portfolio value becomes

$$S(T) = \sum_{i=1}^{n} x_i S_i(0)\big[1 + a_i + b_i\big(\tilde{r}_m(T) - r_0\big) + \varepsilon_i(T)\big] \tag{6}$$

The parameters a_i and b_i are obtained by an ordinary least square method

$$a_i = \bar{r}_i(T) - \beta_i \bar{r}_m(T) \text{ and } b_i = \frac{\operatorname{cov}\big(\tilde{r}_i(T), \tilde{r}_m(T)\big)}{\sigma_m^2} = \beta_i \tag{7}$$

Using CAPM relation we have

$$\bar{r}_i(T) = r_0 + \beta_i\big(\bar{r}_m(T) - r_0\big) \tag{8}$$

Let put

$$\bar{\beta} = \frac{\sum_{i=1}^{n} \beta_i x_i S_i(0)}{\sum_{i=1}^{n} x_i S_i(0)} = \frac{\sum_{i=1}^{n} \beta_i x_i S_i(0)}{S(0)} \tag{9}$$

We get

$$E\big[\Delta S(T)\big] = S(0)\big[r_0 + \bar{\beta}\big(\bar{r}_m(T) - 2r_0\big)\big] \tag{10}$$

and

$$\sigma\left[\Delta S(T)\right]=\left[S(0)\right]^2\left\{\left(\bar{\beta}\sigma_m\right)^2+\sum_{i=1}^{n}\left[\frac{S_i(0)x_i}{S(0)}\right]^2\sigma_{\varepsilon_i}^2\right\} \tag{11}$$

Thus the VaR at the horizon T and the probability level (1- α) with the assumption of normality would be equal to

$$\begin{aligned} VaR_\alpha &= -E\left[\Delta S(T)\right]+\tau_\alpha\sigma\left[\Delta S(T)\right] \\ &= S(0)\left\{\left[-r_0-\bar{\beta}\left(\bar{r}_m(T)-2r_0\right)\right]+\tau_\alpha\sqrt{\left(\bar{\beta}\sigma_m\right)^2+\sum_{i=1}^{n}\left[\frac{S_i(0)x_i}{S(0)}\right]^2\sigma_{\varepsilon_i}^2}\right\} \end{aligned} \tag{12}$$

Next, in order to study the interaction between the VaR and Mean-Variance approach, we're led to introduce a control constraint on the VaR in the Mean-Variance model. This constraint will allow investors to well define their position toward the loss that can undergo their assets in the optimization model.

Assuming that the price of the portfolio is equal to $S(x)=\sum_{j=1}^{n}x_jS_j$ where $x_1,\ldots,x_n$ stands for the n assets in the portfolio and S_j for the price j^{th} item price, the optimization model according to the Mean-Variance approach can be described as follows

$$\begin{aligned} &Min\ \ M(x)=E\left[\Delta S(x)-E\left[\Delta S(x)\right]\right]^2 \\ &subject\ to\ \sum_{j=1}^{n}x_jE\left[\Delta S_j\right]\geq\rho M_0 \\ &\sum_{i=1}^{n}x_j=M_0 \\ &x_j\geq 0\quad j=1,\ldots,n. \end{aligned} \tag{13}$$

where M_0 is the initial capital to invest and ρ is the expected minimum rate of return. The first inequality sets constraint on the minimum expected average return, while the second constraint ensures the completeness of the initial capital to invest. If we insert an additional control constraint on the VaR, the model (13) becomes

$$\begin{aligned} &Min\ \ M(x)=E\left[\Delta S(x)-E\left[\Delta S(x)\right]\right]^2 \\ &subject\ to\ \sum_{j=1}^{n}x_jE\left[\Delta S_j\right]\geq\rho M_0 \\ &VaR_\alpha\leq VaR_0 \\ &\sum_{i=1}^{n}x_j=M_0 \\ &x_j\geq 0\quad j=1,\ldots,n. \end{aligned} \tag{14}$$

where VaR_0 represents the maximum potential loss accepted by the investor. Next, in order to linearize the model (14), we introduce the absolute deviation measure of Kono and Yamazaki given by

$$K(x) = E\{|\Delta S(x) - E[\Delta S(x)]|\} \tag{15}$$

Hence, the model (14) becomes

$$\begin{aligned} &Min\ \ K(x) = E\{|\Delta S(x) - E[\Delta S(x)]|\} \\ &subject\ to\quad \sum_{j=1}^{n} x_j E[\Delta S_j] \geq \rho M_0 \\ &\qquad -E(\Delta S(x)) + \tau_\alpha \sqrt{\frac{\pi}{2}} K(x) \leq VaR_0 \\ &\qquad \sum_{i=1}^{n} x_j = M_0 \\ &\qquad x_j \geq 0, \quad j = 1, \ldots, n. \end{aligned} \tag{16}$$

To practically handle the underlying portfolio parameters, we introduce two estimators $a_j = \frac{1}{T}\sum_{t=1}^{T} \Delta S_{jt}$ $(j = 1, \ldots, n)$ and $\hat{\sigma}_{ij} = \frac{1}{T-1}\sum_{t=1}^{T}(\Delta S_{it} - a_i)(\Delta S_{jt} - a_j)$ $(i, j = 1, \ldots, n)$
This estimation is spread out over an observation period T of the price process related to each asset composing the portfolio $(\Delta S_{it})_{1 \leq t \leq T}$. Hence the model (16) becomes

$$\begin{aligned} &Min\ \ \hat{K}(x) = \frac{1}{T-1}\sum_{t=1}^{T}\left|\sum_{j=1}^{n}(\Delta S_{jt} - a_j)x_j\right| \\ &subject\ to\quad \sum_{j=1}^{n} a_j x_j \geq \rho M_0 \\ &\qquad -\sum_{j=1}^{n} a_j x_j + \frac{\tau_\alpha}{T-1}\sum_{t=1}^{T}\left|\sum_{j=1}^{n}(\Delta S_{jt} - a_j)x_j\right| \leq VaR_0 \\ &\qquad \sum_{i=1}^{n} x_j = M_0 \\ &\qquad x_j \geq 0, \quad j = 1, \ldots, n. \end{aligned} \tag{17}$$

That is equivalent to the following linearized model

$$Min \ \frac{1}{T-1}\sum_{t=1}^{T} y_t \tag{18}$$

$$subject\ to \quad y_t + \sum_{j=1}^{n}\left(\Delta S_{jt} - a_j\right)x_j \geq 0 \qquad t = 1,...,T$$

$$y_t - \sum_{j=1}^{n}\left(\Delta S_{jt} - a_j\right)x_j \geq 0 \qquad t = 1,...,T$$

$$\sum_{j=1}^{n} a_j x_j \geq \rho M_0$$

$$-\sum_{j=1}^{n} a_j x_j + \sqrt{\frac{\pi}{2}}\frac{\tau_\alpha}{T-1}\sum_{t=1}^{T} y_t \leq VaR_0$$

$$\sum_{i=1}^{n} x_j = M_0$$

$$x_j \geq 0, \quad j = 1,...,n.$$

3. Computational Study with Real Stock Market Data Inputs

3.1. Data and Optimization Tool Description

In this section we propose to solve the previous model (18) with real data inputs. A set of 24 stocks out of 73 has been considered, which represents about 33% of the complete set of Moroccan stock market stocks. This was the largest available data set covering the year 2010 and also verifying the normality assumption required by the underlying model. A week has been chosen as time unit.

The remaining 49 stocks have been omitted due to the missing information's within the period under study. In order to check the likelihood of the normality assumption related to changes in equity values, we used the Lilliefors test procedure which provides a more powerful test for normality than the more familiar chi-square goodness-of-fittest (More powerful means that it is more likely to detect non-normality if it exists.). Indeed, it is based on a comparison of the "empirical cdf" and abnormal cdf, where "cdf" stands for cumulative distribution function, showing the probability of being less than or equal to any particular value. For the data used we get the test report shown in figure 1.

As the one may realize, there is no p-value (as in most hypothesis tests), but we see from the statement that the maximum vertical distance is sufficiently large to cast doubt on the normality assumption. More evidence to this effect appears in the cdf's in the included chart. Actually, the fit between the two frontiers appears to be "pretty good, " and it might be good enough for all practical purposes. That is, we might conclude that these data are "close enough" to being normally distributed for our purposes.

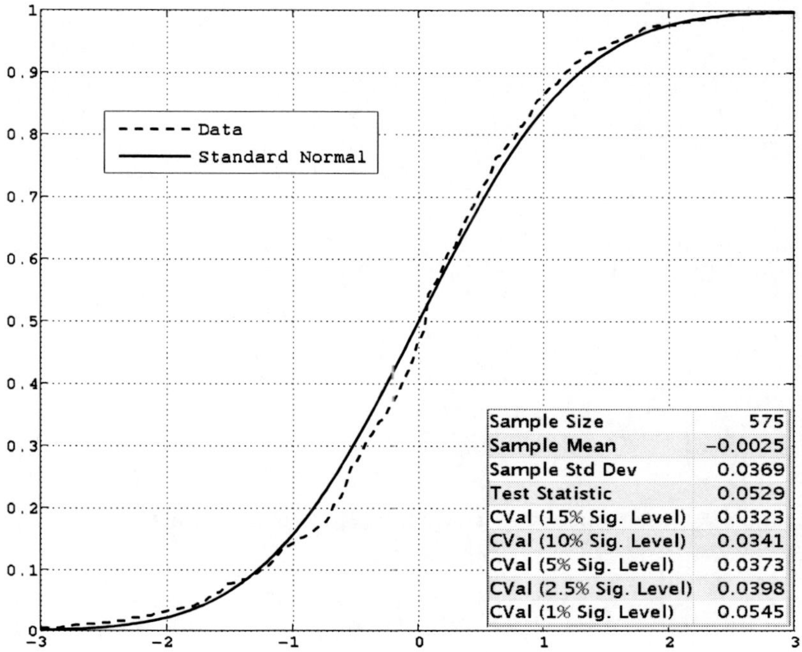

Figure 1. Lilliefors test result.

Next, in order to solve the model (18), The MATLAB optimization package has been used. The following matrical representation (standard form) can be directly set to input

$$\min \ Hz \tag{19}$$

Subject to

$$Az \leq b$$
$$A_{eq} z = b_{eq}$$
$$z \geq 0$$

where z, H, A, b, A_{eq}, and b_{eq} are in matrical notation

$$z = \begin{pmatrix} X \\ Y \end{pmatrix} \quad X = \begin{pmatrix} x_1 \\ . \\ . \\ . \\ x_n \end{pmatrix} \quad Y = \begin{pmatrix} y_1 \\ . \\ . \\ . \\ y_T \end{pmatrix}$$

$$H = \frac{1}{T-1}\left(\underbrace{0.............0}_{n}\underbrace{1.............1}_{T}\right) \quad A = \begin{pmatrix} -R_{T\times n} & -I_{T\times T} \\ R_{T\times n} & -I_{T\times T} \\ -a_1,\dots,-a_n & O_{1\times T} \\ -a_1,\dots,-a_n & \underbrace{\sqrt{\frac{\pi}{2}}\frac{\tau_\alpha}{T-1}\cdots\sqrt{\frac{\pi}{2}}\frac{\tau_\alpha}{T-1}}_{T} \end{pmatrix}$$

$$b = \begin{pmatrix} O_{T\times 1} \\ O_{T\times 1} \\ \rho M_0 \\ VaR_0 \end{pmatrix} \quad A_{eq} = \left(\underset{n}{1....1}\underset{T}{0....0}\right) \quad b_{eq} = M_0$$

$O_{p\times q}$ and $I_{p\times q}$ are respectively $p \times q$ the zero and unity matrices.

$$R_{tj} = \left(\Delta S_{jt} - a_j\right), \quad j = 1,..,n \text{ and } t = 1,..,T.$$

3.2. Results

3.2.1. Efficient Frontier

The mean-variance efficient frontier can be regarded as the solutions such that each point $\left(E\left[\Delta S(T)\right];\sigma\left[\Delta S(T)\right]\right)$ on the frontier corresponds to an efficient portfolio representing that when investing among n assets [6]. Hence, by changing the values of the expected return, we get a set of couples $\left(E\left[\Delta S(T)\right];\sigma\left[\Delta S(T)\right]\right)$ that allows us to draw the efficient frontier in the plan $\left(E\left[\Delta S(T)\right];\sigma\left[\Delta S(T)\right]\right)$. This frontier represents all the feasible portfolios with minimum variance for a given expected return (or maximum expected return for a given variance).

The VaR constraint, on the other hand, can be expressed in this frame as $-E\left(\Delta S(T)\right)+\tau_\alpha\sigma\left(\Delta S(T)\right)\leq VaR_0$.

Figure 2 shows the efficient frontier made of feasible portfolios that are solutions of the linear program (18). The VaR constraint is also represented for the case VaR_0=1.000.000 and α =95%.

We note the following observations: When the expected return is greater than 0.81%, it's not possible to find a feasible solution satisfying the VaR constraint.

We also note the fact that within this interval these solutions are identical to the ones obtained without the VaR constraint i.e. the VaR constraint doesn't affect the optimal compositions but rather limits them. This fact can be understood from the concordance of the two efficient frontiers in this region.

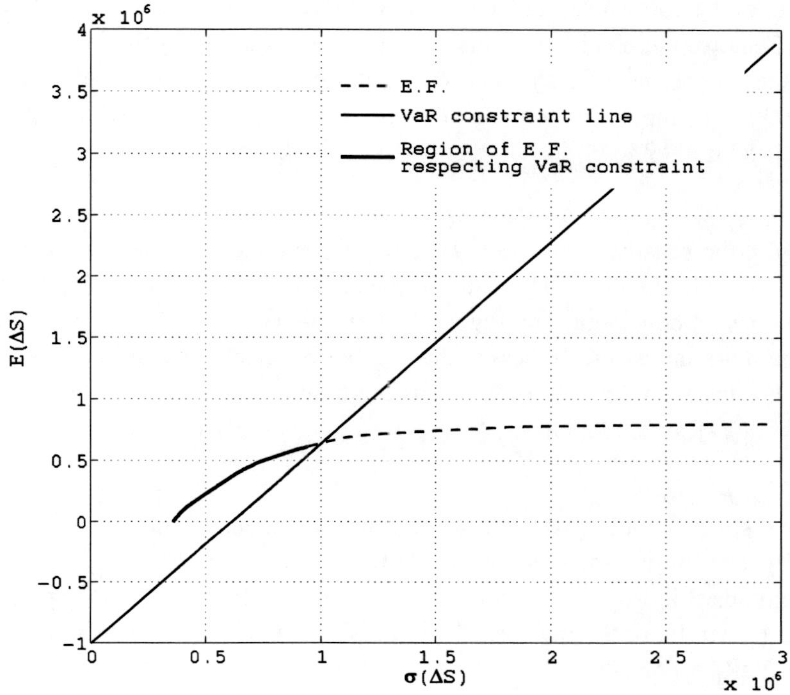

Figure 2. Efficient Frontier with VaR constraint.

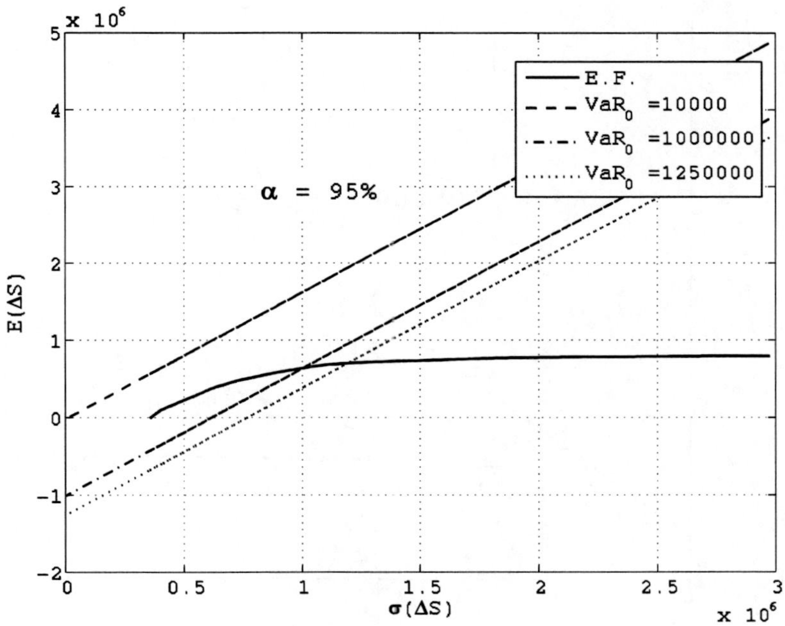

Figure 3. VaR constraint line for different VaR_0.

3.2.2. Sensitivity to VaR_0 Value Change

For a confidence level α set to 95%, the sensitivity to VaR_0 change was testedfor different values: 10.000, 1.000.000 and 1.250.000. This will be graphically interpreted by parallel displacement of the corresponding VaR constraint line.

Figure 3 shows the obtained results. We mention the fact that the more VaR_0 decreases, the less is the number of efficient portfolios fulfilling the VaR constraint. For instance for a VaR_0= 10.000, it is impossible tofind a portfolio respecting the underlying constraint set for a confidence level α = 95%.

3.2.3. Sensitivity to Alpha Value Change

Smilingly, the sensitivity to level was studied for a fixed VaR_0= 1.000.000. Test values are: 90 %, 95% and 99.99 %. This will be graphically interpreted by slope variation of the corresponding VaR constraint line. Figure 4 shows the corresponding results. Here again, we note that the more increases, the less is the number of feasible portfolios respecting the VaR constraint. For instance, for α = 99.99% it is impossible to find a portfolio that meets the set constraint with VaR_0= 1.000.000.

3.2.4. Tangent Portfolio

Here we study the case when the VaR line is tangent to the efficient frontier. We're interested by determining the composition of the underlying portfolio. To find a tangent line there are two possible ways that can be followed; either fixing α, the changing VaR_0 until to get a tangent portfolio or the opposite. Figure 5 shows that for α = 95% the tangent portfolio is found for VaR_0 = 553238.

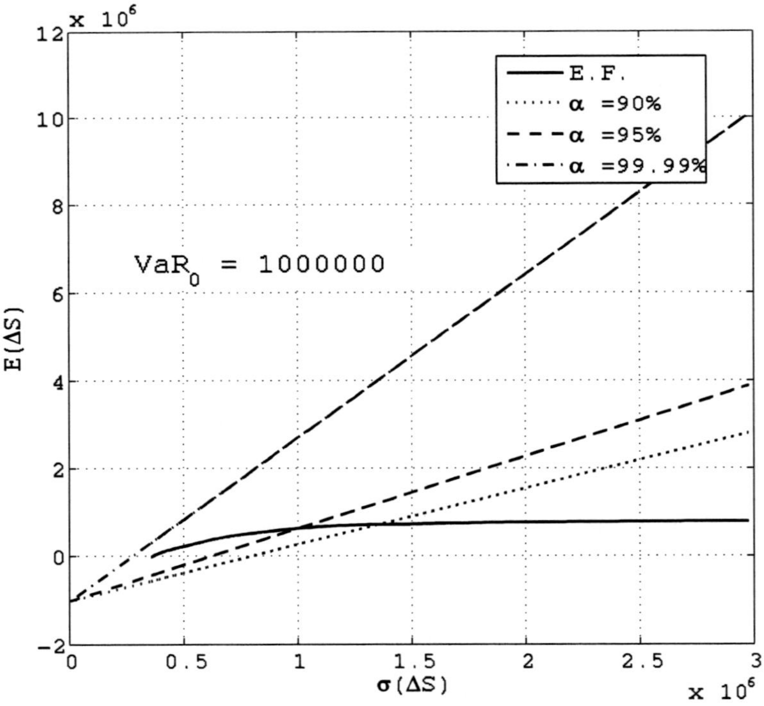

Figure 4. VaR constraint line for different α.

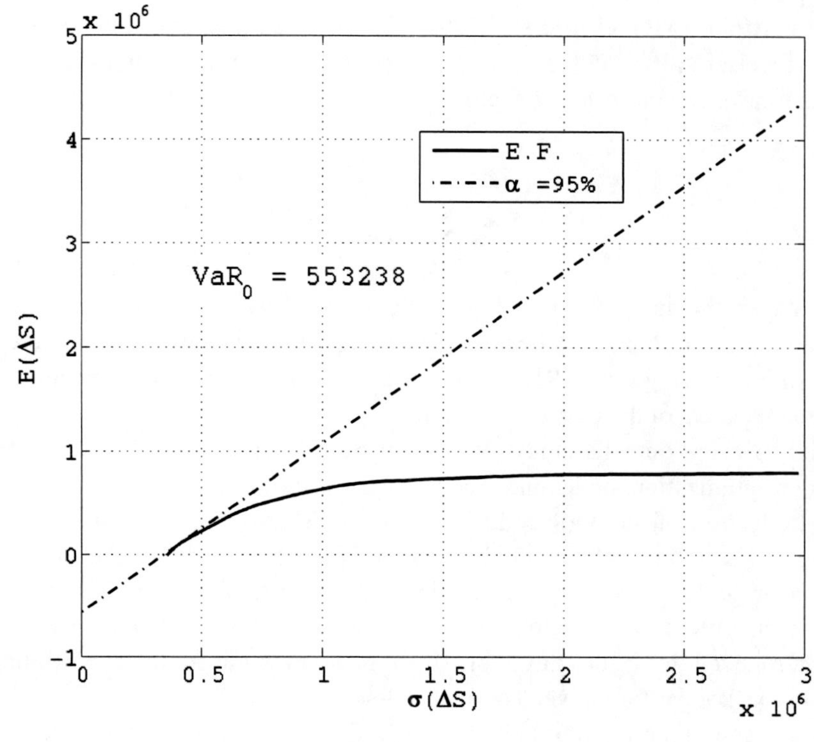

Figure 5. Tangent Portfolio found for a set α value.

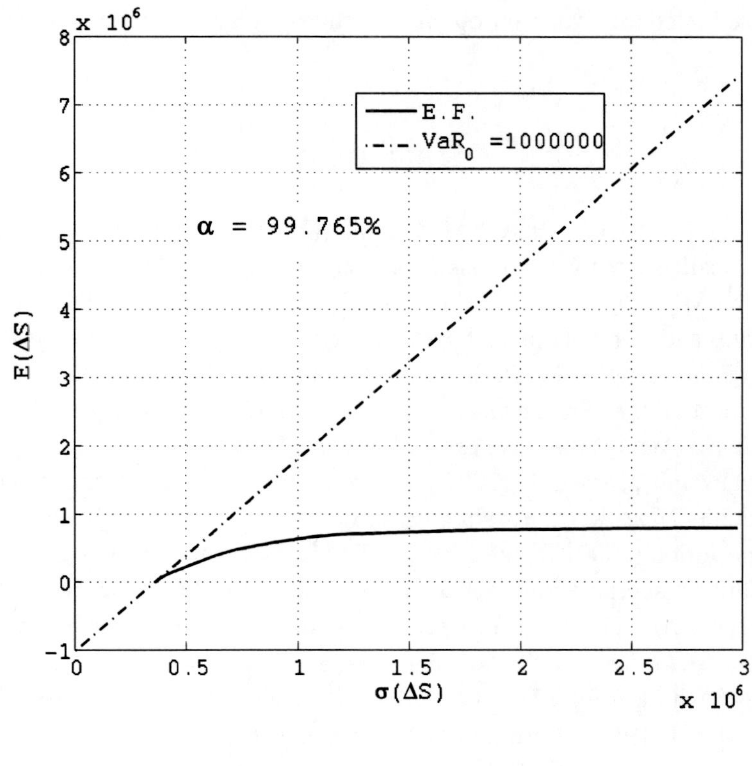

Figure 6. Tangent Portfolio found for a set VaR_0 value.

The expected return of this portfolio is 0.81%. Figure6 shows that for VaR_0= 1.000.000 the tangent portfolio is found forα =99.77%. The expected return of this portfolio is 0.41%. Of course, if we set VaR_0= 553238 (i.e. the same VaR_0found in the first case forset to 95%) we obviously have to find a tangent portfolio for α = 95%. Thing that's been successfully tested.

Conclusion

In this paper, the aim was to study the interaction between the VaR and the Markowitz mean variance approach as it's been discussed in [7], [8] and [4]. Let's recall that the motivation of introducing the VaR constraint was to provide a control element on the loss that can undergo the assets of the portfolio investor.

In order to carry out this study, Moroccan Stock Market (2010) shares were used as inputs for our optimization model under MATLAB environment.

The introduction of the VaR constraint into the Markowitz linear model merely limits feasible portfolios without changing the efficient frontier. Therefore, an efficient portfolio under the linear model without VaR constraint is still an efficient portfolio under the one with VaR constraint, unless we're below the VaR constraint line. Hence, a VaR constraint is therefore introduced to insure investors who have maximized their portfolio, while its maximum loss is known for a given confidence level.

Finally the assumption of normality on which the linear model is considered equivalent to the quadratic model is quite acceptable for our case study. Since the composition of optimal portfolios remains the same, using the equivalent linear model instead of the quadratic one has greatly facilitated the search for optimal solutions with much better performance.

References

[1] Allen L., BoudoukhJ. and Saunders A. (2004), Understanding MarketCredit and OperationalRisk: the value at risk approach, *Blackwell Publishing Ltd.*

[2] Gaivoronski A. A. and G. Pflug (2005), "Value-at-Risk in Portfolio Optimization Properties and Computational Approach", *The Journal of Risk Volume 7* / Number 2.

[3] Hamza F. and Janssen J.(2001), "Mean Variance Portfolio Selection Subject to Value at Risk Constraints". *Proceedings of the Xth ASMDA International Conference of the Quantitative Methods in Business and Industry Society,* VolI.

[4] Hamza F. and Janssen J. (2009), Choix optimal des actifs financiers et gestion de portefeuille, *Hermes Science Publications*.

[5] Philippe Jorion (2000), Value at Risk: The New Benchmark for Tsao C.-Y. and Liu C.-K.(2006), "Incorporating Value-at-Risk in Portfolio Selection: AnEvolutionary Approach", Atlantis Press, Proceedings of the 2006 *Joint Conference onInformation Sciences (JCIS)*, October 8-11, Kaohsiung,

[6] Markowitz H.: Portfolio Selection. *Journal of Finance*, Vol. 7, p. 77-91(1952).

[7] Markowitz H.(1959), Portfolio Selection: *Efficient Diversification of Investments,* John Wiley and Sons, New York.

In: Computational Techniques for Banking and Risk Management ISBN: 978-1-62618-522-7
Editors: C. Zopounidis and M. Doumpos

Chapter 5

EVALUATION OF BANK EFFICIENCY WITH THE DEA APPROACH: A COMPARISON OF EUROPEAN COMMERCIAL BANKS

Ioanna Sfinga[1*] and Dimitrios Niklis[2*]
[1]Msc Business Economics, Finance and Banking,
University of Portsmouth, UK
[2]Financial Engineering Laboratory,
Department of Production Engineering and Management,
Technical University of Crete, University Campus, Chania, Greece

ABSTRACT

This paper investigates the efficiency level of a sample of 30 top European commercial banks (ranked by assets), which operate in Euro area, over the period 2006-2010.

The main goal of this paper is to examine the impact of recent financial crisis on the European commercial banks' efficiency through the Data Envelopment Analysis (DEA) method by using the intermediation approach. The input and output data that have been chosen and used in estimating efficiency for each bank are fixed assets, number of employees and total deposits received as inputs and total loans and securities as outputs respectively.

The results show that the DEA efficiency scores, before the recent financial crisis, characterize more banks as efficient. The main conclusion of this study is that in a dynamic, extremely competitive sector, as the banking sector, the main characteristics of every financial institution need to be the flexibility and the ability of direct adaptation in a rapid changing environment.

Keywords: Banking efficiency, DEA, Europe, financial crisis

* Email: joannasfigga@yahoo.gr.

1. Introduction

Financial Institutions in the Light of the Financial Crisis

The banking system is one of the most significant factors of the economy of all countries around the world. The importance of banking system has led to the necessity of monitoring and evaluation of its efficiency.

Over recent years, the financial sector has rapidly been developed and as a consequence its role has become more complex. This phenomenon appears due to the liberalization of banking sector (deregulation) in 1970 (initially in USA) and due to the adoption of Euro, which accelerated the competition in financial markets. Additional factors are the globalization of financial and banking activities which reinforces the high competitiveness among different financial institutions, mergers and acquisitions, volatility in the banking sector, unexpected fluctuations of the interest rates, high risks and rapid advances achieved in information technology (digitalization, e.g. e-banking) which constitute the recent forces that influence the efficiency of the banking sector.

Banks, compared to other commercial firms, are more susceptible, risky and thereby open to contagion. So, it is obvious, that it is essential for bankers to evaluate the bank's performance through efficiency analysis. For this reason, regulators, bank managers - directors, investors and general public, tend to share best practices so as to mitigate - foresee risks. Then, after gathering such comprehensive practices, each bank can become more efficient and built solidness. Hence, every cause of bank failures need to be indentified and addressed, and especially since such failures often leads to extreme events such as financial crises. In the literature there are studies (using cross-country data) which are related to financial crises. The majority of them either focus on identifying the determinants of the crises and trying to predict the potential crises by looking for "early warning indicators" of trouble (e.g. Demirguc – Kunt and Detragiache, 1998; Heilpern et al., 2009; Demyanyk and Hasan, 2010) or focus on indicating ways to face the crisis successfully (e.g. Demyanyk and Van Hement, 2008; Davis and Karim, 2008; Diamond and Rajan, 2009). Finally, there are researches examining the financial crisis on the economy as well as the efficiency of the financial institutions overall.

Evaluating Bank Efficiency

Bank efficiency can be evaluated by using different methods. Such methods are the traditional financial analysis by using financial indicators (e.g. ROE, ROA etc.) based on balance sheet analysis, parametric methods based on the knowledge of production function and non-parametric methods which do not require such knowledge such as the Data Envelopment Analysis (DEA), (Wozniewska, 2008) This study will attempt to comprehend the non-parametric method Data Envelopment Analysis, known as DEA and assess the efficiency of a sample of 30 top (by assets) European commercial banks through this method, over the period 2006-2010. DEA method has become increasingly popular in measuring bank efficiency in the countries with developed banking systems (Cinca et al., 2011; Altunbas et al., 2007; Drake, 2001). This analysis constitutes a comparison of the evolution of the productivity of financial institutions in areas with different legal and institutional frameworks. Furthermore, our analysis will be completed by commenting our findings.

The main purpose of this research is to explore the banking efficiency over the period 2006-2010 at a group of European commercial banks that belong to different competitive and regulatory environments. In 2007, the dramatic fall in the mortgage loan market in USA was the beginning of a global financial crisis which also affects the European market (Taylor, 2008; Erkens et. al, 2012). The results of the crisis in Europe are getting more obvious from year 2008 and afterwards (Taylor, 2009; Beltratti and Stulz, 2009). We choose to examine this period because we focus on exploring the performance of European commercial banks for the period before and after the crisis, moreover the consequences of crisis in bank's performance. So, the aim is to answer questions such the one followed. How efficient are the examined financial institutions? How the efficiency of every examined bank changed due to the recent financial crisis? Therefore, the main question which derives from this analysis is whether this efficiency analysis will help us to identify the consequences of the recent financial crisis on the examined bank's efficiency.

The majority of a bank's operations or processes include a high or low degree of risk e.g. an asset or a loan will become irrecoverable due to outright default. Moreover, several authors have argued that the aggressive increase in competition could lead to higher bank risk-taking. For this reason, an essential prerequisite is to measure the efficiency of the financial institutions and maintain it at a high level, so as the financial institutions will be secured against a potential failure or bankruptcy. Moreover, it is quite interesting to explore the efficiency of European financial institutions, before financial agitations and then, the consequences of financial crisis in European bank's performance. In addition, the evaluation of financial institutions constitutes one of the most interesting studies, not only for the researchers but also for the financial institutions as well, since such works provide to the banking administration useful information concerning the performance of the financial institution. Furthermore, the results and conclusions of this research are critically for the stability of banking sector, which contribute on the macroeconomic stability globally. Consequently, the results of this analysis are absolutely essential for the viability of the examined European commercial banks under these unstable conditions.

The outline of the paper is as follows. Section II will give an extensive literature overview, which highlights and discusses the frameworks on bank efficiency. Section III, is composed by the presentation of the background of DEA approach, which will be used for the evaluation of the sample commercial banks. Section III continues with the illustration of the data that will be used and the sample of the examined financial institutions. Section IV, comprises a detailed description of the results over the examined period of time. The final section summarizes the conclusions and provides directions for further research.

2. Literature Review

Introduction and Background

Nowadays, new methodologies have been developed for the analysis of institutions' efficiency. Due to the recent events in the finance and banking environment, the study of evaluation and measurement of the efficiency of financial institutions has given rise to a growing body of empirical literature.

According to the literature, there are several studies, which examine the efficiency of financial institutions by using parametric or non-parametric approaches, such as Stochastic Frontier Analysis (SFA), Thick Frontier Approach (TFA), Distribution Free Approach (DFA), and DEA. (Fecher, and Pestieau, 1993; Allen and Rai, 1996; Dietsch and Lozano, 1996; Pastor, Pérez, and Quesada, 1997; Pasiouras, 2006; Wezel, 2010). However, in recent years, the non-parametric DEA has become the most popular efficiency analysis method for the countries with advanced banking systems. As Maudos et al. (2002) support *"among all the techniques for measuring efficiency, the one that requires the smallest number of observations is the nonparametric and determinist data envelopment analysis (DEA), as parametric techniques specify a large number of parameters, making it necessary to have available a large number of observations."* This method was developed in 1978, by Charnes, Cooper and Rhodes (Wozniewska, 2008). Initially, it was used in evaluating activities of non-profit firms which participate in the public sector. However, nowadays, it is widely used by the financial institutions and firms in order to measure their efficiency levels.

The Measuring of Efficiency in Banking Sector - Empirical Studies

In the literature, DEA method is referred as the most effective way of making decisions. Numerous researchers refer to this method and call it as the manager's golden key.

Rangan et al. (1988) in one of the oldest studies were focused on the evaluation of productivity of banks using the non-parametric method DEA. In this study, the researchers assembled data from 215 banks of USA and then, they evaluated their efficiency levels. In addition, Elysiani and Mehdian (1990b) mainly focus on USA countries and tried to establish two separate applications of the method DEA. Specifically, firstly, they apply the method in a data of 144 financial institutions of USA for the period of 1980-1985, whereas the second sample of data concerned 191 banks for the same time of period. Then, in the same year, Aly et al. (1990) and Ferrier and Lowel (1990) used data of 322 USA banks and 575 USA banks, for the years 1986 and 1984, respectively. One additional work with U.S. data is the study of Elyasiani and Mehdian (1995). In this work, the selected years are 1979 and 1986 examining the pre and post-deregulation periods. Through DEA approach, they estimate efficiency levels for examined US banks for these years. (Fernández et al., 2004). Other recent researches, on investigating the efficiency of banks are the work of Wezel (2010) and Cinca et al. (2011). The purpose of the Wezel's research is to investigate the efficiency of domestic and foreign banks in the Central region of America over the period 2002-2007, by using two main empirical approaches, DEA and SFA. The results of this research indicate that the foreign banks are not more efficient than their domestic rivals.

The literature, also, includes several studies which are related to the efficiency of financial institutions of European countries. The research of Berg et al. (1993) used the DEA method and the data from Finland, Norway and Sweden for the year 1990. Altunbas et al. (2001) evaluate the efficiency of European banks during the period 1989 to 1997 and they conclude that *"banks of all sizes can obtain greater cost savings through reducing managerial and other inefficiencies"*. Another research is the study of Casu and Molyneux (2003). In this study, the authors focus on the efficiency of banking system of 5 major

European countries (France, Germany, Italy, Spain and England) having as sample 530 banks, since the creation of the Single Internal Market and the deregulation of financial market by using the DEA method for the period 1993-1997. This study examines three inputs, total costs, total customers and short term funding (total deposits) and two outputs, total loans and other earning assets. According to their results, the DEA efficiency scores are low in average; nevertheless, they discern a slight improvement in the average efficiency scores. Another significant study on European banks' evaluation is Lozano et al. (2002). This study investigates the efficiency of commercial banks across 10 European countries. Their findings suggest that environmental conditions influence strongly the behavior of each country's banking industry. Grigorian and Manole (2002) study the efficiency of banking sector in transition economies (Eastern Europe) with the use of DEA.

Other recent researches consider the examination of efficiency of banking sector for transition and developed countries such as Australia by Sathye (2001); Brazil by Staub et al. (2010); Thailand by Chansarn (2008); England by Drake (2001); Greece by Noulas (1997) and Pasiouras et al. (2008); India by Joshi and Bhalerao (2011); Italy by Resti (1997); Japan by Altunbas et al.(2000); Poland by Wozniewska G. (2008); Taiwan by Chen and Yeh (2000); Turkey by Isik and Hassan (2002, 2003) and Ukraine by Mertens and Urga (2001). This kind of researches are very interesting because not only they offer information of the financial system for every examined countries, but also they focus on various subjects which are connected with the efficiency of financial institutions and finally, such researches offer an absolutely comprehensive analysis.

Furthermore, based on the recent paper of Duygun -Fethi and Pasiouras (2009), a few studies provide cross-country evidence such Field (1990) who applied the DEA method to a cross-section of 71 UK building societies in 1981. Most of them examine banks coming from the large EU banking countries such as Berg et al. (1993) who carry out the examination of the efficiency among Norway, Sweden and Finland. Bukh et al. (1995) and Bergendahl (1998) examine Nordic countries: Denmark, Finland, Norway and Sweden. Altunbas et al. (2001) evaluate financial institutions from 15 European countries, from both North and South Europe and Lozano-Vivas and Pastor (2002) investigate ten commercial European banks. Also, Grigorian and Manole (2002) examine banks from transition countries, Casu and Molyneux (2003) examine selected banks from France, Germany, Italy, Spain, UK and Casu and Ginardone (2006) that developed the research of Altunbas et al. (2001) by studying the same countries. Moreover, Carvallo and Kasman (2005) examine Latin American countries; Hauner (2005) examines large German and Austrian commercial banks; Maudos and Pastor (2001) analyze 14 countries of the European Union, Japan and USA; while Pasiouras (2008) examines an international dataset.

As it is presented by the above mentioned studies, the evaluation of commercial bank performance has been approached from various points of view. Recent DEA studies have examined almost all the banking sectors around the world. Concerning the above and taking into consideration the volatility in financial markets, the high undertaken risks by banks and the competitive environment in which they operate, the globalization of the banking system and the fact that there are no restrictions on the interbank transactions (by using the personal computer and the internet –digitalization), estimation of the banks efficiency is more than necessary. Under such conditions, the present study will try to evaluate the efficiency of European banking sector.

3. DATA AND METHODOLOGY

Data Envelopment Analysis

Earlier referred, in the year 1978, the non-parametric DEA method was first introduced by Charnes, Cooper and Rhodes, known as "CCR model". Few years later, Banker et al. (1984) introduced the "BCC model". Lozano-Vivas and Pastor (2002), evaluate the technical efficiency of the banking industry of different countries through the DEA model. They consider "n" basic banking inputs and "m" basic banking outputs for each bank and apply the BCC input-oriented model. The mathematical formulation of this model is:

$$\begin{aligned} &\text{Min } \theta \text{ subject to } Y_{\tau} \geq Y_0 \\ &\theta,\tau \quad X_{\tau} \leq \theta X_0 \\ &e^T{}_{\tau} = 1 \\ &\tau \geq 0_n \end{aligned} \tag{1}$$

where:

Y is the matrix of output vectors
X is the matrix of input vectors
(X_0, Y_0) is the unit being rated
e^T denotes a row-vector of 1's
τ is the vector of intensity variables and
θ is the so-called efficiency score-a quantity between 0 and 1.

If $\theta < 1$, a proportional decrease of all inputs is required in order to achieve the efficient frontier. This decrease is given by $(1\text{-}\theta)\ X_0$, which means that the projected unit given by $(\theta X_0, Y_0)$ is efficient in Debreu-Farrell terminology or weakly efficient in DEA terminology. No further radial decrease of all inputs is possible given the current amount of outputs. It is possible that, in order DEA to be efficient, further individual reduction in some inputs and/or increase in some outputs is required. To evaluate these mix-inefficiencies we need to resort to a more complex BCC model, in which a non-Archimedean element in the target function is multiplied by the sum of the dummy variables. However, if the dummy variables are not important, we do not need to enhance this model further. The model considered in this first example is called the "basic" model. Additionally, in Mostafa M. (2007b), the "BCC model" focuses on determining the scale efficiency of a set of units (that is a technically efficient unit for the variable returns to scale (VRS) model).

Nowadays, this method has become widely known in measuring efficiency of developed banking systems. Based on Duygun-Fethi and Pasiouras (2009) *"DEA is a mathematical programming technique for the development of production frontiers and the measurement of efficiency relative to these frontiers."* The obvious advantages of DEA approach are that:

- It implies succefully with small samples.
- It does not require undertaking any assumptions concerning the distribution of inefficiency.
- It does not require a specific type of data in order to determine the most efficient banks.

However, in the same research it is mentioned that there are two well-known limitations of this method. "The first is that DEA assumes data to be free of measurement error and the second one, that it is sensitive to outliers."

In this approach the units which convert the inputs to outputs are referred as Decision Making Units (DMUs). In addition, the DEA efficiency value for a Decision-Making Unit (DMU) is not determined by a specific level, but it is determined in comparison to the other DMUs of the examined sample. That characteristic differentiates the DEA approach from the parametric approaches, which require particular functional form (Casu and Molyneux, 2003). According to Pasiouras (2006), DEA can estimate the technical efficiency of each DMU under the hypothesis of constant returns to scale (CRS) or variable returns to scale (VRS). Every unitintheeffectivefrontier is considered to be efficient, which means that the examined unit usesthesuitablesources and it is not possible to increase the production of certain goods, whileitsefficiency is equal to 1. On the other hand, theunits below the efficient frontier line present efficiency less than 1. Consequently, for each unit is considered as efficiency score a value from 0 to 1. (Wozniewska, 2008). So, *"each bank with higher scores indicating a more efficient bank, relatively to other banks in the sample."*Duygun-Fethi and Pasiouras (2009) .

Based on the relevant theory, the implementation of the DEA approach requires the choice of one of the two approaches: Production Approach or Intermediation Approach. In Production Approach a commercial bank's resources produce services to the customers and "under intermediation approach financial institutions are viewed intermediate funds between depositors and borrowers." (Piyu, 1992). Also, DEA model can be either Input-oriented model or Output-oriented model. The input-oriented technical efficiency measures address the question: "By how much can input quantities be proportionally reduced without changing the output quantities produced?" and the output-oriented measures of technical efficiency address the question: "By how much can output quantities be proportionally expanded without altering the input quantities used?" (Coelli et al. , 1999).

Data and Variables

In this study we measure the efficiency of 30 top commercial banks (ranked by assets) from the European banking system (of Euro area) over the period 2006-2010, through the method of Data Envelopment Analysis (DEA), under the intermediation approach (Sealey and Lindley, 1977) of evaluating bank efficiency, which consider banks *"as entities which use labor and capital to transform deposits into loans and securities."* Jemric and Vujcic (2002).

We chose to evaluate commercial banks because this banking category comprises the largest segment of depository institutions in European banking markets, the services they offer are homogeneous and able to be compared among countries (Casu and Girardone, 2006). The geographical coverage of this study is presented in the following table:

However, we have to underline that banks were excluded from the analysis, because either we had not adequate data for analyzing them or other banks did not meet the limitations or the prerequisites we have set. The main limitations and prerequisites that we had set were concerning the selection of the largest European banks by assets and specifically, the top Eurozone banks by assets.

Based on the previous studies of Carbo S. and Williams J. (2002) Beccalli et al. (2006), Pasiouras, F. (2006), Casu, B. and Girardone, C. (2006), and Altunbas Y. et al. (2007) by following the intermediation approach, under the hypothesis of VRS and using Input-oriented model, the inputs and outputs data that have been used are the following:

Inputs	Outputs
1. Input1 (x_{1j}): fixed assets	1. Output1 (y_{1j}): total loans
2. Input1 (x_{2j}): number of employees	2. Output2 (y_{2j}): securities
3. Input1 (x_{3j}): total deposits received	

Table 1. Sample Data, top Eurozone banks by assets

Country	No of banks	Banks' Symbol
Germany	5	B1, B4, B5, B24, B26
France	5	B2, B12, B18, B28, B30
Netherlands	2	B3, B8
Austria	2	B6, B7
Ireland	2	B9, B27
Italy	2	B10, B14
Spain	4	B11, B13, B15, B20
Belgium	2	B16, B19
Greece	4	B17, B23, B25, B29
Luxembourg	1	B21
Portugal	1	B22

This research uses the published annual consolidated financial statement (balance sheet and income statement data) for a sample of European (Euro zone) commercial banks for the years 2006 to 2010 (a period of time of particular interest for the banking sector), obtained from the Bankscope database, one of the biggest databases referred to banks for the efficiency analysis. Also, supplementary data (e.g. staff number) were collected from the official bank's websites. For the efficiency analysis, the software "Frontier Analyst Professional" was used which is provided by Banxia Holdings Ltd.

4. Results

This section reports the results of the DEA efficiency analysis. As it was referred above, the main data set includes annual consolidated financial statements of banks operating in Europe area over the years 2006 to 2010. Also, supplementary data for the banks (e.g. staff number) were collected from the official websites of each bank. The sample includes 30 banks per year and consists of 750 observations in total. The main results of this research will be discussed. In the following table the data of Inputs and Outputs of the 30 examined banks in average per year are depicted.

At first glance, we can see that the values of Loans and Securities (outputs data) and Deposits and Short term funding (inputs data) were sharply increased by 134%, 215% and 137%, respectively, in the year 2010 since 2009. Also, the value of Fixed Assets (input data) was dropped by 51% in the same year.

Table 2. Data (Inputs and Outputs) The data (Inputs and Outputs) of the 30 examined banks is shown in average

	Inputs			Outputs	
Years	Fixed Assets	No of employees	Deposits and Short term funding	Loans	Securities
	mil euro	thousands	mil euro	mil euro	mil euro
2006	12, 470	45, 532	190, 346	146, 453	139, 417
2007	13, 165	50, 233	216, 403	167, 445	151, 575
2008	14, 807	53, 882	223, 489	188, 043	116, 695
2009	17, 056	54, 302	201, 591	190, 453	123, 159
2010	8, 313	56, 841	477, 825	445, 126	387, 884

Efficiency of the Examined European Financial Institutions - DEA Efficiency Scores

In the preliminary analysis, we implied these two models (CRS and VRS model) in order to test the efficiency scores for the examined banks and they come up with quite similar results. We have decided to focus on the BCC, input-oriented model (input minimization). Therefore, the main question which derives is how much the inputs might be reduced while maintaining the current level of outputs. The efficiency scores for each bank are presented in Appendix. Table 3, shows the average DEA efficiency scores over the examined years as well as the annual changes in efficiency results. It should be mentioned here that these results are based on the specific data together with the inputs and outputs used. Therefore, if there is a change on the above parameters, there will be also a change regarding their efficiency.

Table 3. DEA efficiency scores and annual changes in efficiency

years	DEA Efficiency scores	Annual Change in efficiency scores
2010	0.793	-7.67%
2009	0.859	0.51%
2008	0.855	2.76%
2007	0.832	5.38%
2006	0.789	
average	0.826	

According to the above table, over the examined years, the average results of DEA efficiency scores of the examined banks show fluctuations. As it is easily observed in year 2010, the average percentage of efficiency is the lowest (0.793) achieving a decrease of 7.67% compared to the previous year. This means that the number of efficient banks is lower compared to previous years.

Based on the cross-country efficiency results of DEA (Appendix), we observe that throughout the examined years the most productive banks which remain in high levels of scores are the banks B1, B4, B5, B6, B7, B3, B8, B10, B2, B9, which come from Germany (three banks), Austria (two banks), Netherland (two banks), Italy, France and Ireland from one bank respectively.

Concerning the rest of the examined banks, some of them are close to achieve the goal of 100% efficiency and other are far away. As we can observe, although the French bank B12, the Spanish bank B13, the Italian bank B14 and the Greek banks B23 and B17 over the period 2007 to 2009 show 100% efficiency, in 2010 there is a considerable fall of their percentages. Thus, these banks become inefficient.

Examples of other banks which show considerable fall on their efficiency level, in 2010, are the French bank B12, B28, the Spanish banks B13, B20, the Belgian banks B16, B19, the Portuguese bank B22, the German banks B24, B26, the Greek banks B25, B29 and the Irish bank B27. Moreover, the French bank B30 shows the lowest percentage of efficiency level over the years. However, it is considerable the fact that the French bank B18 is characterized as inefficiency bank whereas is the 5th larger bank on our sample and also, the French bank B28 has a low efficiency level whereas is 11th larger bank in Euro zone.

Figures 1 and 2 indicate a summary of the distribution of efficiency scores in different classes for the years 2010 and 2006. A purpose of this selection has to do with the fact that these two years belong in different periods before and after the crisis respectively.

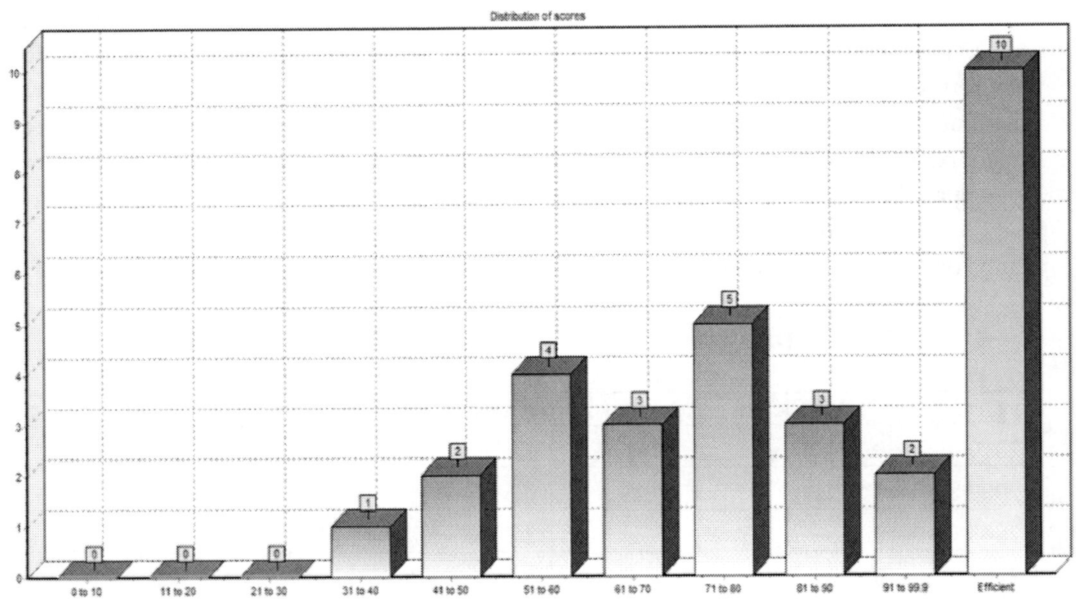

Figure 1. Distribution of scores in 2010.

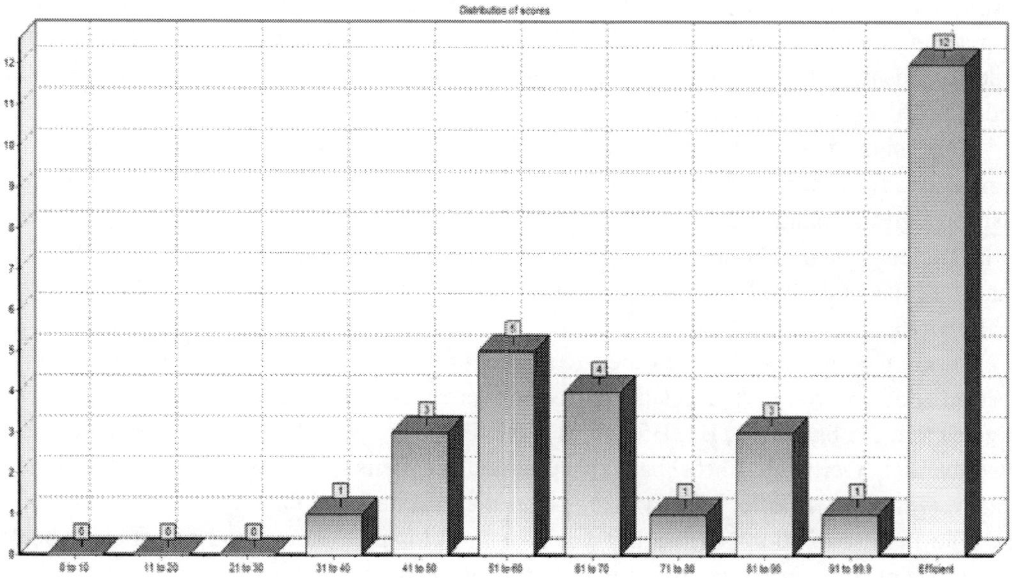

Figure 2. Distribution of scores in 2006.

Figure 1, shows the distribution of the units in eleven classes. There are 10 units (banks) in the efficient range, 2 banks in the 91-99.9 range and the rest of them range between the 31-90 ranges.

In figure 2, we can see that the number of efficient units is 12. Through the period of study there is an increase in the number of efficient banks with 2009 to be the year where 16 out of 30 institutes were efficient. In 2010, there is a decrease in the number of efficient banks, which shows that financial crisis, had a big effect in the performance of the specific financial institutions.

V. Discussion and Further Research

Based on previous studies, we employ the data envelopment analysis (DEA) method on annual data to construct efficiency frontiers. We examine the performance of the largest banks (by assets) which operate in the Euro area, by using a sample of 30 financial institutions of European banking sector. The examined period is the years 2006-2010 and the reference point of recent financial crisis the years 2008-2009.

The results show that the DEA efficiency scores, before the recent financial crisis, characterize more banks as efficient. Specifically, in the year 2006 the efficient banks are 12, in 2007 increases to 15 and remain stable in 2008. Then, in 2009 the number increases by one unit and during 2010, the number of efficient banks becomes lower (10 banks are characterized as efficient).

More precisely, the number of efficient banks is decreased from 16 to 10 banks. The banks which were excluded in 2010, referring to be inefficient, are the Greek banks B17, B23, the Belgian bank B16, the Italian bank B14 and the French bank B12.

In 2008, when the financial crisis began, the Greek economy did not seem to be particularly affected. That happens maybe due to its low exposure to "toxic" financial instruments. However, its deficit was steadily growing and thus, the governance gets support from International Monetary Fund (IMF) and EU which also include austerity measures in order to ensure the payment back. Examples of these measures are the increase in Value-added tax, the reduction of the employees' wages etc.

Also, since the recent crisis is a global crisis, it means that Belgium, Italy and even France as advanced nations undergo an economic recession. One interesting thing is the fact that through the examined years, the efficient scores of the French bank B18 characterized it as inefficiency bank whereas is the 5th larger bank on our sample. Besides, also, the French bank B28 has one of the lowest efficiency scores despite the fact that it is the 11th larger bank in Eurozone.

These topics should be further examined to understand the reasons of their poor performances. Overall, the results based on cross-country efficiency scores (Appendix) suggest that the banks B1, B4, B5, B6, B7, B3, B8, B10, B2, B9, which are from Netherland (two banks), Germany (three banks), Austria (two banks), France, Italy and Ireland are obtaining high levels of efficiency scores over the examined years.

The rapid evolutions of the last years in the global economy and as efficient banking systems contribute in an extensive way for higher economic growth in any country, lead to the conclusion that such analysis is absolutely essential for regulators, banks' managers, investors, borrowers, depositors and everybody else who are interested in the banking sector. In this way, the efficient financial institutions become able to meet the increasing and more sophisticated demands from consumers and businesses, to adapt and adjust to the technological advances, to face the challenges of globalization and liberalization, and to withstand the economic cycle, thereby contributing to the overall economic growth and stability.

The main conclusion of this study is that in a dynamic, extremely competitive sector, as the banking sector, the main characteristics of every financial institution need to be the flexibility and the ability of direct adaptation in any non expectable change.

In the following lines, there are some recommendations about the future research. For instance, the basic DEA model can be extended in order to use environmental variables. In this way, the term "environmental" is used to indicate more qualitative factors which affect the bank's operation and thus, could influence its efficiency level. As it is referred in Casu, B. and Molyneux, Ph. (2003) study, examples of such factors could be the ownership of the financial institution (public or private bank), the location and under which government regulations the examined bank operates.

In addition, we can add factors such as bank's goodwill, the life style, the size of the bank, the years that the bank exists, information about its customer's and investor's profile, the regulation, technology (IT) and strategy under which the bank operates. It would be also interesting the enrichment of the model with more countries or a cross-international comparison of USA banks and EU banks.

In addition, we could use either other set of inputs and outputs or to measure the banking efficiency by using parametric approaches, such as Stochastic Frontier Analysis (SFA), Thick Frontier Approach (TFA), Distribution Free Approach (DFA) and try to compare the results in order to find a better and more comprehensive model for analyzing the bank efficiency and performance.

APPENDIX

DEA efficiency scores (%)

No	Symbol	Country	2010	2009	2008	2007	2006
1.	B1	Germany	100	100	100	100	100
2.	B2	France	100	100	100	100	100
3.	B3	Netherlands	100	100	100	100	100
4.	B4	Germany	100	100	100	100	100
5.	B5	Germany	100	100	100	100	100
6.	B6	Austria	100	100	100	100	100
7.	B7	Austria	100	100	100	100	100
8.	B8	Netherlands	100	100	100	100	100
9.	B9	Ireland	100	100	100	100	100
10.	B10	Italy	100	100	100	100	100
11.	B11	Spain	96, 4	86, 22	81, 87	67, 34	64, 15
12.	B12	France	94, 45	100	100	100	84, 45
13.	B13	Spain	88, 4	100	100	100	100
14.	B14	Italy	84, 64	100	100	100	100
15.	B15	Spain	83, 02	78, 83	77, 5	84, 63	90, 61
16.	B16	Belgium	77, 03	100	91, 62	93, 65	90, 76
17.	B17	Greece	76, 69	100	100	100	58, 22
18.	B18	France	76, 64	74, 76	79, 81	76, 58	68, 82
19.	B19	Belgium	74, 4	81, 3	76, 95	69, 8	79, 89
20.	B20	Spain	71, 9	77, 57	77, 5	81, 3	70, 34
21.	B21	Luxembourg	70, 96	70, 44	70, 67	62, 48	54, 23
22.	B22	Portugal	70, 58	79, 24	79, 22	65, 85	53, 59
23.	B23	Greece	62, 1	100	100	100	50, 26
24.	B24	Germany	58, 53	69, 24	65, 34	61, 25	58, 77
25.	B25	Greece	54, 02	81, 69	81, 31	74	93, 56
26.	B26	Germany	53, 64	61, 87	53, 29	47	44, 76
27.	B27	Ireland	53, 24	63, 75	81, 13	82, 68	70, 17
28.	B28	France	50, 01	56, 93	54, 82	43, 72	37, 59
29.	B29	Greece	49, 2	59, 21	61, 25	53, 08	55, 01
30.	B30	France	35, 65	38, 18	33, 91	33, 99	44, 63

REFERENCES

Allen, L. and Rai, A. (1996) "Operational efficiency in banking: An international comparison", *Journal of Banking and Finance*, Vol. 20, pages 655-672.

Altunbas, Y., Carbo, S., Gardener, E. and Molyneux, P. (2007) "Examining the Relationships between capital, risk and efficiency in European Banking", *European Financial Management*, Vol. 13, No. 1, pages 49–70.

Altunbas, Y., Gardener, E.P.M, Molyneux, P. and Moore, B. (2001) "Efficiency in European banking", European Economic Review, *Elsevier,* Vol.45, No.10, pages 1931-1955.

Altunbas, Y., Ming-Hau, L., Molyneux, P., Rama, S. (2000) "Efficiency and risk in Japanese banking", Journal of Banking and Finance, *Elsevier*, Vol. 24, No. 10, pages 1605-1628.

Aly, H. Y., Grabowski, R., Pasurka, C., Rangan, N. (1990) "Technical, scale, and allocative efficiencies in U.S. banking: An empirical investigation", *Review of Economics and Statistics*, Vol. 72, pages 211-218.

Banker, R., Charnes, A. and Cooper, W. (1984) "Some Models for Estimating Technical and Scale Inefficiencies in Data Envelopment Analysis, " *Management Science*, Vol. 30, pages 1078-1092.

Beccalli, E., Casu, B. and Girardone, C. (2006) "Efficiency and Stock Performance in European Banking", *Journal of Business Finance and Accounting,* Vol. 33, pages 218-235.

Beltratti, A., and Stulz, R., (2009) "The credit crisis around the globe: Why did some banks perform better? Cross-Country *Study of the Impact of Governance and Regulation*", ECGI Working paper series in Finance.

Berg, S., Forsund, F. R., Hjalmarsson, L., and Suominen M. (1993) "Banking efficiency in the Nordic countries", *Journal of Banking and Finance*, Vol. 17, pages 371-388.

Bergendahl, G. (1995) "DEA and Benchmarks for Nordic Banks", *Working paper,* Gothenburg University, Gothenberg, Sweden (December).

Bukh, P. N. D., Berg, S. A., Forsund, F. R. (1995) "Banking Efficiency in the Nordic Countries: A Four-country Malmquist Index Analysis*", Working paper,* University of Aarhus, Denmark.

Carbo, S. and Williams, J. (2002) "Efficiency in banking: Empirical Evidence from the savings banks sector", *The Manchester School*, Vol.70 No.2, ISSN 1463-6786, pages 204-228.

Carvallo, O. and Kasman, A. (2005) "Cost efficiency in the Latin American and Caribbean banking systems", *Int. Fin. Markets, Inst. and Money*, Vol. 15, pages 55–72.

Casu, B. and Girardone, C. (2006) "Bank competition, concentration and efficiency in the single European market", *The Manchester School*, Vol. 74 No. 4, ISSN 1463–6786, pages 441–468.

Casu, B. and Molyneux, Ph. (2003) "A comparative study of efficiency in European banking", *Applied Economics*, Vol.35, No.17, pages 1865 – 1876.

Chansarn, S. (2008) "The Relative Efficiency of Commercial Banks in Thailand: DEA Approach", *International Research Journal of Finance and Economics*, ISSN 1450-2887 Issue 18.

Charnes, A., Cooper, W. W. and Rhodes, E., 1978, "Measuring the efficiency of decision making units", *European Journal of Operations Research,* Vol. 2, pages 429-444.

Chen, Tser-Yieth and Yeh, Tser-Lien (2000) "A Measurement of Bank Efficiency, Ownership and Productivity Changes in Taiwan", *The Service Industries Journal*, Vol.20, No.1, pages 95-109.

Cinca, S., Molinero, M. and F., Callén (2011) "Modeling Banking Efficiency with DEA", *Kent Business School: Working Paper Series,* No. 242, University of Kent.

Coelli T., Prasada Rao D.S., Battese G.E., (1999) *"An introduction to efficiency and productivity analysis",* US: *Kluwer Academic Publishers*.

Davis, E. and Karim, D. (2008) "Comparing early warning systems for banking crises", *Journal of Financial Stability* 2008, Vol. 4, pages 89-120.

Demirguc-Kunt, A. and Detragiache, E. (1998) "The determinants of banking crises in developing and developed countries", *IMF staff papers*, Vol. 45, pages 81-109.

Demyanyk, Y. and Hasan, I. (2010) "Financial crises and bank failures: A review of prediction methods", *Omega*, Vol. 38, pages 315-324.

Demyanyk, Y. and Van Hement, O. (2008) "Understanding the subprime mortgage crisis", St. Louis, MO: *Federal Reserve Bank of St. Louis*, pages 1-39.

Diamond, D. and Rajan, R. (2009) "The credit crisis: conjectures about causes and remedies", NBER Working papers 14739, *National Bureau of Economics Research, Inc.*

Dietsch, M. and Lozano, A. (1996) "How the Environment Determine the Efficiency of Banks: A Comparison between French and Spanish Banking Industry", paper presented at the II Georgia Productivity Workshop, *Georgia University*, USA.

Drake, L. (2001) "Efficiency in UK Banking", *Applied Financial Economics*, Vol. 11, pages 557-571.

Drake, L., Howcroft, B. (1994) "Relative efficiency in the branch network of a U.K. bank: an empirical study", *OMEGA International Journal of Management Science*, Vol. 22, pages 83-90.

Duygun-Fethi, M. and Pasiouras, F. (2009) "Assessing Bank Performance with Operational Research and Artificial Intelligence Techniques: A Survey", SSRN database: *Working Paper Series*.

Elyasiani, E., and S.M. Mehdian, (1995) "The Comparative Efficiency Performance of Small and Large U.S. Commercial Banks in the Pre- and Post-Deregulation Eras, " *Applied Economics,* Vol. 27, pages 1069-1079.

Elysiani E., Mehdian S., (1990b) "A non-parametric approach to measurement of efficiency and technological change: the case of large US banks", *Journal of Financial Services Research*, Vol. 4, pages 157-168.

Erkens, D., H., Hung, M. and Matos, P., P. (2012) "Corporate Governance in the 2007-2008 Financial Crisis: Evidence from Financial Institutions Worldwide", *Journal of Corporate Finance*, Vol. 18.

Fecher, F. and Pestieau, P. (1993) "Efficiency and Competition in O.E.C.D. Financial Services", in H.O. Fried, C.A.K. Lovell, and S.S. Schmidt, eds., The Measurement of Productive Efficiency: *Techniques and Applications*, (Oxford University Press), U.K., pages 374-385.

Fernández, A., I., Gascón, F. and González, E. (2004) "Economic Efficiency and Value Maximization in Banking Firms", Universidad de Oviedo.

Ferrier, G., and Lovell, K. (1990) "Measuring cost efficiency in banking: Econometric and linear programming evidence", *Journal of Econometrics*, Vol. 46, pages 229-245.

Field, K. (1990) "Production efficiency of British building societies", *Applied Economics*, Vol. 22, pages 415-426.

Grigorian, D., and Manole, V. (2002) "Determinants of Commercial Bank Performance in Transition: An Application of Data Envelopment Analysis", *World Bank Policy Research Working Paper*, series 2850.

Hauner, D. (2005) "Explaining efficiency differences among large German and Austrian banks", *Applied Economics,* Vol. 37, pages 969–980.

Heilpern, E., Haslam, C. and Andersson, T. (2009) "When it comes to the crunch: What are the drivers of the U.S banking crisis", Accounting Forum, Vol. 33, pages 99-113.

Isik I., Hassan M.K., (2002) "Technical scale and allocative efficiencies of Turkish banking industry", *Journal of Banking and Finance*, Vol. 26, pages 719-766.

Isik I., Hassan M.K., (2003) "Financial deregulation and total factor productivity change: An empirical study of Turkish commercial banks", *Journal of Banking and Finance, Elsevier*, Vol. 27, No. 8, pages 1455-14485.

Jemric, I. and Vujcic, B. (2002) "Efficiency of Banks in Croatia: A DEA Approach", Croatian National Bank Working Papers, No 7.

Joshi, P. and Bhalerao, J., V. (2011) "Efficiency evaluation of banking sector in India based on data envelopment analysis", *Indian Journal of Commerce and Management Studies*, Vol–II, Issue -3.

Lozano-Vivas, A., J. and Pastor, J. (2002) "An Efficiency Comparison of European Banking Systems Operating under Different Environmental Conditions", *Journal of Productivity Analysis,* Vol. 18, pages 59–77.

Maudos, J. and Pastor, J. (2001) "Cost and profit efficiency in banking: an international comparison of Europe, Japan and the USA", *Applied Economics Letters*, Vol. 8, pages 383- 387.

Maudos, J., Pastor, J., Perez, F. and Quesada, J. (2002) "Cost and profit efficiency in European banks", *Journal of International Financial Markets, Institutions and Money*, Vol. 12, pages 33–58.

Mertens A., Urga G., (2001) "Efficiency, scale and scope economies in the Ukrainian banking sector in 1998", *Journal of Emerging Markets Review,* Vol.2, pages 292-308.

Mostafa, M., (2007b) "Modeling the efficiency of GCC banks: a data envelopment analysis approach", *International Journal of Productivity and Performance Management,* Vol.56, No.7, pages 623-643.

Noulas, A. (1997) "Productivity growth in the Hellenic Banking Industry: State versus private banks", *Applied Financial Economics*, Vol.7, pages 223-228.

Pasiouras, F. (2006) "Estimating the technical and scale efficiency of Greek commercial banks: the impact of credit risk, off-balance sheet activities, and international operations", SSRN database: *Working Paper Series*.

Pasiouras, F. (2008) "International evidence on the impact of regulations and supervision on banks' technical efficiency: an application of two-stage data envelopment analysis", Review of Quantitative Finance and Accounting, *Springer*, Vol. 30, No.2, pages 187-223.

Pasiouras, F., Liadaki, A., and Zopounidis, C. (2008) "Bank efficiency and share performance: evidence from Greece", *Applied Financial Economics,* Vol.18, No.14, pages 1121 – 1130.

Pastor, J.M., Pérez, F. and Quesada, J. (1997) "Efficiency Analysis in Banking Firms: An International Comparison", *European Journal of Operational Research,* Vol.98, pages 395-407.

Piyu, Y., (1992) "Data envelop analysis and commercial bank performance: A primer with applications to Missouri Banks", *Federal Reserve Bank of St. Louis,* Vol. 74, No.1, pages 31-45.

Rangan, N., Grabowski, R., Aly, H., Pasurka, C. (1988) "The technical efficiency of U.S. banks", *Economic Letters*, Vol. 28, No. 2, pages 169-175.

Resti, A. (1997) "Evaluating the Cost-Efficiency of the Italian Banking System: What Can Be Learned from the Joint Application of Parametric and Non-Parametric Techniques?" *Journal of Banking and Finance,* Vol. 21, pages 221-250.

Sathye M., (2001) "X-efficiency in Australian banking: An empirical investigation", *Journal of Banking and Finance*, Vol. 25, pages 613-630.

Sealey, Jr. C. W. and Lindley, J. T. (1977) "Inputs, outputs and theory of production and cost at depository financial institutions", *Journal of finance* Vol.4, pages 1251-1266.

Staub R., Souza, G. and Tabak, M., B. (2010) "Evolution of bank efficiency in Brazil: A DEA approach", European Journal of Operational Research, Vol. 202 No. 1, pages 204–213.

Taylor, J. (2008). The Financial Crisis and the Policy Responses: An Empirical Analysis of What Went Wrong. *NBER Working Paper* No. 14631

Taylor, J. (2009) The financial crisis and the policy responses: An analysis of what went wrong, unpublished working paper, *Stanford University*, Palo Alto, CA.

Wezel, T. (2010) "Bank Efficiency amid Foreign Entry: Evidence from the Central American Region", IMF Working Paper, No. 10/95, Washington: *International Monetary Fund.*

Wozniewska, G. (2008) "Methods of measuring the efficiency of commercial banks: an example of Polish banks, " *Economika,* Vol. 84, pages 81-91.

In: Computational Techniques for Banking and Risk Management ISBN: 978-1-62618-522-7
Editors: C. Zopounidis and M. Doumpos

Chapter 6

CASH WITHDRAWALS FORECASTING BY NEURAL NETWORKS

Ioanna G. Atsalaki[1*], George S. Atsalakis[2] and Constantinos D. Zopounidis[2]

[1]Department of Business Administration of Food and Agricultural Products
University of Western Greece, Agrinio, Greece
[2]Department of Production Engineering and Management
Technical University of Crete, Chania, Greece

ABSTRACT

Forecasting daily cash withdrawals at automatic teller machines (ATMs) cause several difficulties to arise due to the volatility of such a time series. This paper deals with the application of neural networks in order to forecast cash withdrawals one-step-ahead. Fifty multi layer feed foreword neural network models have been developed and tested using a range of a number of hidden layers (one to ten) and a range of a number of lags (one to five). A time series data of 735 daily observations has been implemented as inputs to feed the models. Fifty five percent (85%) of the observations (raw data) has been used to train the neural network models. The remaining 15% has been used for out of sample validation of the accuracy of the suggested neural network forecasting model. The accuracy of the model has been tested by using the well known statistical error measure of Root Mean Square Error (RMSE). Further tests have been applied to one hundred time series data of different ATMs that have been located in different locations. In total, 5, 000 neural network models have been developed and tested.

Finally one hundred models (the best model for each ATM) have been chosen and their RMSEs are presented in a table. The results indicate that the lowest root mean square error (0.0469) arises with a neural network consisted of five lags and seven hidden layers.

Keywords: Cash withdrawals forecasting, cash machines forecasting, cash demands, neural network forecasting, time series forecasting

[*] E-mail: joanna_atsa@hotmail.com.

1. Introduction

Based on the forecasts, an inventory of cash money needs to be ordered and each has to be ATM replenished by a set period of time beforehand. If the forecasts are too high, the unused money stored in the ATMs incurs costs. If the ATMs run out of cash, customers will be dissatisfied.

Modeling and forecasting financial time series is challenging due to their volatile behavior. The development of empirical models based on the observed characteristics of the historical data is required. Assuming y is a time series of daily cash withdrawals, the future values can be forecasted by the following formula:

$$y_{t+1} = f(y_{t-k}, \ldots\ldots, y_t) \tag{1}$$

where y_{t+1} is the value to be predicted and y_{t-k} is the influence factor that denote the time-ordered sequence of historical values characterizing the movements of a data series up to the current time y_t.

The forecasting objective is therefore to minimize the error between the forecasting value $\hat{y}_{t+1}$ and the subsequently observed actual time series value y_{t+1}.

Traditional models have been used to forecast financial time series such as linear regression, stochastic regression, statistical regression, etc. These models are based on probability theory and statistical analysis with a certain number of distributions assumed in advance. In most cases these assumptions are unreasonable and non-realistic.

The latest computational intelligence techniques have been applied to forecast financial time series such as fuzzy, neuro-fuzzy, neural network, genetic algorithm etc. These techniques are model based approaches with promised results due to the significant properties of handling non-linear data with self learning capabilities (Atsalakis, 2009a, 2009b; Hornik, 1991; Jain, 1997; Skapura, 1996).

During the past few years a noteworthy effort by many researchers has been carried out, aiming at making forecasts using neural networks. Neural networks are a part of Artificial Intelligence, a multidisciplinary field which aims not only to replicate human reasoning and brain activity but also to improve decision making by enhancing consistency.

According to Wen (2000), "Artificial Neural Networks (ANNs) are an information processing technology pertaining to the area of machine learning in artificial intelligence. A neural network employs an adaptive structure that can be trained with application data to capture complex relationships between input and out variables."

Neural networks are being used in widespread areas such as stock market prediction, medical diagnostics, product selection, system control, pattern recognition, functional synthesis and forecasting due to their ability to combine accuracy with common-sense performance and ease of use.

They have been found useful in many different types of applications in economics, finance and business, because they have been particularly effective in capturing complex relationships, outperforming linear models in a variety of circumstances.

Neural networks have several advantages, the most important one being their ability to learn from data, thereby acquiring the potential to generalize, i.e. produce an acceptable output for previously unseen input data which is very important in prediction tasks. This even holds, to a certain extent, when input series contain low-quality or missing data. Another valuable quality is the non-linear nature of a neural network. Furthermore, no expert system, such as a typical programmer coding rules in a computer program, is needed. This makes the network extremely flexible to changes in the environment. One only has to retrain the system.

Regarding downsides, the black-box-property first springs to mind. Relating one single outcome of a network to a specific internal decision known as the credit assignment problem (Grothman, 2002; Haykin, 1994) is very difficult. Noisy data also reinforce the negative implications of establishing incorrect causalities, overtraining or over fitting, which will harm generalization. Finally, a certain degree of knowledge in the current subject is required as it is not trivial to assess the relevance of chosen input series.

Many of the studies on early warning failure prediction studies compared the predictive powers of neural networks and conventional statistical models like multiple discriminant analysis and logistic regression. A number of studies found neural networks to be superior to these models (e.g., Coats and Fant, 1993; Lenard, et al., 1993; Salchenberger, et al., 1992). Yet other studies found both approaches yield a balanced degree of accuracy (Altman, et al., 1994; Boritz, et al., 1995; Yang, et al., 1999). Boritz (1995) showed that the performance of neural networks is sensitive to the choice of variables selected and that the networks cannot be relied upon to evaluate and focus on the most important variables. Zurada, et al. (1998) found that neural networks are not superior to logistic regression models for traditional dichotomous response variables, but are superior for more complex financial distress response variables. Zhang (2001) found that neural networks are quite effective in linear time-series modeling and forecasting. This implies that the technology can compete with linear models for linear problems.

Computer intelligent techniques to forecast ATM cash withdrawals have been used by: Balkin and Ord, 2000; De Gooijer and Hyndman, 2006; De Menezes and Nikolaev, 2006; Terasvirta, van Dijk and Medeiros, 2005.

The rest of the paper is organized as follows: Section 2 presents the neural network architecture. Section 3 describes the data and the training of the models. Section 4 presents the out of sample evaluation of the suggested forecasted models. Section 5 presents the conclusion of the paper with a summary and a discussion of potential future work.

2. Neural Network Architecture

A typical neural network consists of layers. In a single layered network there is an input layer of source nodes and an output layer of neurons. Moreover, a multi-layer network has one or more hidden layers of hidden neurons. Extra hidden neurons raise the network's ability to extract higher-order statistics from (input) data. This is a crucial quality, especially if there is a large input layer.

The building block of a neural network is a simple computational device and the connections between neurons determine the function of the network. Neural network architecture employs multiple layers of nodes. A 'node' is where the data is converted into values between 0 and 1 using sigmoid transfer function in a network. Its technology is inspired by the architecture of the human brain. Similarly, it is composed of many neurons operating in parallel whose function is determined by network structure, connection strengths and the processing performed at computing elements or nodes. The difference between a neural network and other approximation methods is that the neural network makes use of one or more hidden layers, in which the input variables are squashed or transformed by a special function, known as a logistic or log sigmoid transformation (McNelis, 2005). In addition to the sequential processing of typical linear systems, the neurons in the hidden layer process the inputs in a parallel fashion to improve the predictions. The connectors between the input variables, often called input neurons, and the neurons in the hidden layers, as well as the connectors between the hidden-layer neurons and the output variable, or output neuron, are called synapses (McNelis, 2005). This paper uses a feedforward network with hidden layers, the architecture of which is illustrated in Figure 1:

It can be observed that the first layer is the input layer that presents data into the network and has as many neurons as there are input categories. Moreover, the next layer is called the hidden layer because it creates an internal mapping of the input data and explores hidden patterns, correlations and causal relationships in the data set in order to make generalizations. A network may have more than one hidden layer depending on the complexity of the problem. The final layer is the output layer, where each neuron in it receives input from each neuron in the hidden layer immediately proceeding. The number of neurons in the output layer will equal the number of output categories the researcher wants. Finally, a neural network involves large numbers of nodes that continuously interact with each other. Between each set of nodes there is a nonlinear transfer function, such as a numerical weight, that helps determine the final solution. As the neural network learns or is trained through the input of data, the weights are varied for a better solution and the inputs are thus transformed by the squasher function before transmitting their effects on the output. Ultimately, the network is trained and learns the solution for itself.

With a description of the network structure at hand, training matters have to be settled. The overall objective in training is to minimize the discrepancy between real data and the output of the network. In a step-by-step manner the error guides the network in the direction towards the target data.

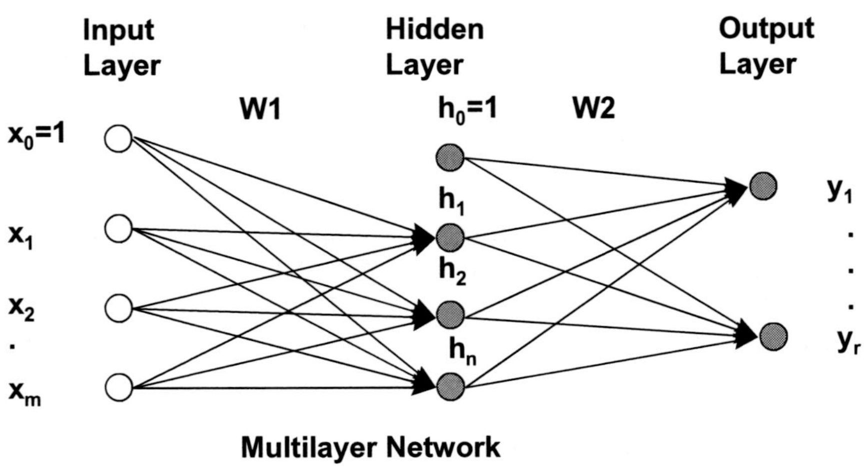

Figure1. Architecture of a feedforward multilayer neural network.

The backpropagation algorithm belongs to this class and can be described as "an efficient way to calculate the partial derivatives of the network error function with respect to the weights" (Grothmann, 2002).

3. Data Series and Model Training

The time series data concerns the cash withdrawals of one hundred ATM that are located in different areas. The data consists of 100 different time series (one for each ATM). Each time series is comprised of 735 daily samples. Eighty five percent (85%) of the data have been used to train the models. The remaining 15% of the data have been used for out of sample evaluation of the models.

The neural network structure consists of one to five inputs and one output. The model is a feedforward multilayer network and uses the 'tansig' as a transfer function for hidden layers and the 'purelin' for the output layer.

Table 1. Key neural network model parameters for the back-propagation model

Hidden layers: 1-10	Cases in training : 624
Process Elements in hidden layer: 3	Cases in testing : 111
Process Elements in input layer : 1-5	Epoch size :1, 000
Process Elements in output layer: 1	Learning coefficient (HL): 0.1
Learn rule: learnlm	Learning coefficient (OL) :0.1
Learn sequence: Random	Learning coefficient ratio :1.05
Learn cycles: 300, 000	Number of lags : 1-5
Transfer mode: tansig , purelin	Performance goal :0.00001

The back propagation network training function is 'learnlm'. The learning rate is 0.1, the ratio to increase the learning rate is 1.05 while the ratio to decrease the learning rate is 0.7. The maximum number of epochs to train is 1, 000 and the performance goal is 0.00001. Table 1 summarizes the parameters of the model.

4. Out of Sample Model Evaluation

In this section the optimal network configuration for forecasting the time series data is determined. Due to the nature of the data, fifty neural network models have been applied for each of the one hundred different data sets (each ATM). Five thousand neural network models have been developed and tested using a varying number of hidden layers (up to ten) and a different number of lags (up to five).

Each of these models has been trained using the training set, and their one-step-ahead forecasting performances have been evaluated by using the corresponding out of sample validation test.

A crucial part of time series forecasting is the evaluation of the forecasting model which is carried out once widely used performance measures have been applied.

The objective here is to determine the optimal configuration of each time series model. The Root Mean Square Error (RMSE) metric has been employed to measure the forecasting performance of each of the 5, 000 models. The RMSE is computed as follows (equation 2):

$$RMSE = \sqrt{\frac{\sum_{\delta-1}^{N} e_t^2}{N}} \tag{2}$$

The lower RMSE value corresponds to the better forecasting performance. Based on the computed RMSE results, the optimal network configuration has been identified as the one that yields the lowest RMSE value. In this way an optimal neural network for each time series has been obtained. The results shown in Table 2 clearly demonstrate the best configuration of each one of the 100 data set models.

Each column corresponds to a different ATM data set. The first row shows the lags (the number of inputs) of the model. The second row shows the number of hidden layers of the neural model. The best performance (RMSE: 0.0469) is obtained by the data set of the ATM60 which is modeled by a neural network with the follow configuration:

a) input layers: number of inputs 5 (number of lags)
b) hidden layers: seven
c) output layer: one-step-ahead forecast

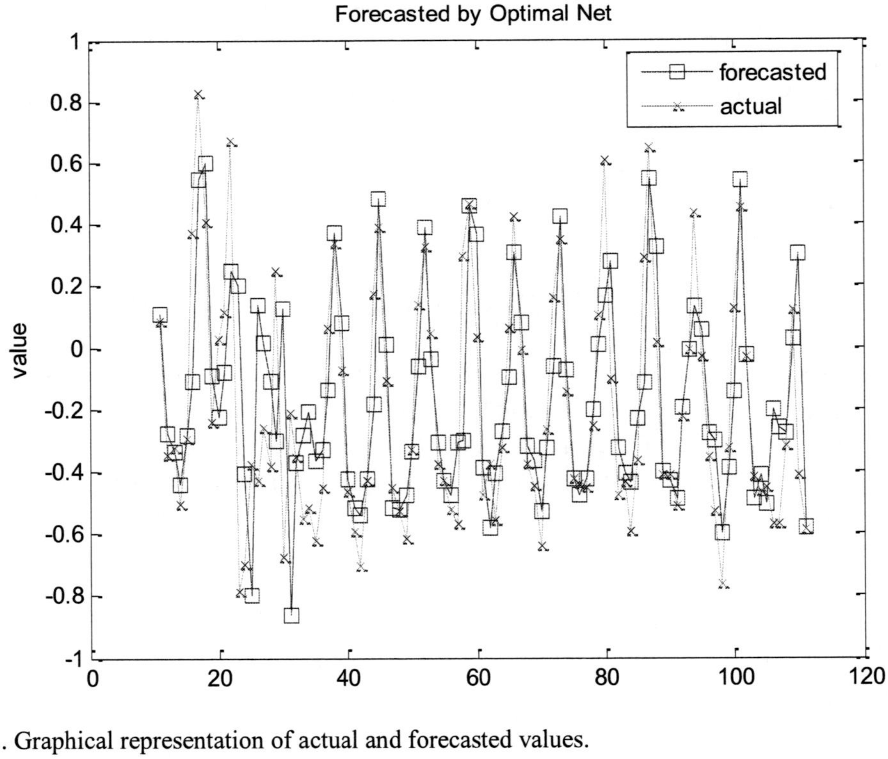

Figure 2. Graphical representation of actual and forecasted values.

Table 2. RMSE performance of the fifty neural networks

	ATM1	ATM2	ATM3	ATM4	ATM5	ATM6	ATM7	ATM8	ATM9	ATM10
Lags	5	5	5	5	5	4	4	4	5	4
Hidden Layers	7	4	8	2	7	10	5	2	7	4
RMSE	0.1038	0.0879	0.0985	0.1095	0.0799	0.1220	0.1123	0.1108	0.0907	0.1464
	ATM11	ATM12	ATM13	ATM14	ATM15	ATM16	ATM17	ATM18	ATM19	ATM20
Lags	4	4	4	4	4	5	4	3	4	3
Hidden Layers	8	8	5	9	7	7	3	8	4	4
RMSE	0.1046	0.1194	0.1149	.0860	0.1051	0.0866	0.1157	0.1100	0.1133	0.0995
	ATM21	ATM22	ATM23	ATM24	ATM25	ATM26	ATM27	ATM28	ATM29	ATM30
Lags	4	4	3	5	3	2	2	3	4	5
Hidden Layers	8	8	9	8	8	9	2	10	6	10
RMSE	0.1265	0.1067	0.0918	0.0960	0.1104	0.1233	0.1252	0.1087	0.0889	0.0680
	ATM31	ATM32	ATM33	ATM34	ATM35	ATM36	ATM37	ATM38	ATM39	ATM40
Lags	2	5	5	2	2	5	5	4	4	5
Hidden Layers	2	9	8	5	6	3	4	9	3	10
RMSE	0.1240	0.1157	0.1018	0.1054	0.0975	0.1140	0.0951	0.0892	0.0908	0.0973
	ATM41	ATM42	ATM43	ATM44	ATM45	ATM46	ATM47	ATM48	ATM49	ATM50
Lags	2	5	5	5	5	4	5	5	4	4
Hidden Layers	2	7	4	4	6	10	4	7	10	4
RMSE	0.1153	0.0837	0.1169	0.1057	0.1000	0.0861	0.1124	0.1188	0.0545	0.1135
	ATM51	ATM52	ATM53	ATM54	ATM55	ATM56	ATM57	ATM58	ATM59	ATM60
Lags	5	5	5	5	4	4	5	4	5	5
Hidden Layers	8	4	10	3	10	5	6	7	4	7
RMSE	0.1290	0.1378	0.0858	0.0822	0.1323	0.0860	0.1182	0.0933	0.0974	0.0469
	ATM61	ATM62	ATM63	ATM64	ATM65	ATM66	ATM67	ATM68	ATM69	ATM70
Lags	5	5	5	5	5	5	4	2	3	5
Hidden Layers	4	10	7	8	6	8	5	6	8	9
RMSE	0.1114	0.0875	0.1103	0.0996	0.1144	0.1020	0.0740	0.0817	0.1236	0.0941

Table 2. (Continued)

	ATM71	ATM72	ATM73	ATM74	ATM75	ATM76	ATM77	ATM78	ATM79	ATM80
Lags	4	5	5	4	2	5	5	4	5	5
Hidden Layers	5	5	7	10	9	9	4	6	3	2
RMSE	0.1199	0.1054	0.1067	0.1110	0.1007	0.0904	0.1033	0.1114	0.0608	0.0881
	ATM81	ATM82	ATM83	ATM84	ATM85	ATM86	ATM87	ATM88	ATM89	ATM90
Lags	5	3	5	2	5	1	3	5	4	4
Hidden Layers	4	7	3	6	8	8	10	2	5	10
RMSE	0.1166	0.0882	0.1131	0.1071	0.1094	0.1279	0.0950	0.1178	0.0785	0.0715
	ATM91	ATM92	ATM93	ATM94	ATM95	ATM96	ATM97	ATM98	ATM99	ATM100
Lags	4	2	4	5	1	5	5	5	5	5
Hidden Layers	6	5	7	8	8	2	9	8	5	8
RMSE	0.1022	0.1217	0.0842	0.0801	0.0760	0.1068	0.0744	0.1076	0.0847	0.0900

Figure 2 illustrates the graphical representation of the performance of the optimal neural network model that uses 7 hidden layers and 5 inputs. The dotted red line with the asterisks depicts the actual values and the blue continuous line with the square indicates the forecasted out of sample values derived by the neural network model. It is clearly demonstrated that the two lines almost coexist.

CONCLUSION

In this paper, a multi-layer feed forward neural network model has been used to model and forecast the unknown future values of a set of 100 time series of daily ATM cash withdrawals. The forecasting model results portray the complex dynamics of the times series data which have effectively been modeled. After testing 5, 000 models, the optimal one is that which has five inputs and seven hidden layers that models the ATM60 data set.

Despite the fact that no preprocessing has been carried out on the data sets, the results are very satisfactory.

Future research, must incorporate seasonality adjustments in the forecasting models. In addition, the use of other modeling techniques should be investigated to further improve the forecasting accuracy.

REFERENCES

Altman, E. I., Marco, G., and Varetto, F. (1994) Corporate Distress Diagnosis: Comparisons Using Linear Discriminant Analysis and Neural Networks (the Italian Experience). *Journal of Banking and Finance* 18 (May): 505-529.

Atsalakis, G. (2009a). Wind energy production forecasting. In Mastorakis N., Mladenov, V., Vasiliki, T. (Eds.) *Lecture notes in electrical engineering* (vol. 2, pp. 1-13). New York: Springer.

Atsalakis, G., and Valavanis, K. (2009b). Forecasting stock Market short-term trends using a neuro-fuzzy based methodology. *Journal of Expert Systems with Applications*, 36, 10696-10707.

Balkin, S. D., and Ord, J. K. (2000). Automatic neural network modeling for univariate time series. *International Journal of Forecasting*, 16, 509–515.

Boritz, J. E., Kennedy, D. B., and de Mirande e Albuquerque, A. (1995) Predicting Corporate Failure Using a Neural Network Approach. *International Journal of Intelligent Systems in Accounting, Finance and Management* 4(2) (June): 95 –111.

Coats, P. K., and Fant, L. F. (1993) Recognizing Financial Distress Patterns Using a Neural Network Tool. *Financial Management*: 142-155.

De Gooijer, J. G., and Hyndman, R. J. (2006). 25 years of time series forecasting. *International Journal of Forecasting*, 22, 443–473.

De Menezes, L. M., and Nikolaev, N. Y. (2006). Forecasting with genetically programmed polynomial neural networks. *International Journal of Forecasting*, 22, 249–265.

Fletcher, D., and Goss, E. (1993) Forecasting With Neural Networks: An Application Using Bankruptcy Data. *Information and Management* 24(3): 159-167.

Grothmann R. (2002) *Multi-Agent Market Modeling based on Neural Networks*, Ph.D. thesis, Faculty of Economics, University of Bremen, Germany.

Haykin S. (1994) *Neural Networks.* A Comprehensive Foundation, Macmillan College Publishing, New York.

Hornik K., (1991), Approximation capabilities of multi-layer feed- forward networks, *Neural Networks* 4, 251-257.

Jain B.A. and Nag B.N., (1997), Performance evaluation of neural network decision models, *Manage Information Systems* 14, 201-216.

Lenard, M. J., Alam, P., and Madey, G. R. (1995) The Application of Neural Networks and A Qualitative Response Model to the Auditor's Going Concern Uncertainty Decision. *Decision Sciences* 26(2), 209 –227.

McNelis, Paul, D., (2005), N*eural Networks in Finance: Gaining Predictive Edge in the Market,* Elsevier Academic Press, New York.

Salchenberger, L. M., Cinar, E. M, and Lash, N. A. (1992) Neural networks: A New Tool for Predicting Thrift Failures. *Decision Sciences*. 23(4), 899-916.

Skapura D., (1996), *Building Neural Networks*, Addison Wesley, New York (1).

Terasvirta, T., van Dijk, D., and Medeiros, M. C. (2005). Linear models, smooth transition autoregressions and neural networks for forecasting macroeconomic time series: a re-examination. *International Journal of Forecasting*, 21, 755–774.

Wen, Kuang-Wei et al.(2002) "Market segmentation via structured click stream analysis", *Industrial Management and Data Systemes*; MCB UP Limited; Vol. 102/9; 2002.

Yang, Z. R, Platt, M. B., and Platt, Harlan D. (1999) Probabilistic Neural Networks in Bankruptcy Prediction. *Journal of Business Research*44(2), 67-74.

Zhang, G. P. (2001) An investigation of neural network for linear time-series forecasting. *European Computers and Operational Research* 28(12), 1183-1202.

Zurada, J. M., Foster, B. P., Ward, T. J., and Barker, R. M. (1998-1999) Neural Networks Versus Logit Regression Models for Predicting Financial Distress Response Variables. *The Journal of Applied Business Research* 15(1), 21-29.

In: Computational Techniques for Banking and Risk Management ISBN: 978-1-62618-522-7
Editors: C. Zopounidis and M. Doumpos

Chapter 7

COMPUTING OPTIMALITY CONDITIONS IN ECONOMIC PROBLEMS

George E. Halkos and Kyriaki D. Tsilika*

Department of Economics, University of Thessaly,
Korai, Volos, Greece

ABSTRACT

This chapter proposes optimization analysis using functions programmed in the free computer algebra system (CAS) Xcas. The theoretical basis of the chapter follows classical deterministic optimization methods, with focus on necessary and sufficient conditions of an objective function *f(x)* when vector variable *x* is unconstrained and when *x* satisfies equality and inequality constraints. The computer codes presented are based on the Lagrange Multiplier Method and the Fritz-John, Kuhn-Tucker necessary conditions. The output generated is both symbolic and numerical. By our computational approach, multivariable optimization problems are solved by applying - not substituting - theoretical methodology while, at the same time, acquainting the reader with a powerful digital mathematical tool, CAS software Xcas. The applications presented are aimed at students and scientists with an economics and mathematics background.

Keywords: Optimization; optimality conditions; mathematical programming; computer software

1. INTRODUCTION

Different software packages assume different formulations of optimization applications (linear, nonlinear, geometric programming). Most efficient and robust software packages compute minimum and maximum of an objective function that depends on a set of variables while satisfying some constraints.

* Corresponding Author: E-mail: ktsilika@econ.uth.gr; Phone: 0030 24210 06351.

Moré and Wright (1993), Kendrick and Amman (1999), discuss in details a list of optimization software. Specialized algorithms for optimization problems are proposed in various different studies (Gupta et al. 1993; Levi 2001; Ferris et al. 2000; Miranda and Fackler 2002; Pál and Csendes 2009).

In (Baiocchi 2007; Wang 1998; Judd 1997) potential usefulness of software tools in economics is discussed. Optimization and certain optimality conditions with Mathematica as software tool are discussed in (Varian 1996 chapter 3; Huang and Crooke 1997 chapters 11, 12).

While mathematical programming software is considered efficient in numerical computations, it generates results in a black box mode and cannot reproduce methodology of optimization theory.

As for software tools suitable for symbolic processing applications, concerning the issue of optimality conditions, the contribution of typical mathematical software is limited in presenting and computing jacobian and hessian matrices.

The computer codes presented in this chapter create functions in Xcas that generate and check necessary and sufficient optimality conditions for problems of unconstrained and constrained optimization. Xcas is accessible to all users interested, free of any charges, available at http://www-fourier.ujf-grenoble.fr/~parisse/giac.html. Xcas is compatible with Mac OS X, Windows (except possibly for Vista) and Linux/Ubuntu. Our computational approach emphasizes in mathematical methodology and aims at both symbolic and numerical results. The computer codes presented are written in Xcas version 0.9.9.

We do not intend to give immediate answers of the «True / False» type while testing optimality conditions and we expect users and readers to be acquainted with optimization theory and methods.

The functions that we programmed in Xcas take the advantage when the number of variables and constraints increase and, apart from the calculative difficulty, the low of formation of optimality conditions becomes complex.

The chapter is organized as follows. Section 2 introduces the basis of optimization in Economics. Section 3 presents classical optimization methods based on Hessian and bordered Hessian determinental expressions.

Section 4 uses determinental computations to create Xcas functions that generate and test automatically sufficient optimality conditions. The computer codes are then tested on several economic applications.

Section 5 uses the mathematical programming approach and presents the Fritz-John and Kuhn-Tucker necessary and sufficient conditions for local minima. Section 6 used Fritz-John and Kuhn-Tucker necessary conditions to create Xcas functions that generate and test automatically necessary optimality conditions. Some numerical applications are used to perform the functional programming output. The final section concludes the paper.

2. Ordinary Symbolic Computations in Economics

Optimization is a mathematical issue with wide economic applications. Optimization problems are needed in Economics as various economic problems require solutions that are subject to constraints.

Such problems are the utility maximization subject to budget constraint, the cost minimization subject to some minimal requirement of output as a production quota, maximization of profit for firms in competitive markets and subject to a firm's joint output level.

The constraints may be formalized either as equalities or inequalities, which may represent wage, budget or production levels constraints.

3. Theoretical Background of Classical Optimization Theory

3.1. Optimality Conditions for Unconstrained Optimization

Suppose f(x): $R^n \to R$ is a twice differentiable function and consider the problem of minimizing/maximizing f(x). The necessary condition for c to be a relative extremum:

$$\nabla f(c) = 0, \tag{1}$$

$\nabla f(c)$ denotes the gradient vector evaluated at c. The sufficient conditions for relative extremum c are:

c is a critical point and $|H_k(c)| > 0, k = 1,2,\ldots,n$, then c is a relative minimum

c is a critical point and $(-1)^k |H_k(c)| > 0, k = 1,2,\ldots,n$, then c is a relative maximum,

where $|H_k|$ denote the leading principal minors of the Hessian determinant:

$$|H| = \begin{vmatrix} f_{11} & f_{12} & \cdots & f_{1k} \\ f_{21} & f_{22} & \cdots & f_{2k} \\ \cdots & \cdots & \cdots & \cdots \\ f_{k1} & f_{k2} & \cdots & f_{kk} \end{vmatrix} \tag{2}$$

3.2 Optimality Conditions for Constrained Optimization. The Case with m Equality Constraints

Suppose f(x), $g_j(x)$: $R^n \to R$ are twice differentiable functions on R^n and consider the problem of optimizing f(x) subject to $S = \{x \in R^n / g_j(x) = 0, j = 1,2,\ldots,m\}$, where m<n. The necessary conditions for c to be a relative extremum:

$$\nabla L(c) = 0, \left.\frac{\partial L}{\partial \lambda_j}\right|_{(c)} = 0 \tag{3}$$

where L denotes the Lagrangian function, $\lambda_j, j = 1,2,\ldots,m$ are m Lagrange multipliers and $\nabla L(c)$ denotes the gradient vector evaluated at c.

Sufficient conditions: Suppose c satisfies necessary conditions (3) for a relative extremum.

If $(-1)^m |B_r(c)| > 0, r = m+1,\ldots,n$, then c is a relative minimum point

If $(-1)^r |B_r(c)| > 0, r = m+1,\ldots,n$, then c is a relative maximum point

where n is the number of variables and $|B_r|$ the r-th order bordered Hessian determinant:

$$|B_r| = \begin{vmatrix} L_{\lambda_1\lambda_1} & \cdots & L_{\lambda_1\lambda_m} & L_{\lambda_1 1} & \cdots & L_{\lambda_1 r} \\ \cdots & \cdots & \cdots & \cdots & \cdots & \cdots \\ L_{\lambda_m\lambda_1} & \cdots & L_{\lambda_m\lambda_m} & L_{\lambda_m 1} & \cdots & L_{\lambda_m r} \\ L_{1\lambda_1} & \cdots & L_{\lambda_1\lambda_m} & L_{11} & \cdots & L_{1r} \\ \cdots & \cdots & \cdots & \cdots & \cdots & \cdots \\ L_{r\lambda_1} & \cdots & L_{r\lambda_m} & L_{r1} & \cdots & L_{rr} \end{vmatrix} \tag{4}$$

For more details see Bertsekas (2003, chapter 5), Nash Sofer (1996, chapters10, 14), Nocedal and Wright (1999, chapters 2, 12), Pardalos and Rosen (1987). For nonconvex functions see Mistakidis and Stavroulakis (1998).

4. Computer Codes for Sufficient Optimality Conditions

The computer codes presented in this section use Hessian determinental expressions for problems of unconstrained optimization and Lagrange multiplier method for problems of constrained optimization.

4.1. The Case of Unconstrained Optimization

In the general case of unconstrained optimization, we present analytically and check numerically the sufficient conditions (2) by programming hessianseries and signseries functions in Xcas. By hessianseries function we create the series of the leading principal minors of Hessian determinant. hessianseries(f, vars) takes the objective function (f) as the first argument and the function variable vector (vars) as the second argument. The code in Xcas is:

```
hessianseries(f, vars):=seq(hessian(f, vars)[0..k, 0..k], k=0..length(hessian(f, vars))-1)
```

By signseries function we compute the signs of the leading principal minors of Hessian determinant. Signseries function's output gives the result needed to characterize the critical point as relative minimum, maximum or saddle point. signseries(f, vars, criticalvalue) takes the objective function (f) as the first argument, the function variable vector (vars) as the second argument and the critical point (criticalvalue) as the third argument. signseries generates the signs of the leading principal minors of Hessian determinant and can be defined in Xcas as follows:

```
signseries(f, vars, criticalvalue):=[seq(sign(subst(det(hessian(f, vars)[0..k, 0..k]),
    vars=criticalvalue)), k=0..length(hessian(f, vars))-1)]
```

4.2. The Case of Constrained Optimization

In the general case of constrained optimization of an n-variable function subject to m constraints where m<n, we present analytically and check numerically the sufficient conditions (4) by programming borderhessian and signborderhessian functions in Xcas. By borderhessian function we create the series of bordered Hessian determinants that sufficient conditions (4) require. borderhessian(f, varvector, #const) takes the Lagrangian function (f) as the first argument, the vector with Lagrange multipliers and function variables (varvector) as the second argument and the number of constraints (#const) as the third argument. The code in Xcas is:

```
borderhessian(f, varvector, #const):=seq(hessian(f, varvector)[0..t, 0..t],
    t=2*#const..length(hessian(f, varvector))-1)
```

By signborderhessian function we compute the signs of bordered Hessian determinants that sufficient conditions (4) require. signborderhessian function's output gives the result needed to characterize the critical point as relative minimum, maximum or saddle point. signborderhessian(f, varvector, #const, criticalvalue) takes the Lagrangian function (f) as the first argument, the vector with Lagrange multipliers and function variables (varvector) as the second argument, the number of constraints (#const) as the third argument and the critical point (criticalvalue) with critical Lagrange multipliers' values and critical variables' values as the forth argument. signborderhessian can be defined in Xcas as follows:

```
signborderhessian(f, varvector, #const, criticalvalue):=[seq(sign(subst(det(hessian(f,
    varvector)[0..t, 0..t]), varvector=criticalvalue)), t=2*#const..length(hessian(f,
    varvector))-1)]
```

4.3. Computational Performance in Economic Problems

Let us examine a number of examples.

Example 4.1.

Find the extrema of a production of a renewable natural resource of the form

$$f(x,y,z) = (x^2 + 2y^2 + 3z^2)e^{-(xz^2+y^2+z^2)}$$

in the first quadrant of the xy-plane.

In Xcas' environment we define

f(x, y, z):=(x^2+2*y^2+3*z^2)*exp(-(x*z^2+y^2+z^2))

We first calculate the critical points using the necessary condition (1). We use Xcas's function grad(Expr(expr), LstVar) to solve necessary condition (1) and get nine critical points. The nonnegative ones are selected:
criticalpoint:=[[0.54, -0.0, 0.74], [1/2, (sqrt(2))/4, (sqrt(2))/2], [0, 1, 0], [0, 0, 0]]

Next we check the signs of the sequence of the leading principal minors of Hessian determinant, evaluated at every nonnegative critical point:

signseries(f(x, y, z), [x, y, z], [0.54, -0.0, 0.74])
[1, 1, -1] (1 stands for sign (+) and -1 stands for sign (-))
signseries(f(x, y, z), [x, y, z], [1/2, (sqrt(2))/4, (sqrt(2))/2])
[1, -1, 1]
signseries(f(x, y, z), [x, y, z], [0, 1, 0])
[1, -1, -1]
signseries(f(x, y, z), [x, y, z], [0, 0, 0])
[1, 1, 1]

Alternatively, we generate the signs of the leading principal minors of Hessian determinant for all four critical points together:

map([1, 2, 3, 4], j->signseries(f(x, y, z), [x, y, z], criticalpoint[[j]])
[[1, 1, -1], [1, -1, 1], [1, -1, -1], [1, 1, 1]]

Results: the critical point (0, 0, 0) (or for Xcas criticalpoint[[3]]) satisfies sufficient conditions (2) for relative minimum.

Example 4.2.
Find the relative extrema of the following utility function of the consumption of four goods

$$f(x,y,z,w) = 0.3\log(x-2) + 0.4\log(y-3) + 0.2\log(z-4) + 0.1\log(w-5)\,,$$

subject to the budget constraint $g(x,y,z,w) = 2x + 3y + 4z + 5w - 100 = 0$.

We define the Lagrangian function l
l(x, y,z,w,λ):=0.3*log(x-2)+0.4*log(y-3)+0.2*log(z-4)+0.1*log(w-5) +λ*(2*x+3*y+4*z+5*w-100)

We calculate a critical point of the Lagrangian function:

criticalpoint:=solve(grad(l(x, y, z, w, λ), [x, y, z, w, λ])=[0, 0, 0, 0, 0], [λ, x, y, z, w])
[[-0.022, 8.9, 9.1, 6.3, 5.9]]

We compute the leading principal minors of the bordered Hessian determinant starting from $|B_2|$:

borderhessian(l(x, y, z, w, λ), [λ, x, y, z, w], 1)

$$\left(\begin{vmatrix} 0, & 2, & 3 \\ 2, & \frac{0.3\cdot(-1)}{(x-2)^2}, & 0 \\ 3, & 0, & \frac{0.4\cdot(-1)}{(y-3)^2} \end{vmatrix}, \begin{vmatrix} 0, & 2, & 3, & 4 \\ 2, & \frac{0.3\cdot(-1)}{(x-2)^2}, & 0, & 0 \\ 3, & 0, & \frac{0.4\cdot(-1)}{(y-3)^2}, & 0 \\ 4, & 0, & 0, & \frac{0.2\cdot(-1)}{(z-4)^2} \end{vmatrix}, \begin{vmatrix} 0, & 2, & 3, & 4, & 5 \\ 2, & \frac{0.3\cdot(-1)}{(x-2)^2}, & 0, & 0, & 0 \\ 3, & 0, & \frac{0.4\cdot(-1)}{(y-3)^2}, & 0, & 0 \\ 4, & 0, & 0, & \frac{0.2\cdot(-1)}{(z-4)^2}, & 0 \\ 5, & 0, & 0, & 0, & \frac{0.1\cdot(-1)}{(w-5)^2} \end{vmatrix} \right)$$

Next, the determinants' signs at the critical point are evaluated:
signborderhessian(l(x, y, z, w, λ), [λ, x, y, z, w], 1, [-0.022, 8.9, 9.1, 6.3, 5.9])
[1, -1, 1]

Sufficient conditions (4) for critical point (8.9, 9.1, 6.3, 5.9) are satisfied for relative maximum.

Example 4.3.

Consider the constrained optimization problem

$\min u(x, y, z, w) = x^2 + 2y^2 + 2z^2 + w^2 - 2xy - 2yz - 2zw$ subject to

$$g^1(x, y, z, w) = 2x + y + z + w - 10 = 0, g^2(x, y, z, w) = 4x - z + w - 12 = 0$$

In Xcas' environment we define

u(x, y, z, w, λ, μ):=x^2+2*y^2+2*z^2+w^2-2*x*y-2*y*z-2*z*w+λ*(2*x+y+z+w-10)+μ*(4*x-z+w-12)

borderhessian(u(x, y, z, w, λ, μ), [λ, μ, x, y, w, z], 2)

$$\left(\begin{bmatrix} 0, & 0, & 2, & 1, & 1 \\ 0, & 0, & 4, & 0, & 1 \\ 2, & 4, & 2, & -2, & 0 \\ 1, & 0, & -2, & 4, & 0 \\ 1, & 1, & 0, & 0, & 2 \end{bmatrix}, \begin{bmatrix} 0, & 0, & 2, & 1, & 1, & 1 \\ 0, & 0, & 4, & 0, & 1, & -1 \\ 2, & 4, & 2, & -2, & 0, & 0 \\ 1, & 0, & -2, & 4, & 0, & -2 \\ 1, & 1, & 0, & 0, & 2, & -2 \\ 1, & -1, & 0, & -2, & -2, & 4 \end{bmatrix}\right)$$

The critical point of the Lagrangian function u is:

approx(solve(grad(u(x, y, z, w, λ, μ), [x, y, z, w, λ, μ])=[0, 0, 0, 0, 0], [λ, μ, x, y, z, w]))

[[0.766, -0.957, 2.98, 1.83, 1.06, 1.16]]

Evaluating determinant's signs at the critical point:

signborderhessian(u(x, y, z, w, λ, μ), [λ, μ, x, y, z, w], 2, [0.766, -0.957, 2.98, 1.83, 1.06, 1.16])

[1, 1]

Positive determinants' signs for (2.98, 1.83, 1.06, 1.16) satisfy sufficient conditions for a relative minimum.

5. Theoretical Background of Mathematical Programming Approach

5.1. Optimality Conditions for Constrained Optimization Problems. The Case with m Inequality Constraints

5.1.1. Fritz – John Necessary Condition

Suppose f(x), $g_i(x): R^n \to R$ are differentiable functions on R^n and consider the problem of minimizing f(x) subject to $S = \{x \in R^n / g_i(x) \le 0\}$. Suppose α is a local minimum point. Let $J(a) = \{j / g_j(a) = 0\}$ be an index of binding constraints. Then there is a set of nonnegative scalars, λ_0, λ_j for j ∈ J(α(, not all zero, such that $\lambda_0 \nabla f(a) + \sum_{j \in J(a)} \lambda_j \nabla g_j(a) = 0$.

5.1.2. Kuhn-Tucker Necessary Conditions

Suppose f(x), $g_i(x): R^n \to R$ are differentiable functions on R^n and consider the problem of minimizing f(x) subject to $S = \{x \in R^n / g_i(x) \le 0\}$. Suppose α is a point where f(x) has a local minimum. Let $J(a) = \{j / g_j(a) = 0\}$ be an index of binding constraints. Suppose that the gradient vectors of the binding constraints $\{\nabla g_i(\alpha)=0 / j \in J(a)\}$ are linearly independent. Then there is a set of nonnegative scalars, $\{\lambda_j / j \in J(a)\}$ such that $\nabla f(a)+\sum_{j\in J(a)} \lambda_j \nabla g_j(a)=0$.

5.1.3. Kuhn-Tucker Sufficient Conditions

When there are no binding constraints and α satisfies the Kuhn Tucker necessary conditions the sufficient conditions for α to be a local extremum point are the same as in the case of unconstrained optimization.

When there are m binding constraints and α satisfies the Kuhn Tucker necessary conditions, the sufficient conditions are the sufficient conditions of constrained optimization theory using hessian and bordered hessian determinental expressions presented in section 3.

For more details see Jeter (1986 chapter 7), Bazaraa et al. (2006 chapter 4), Boyd and Vandenberghe (2004 chapter 5), Nocedal and Wright (1999 chapter 16), Pardalos and Chinchuluun (2004).

6. Computer Codes for Necessary Optimality Conditions

The computer codes presented in this section use the mathematical programming approach for problems of constrained minimization with inequality constraints. In case of maximizing an objective function f(x), we use the following procedure replacing f(x) with -f(x).

6.1. Fritz John Necessary Conditions

We create the function bindingtest(g1, vars, testvalue, λ) with constraint g_j as the first argument, its variable vector (vars) as the second argument, the test value as the third argument and parameter (λ) as the forth argument. bindingtest generates the term $\lambda_j \nabla g_j(a)$ if only g_j constraint is binding at testvalue, else 0:

```
bindingtest(g1, vars, testvalue, λ):=if(approx(subst(g1, vars=testvalue), 4)=0)λ
*subst(grad(g1, vars), vars=testvalue); else 0;
```

Next we create the function fritzjohn(f, g1, g2, g3, vars, testvalue) with arguments the objective function (f), the constraints g_i, variable vector (vars) and the testvalue. fritzjohn generates the expression $\lambda_0 \nabla f(a)+\sum_j \lambda_j \nabla g_j(a)$ only for binding constraints g_j at testvalue α:

```
fritzjohn(f, g1, g2, g3, vars, testvalue):=subst(λ0*grad(f, vars), vars= testvalue)
    +bindingtest(g1, vars, testvalue, λ1)+bindingtest(g2, vars, testvalue,
    λ2)+bindingtest(g3, vars, testvalue, λ3)
```

fritzjohn function can be modified for less or more constraints by removing or adding bindingtest functions.

6.2. Kuhn Tucker Necessary Conditions

We create the function bindinggrad(g1, vars, testvalue), with constraint g_j as the first argument, its variable vector (vars) as the second argument and the test value as the third argument. bindingrad generates $\nabla g_j(a)$ if only g_j is binding at testvalue α, else the zero vector:

bindinggrad(g1, vars, testvalue):=if(approx(subst(g1, vars=testvalue), 4)=0)subst(grad (g1, vars), vars=testvalue); else makelist(0, 1, ncols([vars]));

We create the function kuhntucker1, with arguments the objective function name (f), the constraints, the variable vector (vars) and the test value. kuhntucker1 generates the expression $\nabla f(a) + \sum_j \lambda_j \nabla g_j(a)$ if only g_j is binding at testvalue α:

kuhntucker1(f, g1, g2, vars, testvalue):=subst(grad(f, vars), vars=testvalue) +bindingtest(g1, vars, testvalue, λ1) +bindingtest(g2, vars, testvalue, λ2)

kuhntucker1 function can be modified for less or more constraints by removing or adding bindingtest functions.

For the linear dependence test of the gradient vectors of the binding constraints at test value, we define the function kuhntucker2. The first arguments contain the constraints while the following arguments contain the variable vector (vars) and the test value. kuhntucker2 computes the rank of the matrix consisting of rows filled by the gradient vectors when the constraints are binding and rows filled by zeros when the constraints are nonbinding:

kuhntucker2(g1, g2, vars, testvalue):=rank(bindinggrad((g1, vars, testvalue)), bindinggrad((g2, vars, testvalue))

The output of kuhntucker2 function checks the property of linear independence of the gradient vectors of the binding constraints. kuhntucker2 function can be modified for less or more constraints by removing or adding bindinggrad functions.

6.3. Computational Performance in Economic Problems

Example 6.1.

Consider the optimization problem where a company wants to find the combinations of commodities X and Y that may minimize costs when the firm has three production quotas g1, g2 and g3. Specifically:

minimize $f(x, y) = (x-8)^2 + (y-6)^2$

subject to
$g_1(x, y) = x + y - 7 \le 0, g_2(x, y) = 4x + y - 16 \le 0, g_3(x, y) = -x + y - 5 \le 0, x \ge 0, y \ge 0$
Check whether the points (3, 4) and (1, 6) satisfy the Fritz – John necessary condition.

We create the Fritz-John expression $\lambda_0 \nabla f(a) + \sum_j \lambda_j \nabla g_j(a)$ for α=(3, 4):

```
fritzjohn(f(x, y), g1(x, y), g2(x, y), g3(x, y), [x, y], [3, 4])
[-10*λ0+λ1+4*λ2, -4*λ0+λ1+λ2]
```

We check the validity of Fritz-John necessary condition for local minimum at (3, 4):

```
solve([-10*λ0+λ1+4*λ2=0, -4*λ0+λ1+λ2=0], [λ1, λ2])
[[2*λ0, 2*λ0]]
```
(we show that nonnegative parameters λ0, λ1, λ2 exist)

The same procedure at (1, 6) does not prove validity of Fritz-John necessary condition:

```
fritzjohn(f(x, y), g1(x, y), g2(x, y), g3(x, y), [x, y], [1, 6])
[-14*λ0+λ1-λ3, λ1+λ3]
```

```
solve([-14*λ0+λ1-λ3=0, λ1+λ3=0], [λ1, λ3])
```

[[7*λ0, -7*λ0]] (we show that there are no parameters λ0, λ1, λ2≥0 as Fritz-John necessary condition assumes for local minimum)

Example 6.2.

Consider the optimization problem of a monopoly firm that wants to minimize its costs subject to two different production quotas in two different markets. That is:

minimize $f(x, y, z) = x - y^2$

subject to $g_1(x, y, z) = x^2 + y^2 + z^2 - 9 \le 0, g_2(x, y, z) = -x + 3y + z - 6 \le 0$.

Check whether the points (0.143426, 2.5645, -1.55008), (-0.5, -2.95804, 0) satisfy Kuhn-Tucker necessary conditions.

We prove validity of the Kuhn-Tucker condition at point (0.143426, 2.5645, -1.55008). We create the Kuhn-Tucker expression $\nabla f(a) + \sum_j \lambda_j \nabla g_j(a)$:

```
kuhntucker1(f(x, y, z), g1(x, y, z), g2(x, y, z), [x, y, z], [0.143426, 2.5645, -1.55008])
[1+0.286852*λ1-λ2, -5.129+5.129*λ1+3*λ2, -3.10016*λ1+λ2]
```

By writing

```
solve([1+0.286852*λ1-λ2=0, -5.129+5.129*λ1+3*λ2=0], [λ1, λ2])
[[0.35545205688, 1.10196213342]]
```
(nonnegative values for λ1, λ2 exist)

kuhntucker2(g1(x, y, z), g2(x, y, z), [x, y, z], [0.143426, 2.5645, -1.55008])

2 (the result proves linear independence of $\nabla g_1(a), \nabla g_2(a)$ at (0.143426, 2.5645, -1.55008)

We prove validity of the Kuhn-Tucker condition at point (-0.5, -2.95804, 0):

kuhntucker1(f(x, y, z), g1(x, y, z), g2(x, y, z), [x, y, z], [-0.5, -2.95804, 0])

[1-1.0*λ1, 5.91608-5.91608*λ1, 0]

solve([1-1.0*λ1=0, 5.91608-5.91608*λ1=0], λ1]

[1] (nonnegative value for λ1 exists)

kuhntucker2(g1(x, y, z), g2(x, y, z), [x, y, z], [-0.5, -2.95804, 0])

1

CONCLUSION

In this chapter, we propose functional programming techniques to represent and compute optimality conditions in a user-friendly software. Our contribution includes the following results: I) In the fields of unconstrained optimization, hessianseries function generates the series of the leading principal minors of Hessian determinant. signseries function extracts the signs of the leading principal minors of Hessian determinant evaluated at the critical point(s), testing sufficient conditions for local extrema. II) In the fields of constrained optimization under equality constraints, borderhessian function generates the series of bordered Hessian determinants according to sufficient optimality conditions law. signborderhessian function extracts the signs of bordered Hessian determinants evaluated at the critical point(s) according to sufficient conditions law, testing sufficient conditions for local extrema. III) In the fields of constrained optimization under inequality constraints, fritzjohn function tests Fritz- John necessary condition for local minima. kuhntucker1, kuhntucker2 functions test Kuhn-Tucker necessary conditions for local minima.

The reader can reproduce the results without serious programming skills and use them in research, practice and teaching. Working with our programmed Xcas functions has the advantage of less and simpler computations compared to working manually or working using built-in software functions. The use of the proposed functions also prevents the user from possible mistakes while formulating optimality conditions in multivariable optimization.

REFERENCES

Baiocchi, G. (2007), «Reproducible research in computational economics: guidelines, integrated approaches, and open source software», *Computational Economics*, 30, 19–40, DOI: 10.1007/s10614-007-9084-4.

Bazaraa, M.S., Sherali, H.D. and Shetty, C.M. (2006), *Nonlinear Programming Theory and Algorithms* (3rd edition), John Willey, New Jersey.

Bertsekas, D.P., Nedic, A. and Ozdaglar, A.E. (2003), Convex Analysis and Optimization, Athena Scientific, Belmont, Massachusetts.

Boyd, S. and Vandenberghe, L. (2004), Convex Optimization, *Cambridge University Press,* Cambridge.

Ferris, M.C., Mesnier, P.M. and Moré, J.J. (2000), «NEOS and condor: solving optimization problems over the internet», ACM Transactions on Mathematical Software, 26(1), 1-18.

Gupta, I., Bassin, K., Gupta, A. and Khanna, K. (1993), *«Optimization of water distribution system», Environmental Software*, 8, 101-113.

Huang, C. and Crooke, P. (1997), Mathematics and Mathematica for Economists, Oxford Blackwell Publishers, Massachusetts.

Jeter, M. (1986), Mathematical Programming An Introduction to Optimization, Marcel Dekker, New York.

Judd, K.L. (1997), «Computational economics and economic theory: substitutes or complements?», *Journal of Economic Dynamics and Control*, 21, 907-942.

Kendrick, D.A. and Amman, H.M. (1999), «Programming languages in economics», *Computational Economics*, 14, 151-181.

Levi V. (2001), «Application of the optimal power flow model in power system education», *IEEE Transactions on Power Systems*, 16(4), 572-580.

Miranda, M.J. and Fackler, P.L. (2002), Applied Computational Economics and Finance, The MIT Press, Cambridge, Massachusetts, London.

Mistakidis, E. and Stavroulakis, G. (1998), Nonconvex Optimization in Mechanics, Kluwer Academic Publishers, Boston.

Moré, J.J. and Wright, S.J. (1993), *Optimization Software Guide*, SIAM Publications, Philadelphia.

Nash, S.G. and Sofer, A. (1996), *Linear and Nonlinear Programming*, McGraw Hill, New York.

Nocedal, J. and Wright, S. (1999), Numerical Optimization, Springer, New York.

Pál, L. and Csendes, T. (2009), «INTLAB implementation of an interval global optimization algorithm», *Optimization Methods and Software,* 24(4), 749-759.

Pardalos, P.M. and Rosen, J.B. (1987), Constrained Global Optimization: algorithms and applications, Springer Verlag, New York.

Pardalos, P.M. and Chinchuluun, A. (2004), «Some recent developments in deterministic global optimization», *Operational Research An International Journal,* 4(1), 3-28.

Varian, H.R. (Ed.). (1996), «Computational economics: Economic and financial analysis with mathematica», TELOS/Springer, New York.

Wang, J. (1998), «Computer-aided economic optimization of end-milling operations», *International Journal of Production Economics*, 54, 307-320.

In: Computational Techniques for Banking and Risk Management ISBN: 978-1-62618-522-7
Editors: C. Zopounidis and M. Doumpos

Chapter 8

MEASURING WORKFLOW KNOWLEDGE-BASE EFFECTIVENESS FOR AN *IN-HOUSE* BANKING CUSTOMER SERVICE CALL CENTER

***Angelos Karakerezis*[1] *and Konstantinos Nakos**[*2]

[1]Household Lending Business Unit, EFG Eurobank Ergasias SA, Athens, Greece
[2]Credit Control Sector – International Subsidiaries Division, EFG Eurobank Ergasias SA, Athens, Greece

ABSTRACT

The measurement of the effects of information technology initiatives on organizational productivity has long been considered a difficult and complex topic, leading some prominent scholars to what has been known as the 'IT productivity paradox'. This paper contributes to this topic by suggesting a concise and robust methodology for the measurement of the effects of such initiatives and by demonstrating this methodology using a particular example from the implementation of an IT-based workflow knowledge-base on the increased efficiency of a Bank's call centre.

The ultimate objective then is to demonstrate that through consistent and thorough application of appropriate and systematic analysis, scholars and practitioners alike are able to answer such pivotal questions with accuracy and confidence. In the particular context of study, we investigate the increase in productivity (reduction of credit application-related calls) of a Bank customer service centre by the establishment of an intelligent application workflow system which provides on-line, real-time guidance and alerts to distribution networks as to the next actions required for disbursement. We do so by defining a measure of "counter-productivity" – the number of service calls generated per application received in an appropriate previous period and provide an inter-temporal comparison of its evolution before and after the implementation of the intelligent workflow system, taking also into account potential adoption (learning curve) effects by system actors.

[*] 10 Panepistimiou str.; GR 10671, Athens; Tel.: (+30) 210 3635420 (ext. 31); E-mail: akarakerezis@ eurobank.gr | knakos@hfsf.gr.

Through our analysis we demonstrate that significant service productivity improvements can be documented using our methodology (of above 10%) which ultimately lead towards either service level improvement and/or respective cost reductions (through the release of FTEs to other activities). In addition, we highlight a methodology for determining and actively managing learning curve effects and identify such effects in the context of this study. Finally, we demonstrate in practice that Bank service management is an area well-suited for further optimization / cost minimization through insightful application of thorough scientific analysis.

INTRODUCTION

In recent years, the growth of the retail banking sector in Greece has been remarkable: consumer and mortgage lending activities have increased at least tenfold in terms of both disbursed funds as well as customers served in comparison to ten years ago (Eurobank EFG, 2006). Although this development has had a number of economic, financial and societal implications – some of which are yet probably to be revealed– it has also had some quite unique implications for the management of banking operations: Greek retail banks (and especially leading ones) have been faced with a previously unthinkable number of consumer and mortgage loan applications to be assessed in terms of the risk they represented. Given typical retail banking application approval ratios, it becomes evident that such assessment systems are faced *prima facie* with approximately 50% additional "traffic" (in terms of applications) than what was ultimately reported as disbursed number of loans. Adding to this the number of "negotiated" applications (i.e., applications where a counter-offer rather than a rejection was made or applications where the client has changed his or her mind thus requesting a higher amount or better terms than were previously granted) it is not difficult to grasp the enormous demands placed upon loan application processing systems[1].

Within this context, Greek retail banking units have (explicitly or implicitly) chosen one of two broad types of operational models: (1) a "decentralized model" where local Branch Officers (Managers, Deputy Managers or other employees) were given authority to grant or reject the majority of consumer and / or mortgage loan applications or (2) a "centralized model" where all (or most) applications where channeled (physically or electronically) towards specialized credit underwriting units who were then solely responsible for accepting or rejecting the application through the application of pre-specified credit policy criteria and / or some degree of judgment.

There are several advantages and disadvantages to each model, related primarily to the degrees of undertaken operational risk (primarily, risk of fraud) and credit risk, as well as to operational efficiency levels achieved. The former model then seems to be preferable in terms of operational efficiency as it allows for the loan granting, rejection or negotiation decisions to take place almost "on the spot", with minimal customer wait time and with minimal additional staffing and infrastructure required. However, the increased operational efficiency does come at a cost: the "decentralized" model presents also some very serious problems in terms of increased operational risk levels (e.g., risk of internal fraud through collusion of Bank employees with customers) as well as significant inconsistencies in terms of credit risk undertaking (e.g. not all Branches perceive and employ credit policy in a consistent and

[1] Used here in the broader sense to signify infrastructure, processes as well as participating employees.

uniform manner nor are they faced with the same population of customers so as to employ a common reference). In most major Banks then, the decision was gradually made to employ the "centralized" model for loan applications processing and, subsequently, to optimize the respective processes and infrastructure so as to promote its internal efficiency and external customer responsiveness to the greatest possible extend (Attica Bank, 2007; Alpha Bank, 2009; Eurobank EFG, 2009, Emporiki Bank, 2009).

One key aspect then of process optimization and customer responsiveness is the ability of Branches to be aware of the status of the loan applications they have forwarded to the central underwriting units as well as of any necessary next steps required by them or by the customer (e.g., additional documentation required, verification of customer signature, ordering a property appraisal etc.). Typically, Branches do receive detailed instructions as to the sequence of process steps they need to follow, but the issuance of such guidelines presents at least the following problems from an operational efficiency perspective:

- Actual loan application workflow might not follow these steps precisely: for example, a customer might have his or her property appraised before or after submitting a formal application.
- Such process guidelines are not – typically – written from an operational efficiency standpoint but, rather, from an auditing and control standpoint. To understand why these might be widely different standpoints (always from an operational efficiency perspective) it suffices to mention that the latter does not consider the critical path of processes and required documentation.

Several solutions have subsequently been suggested and implemented in order to address this source of inefficiency: for some Banks, the "natural" solution has been to allow for direct communication between the front-line and back-office, while others – as in the case examined in this paper – introduced specialized "internal customer service" departments which aimed to support the front-line in terms of the current status of the application, pending items, current credit policies and criteria, etc. One pivotal question then for senior management of consumer- and mortgage-lending units became the measurement of the effectiveness of those departments: which initiatives (if any) did truly add value and how much?

This paper then presents a formal methodology employed to address this exact question within the context of a specific initiative: the introduction of "application-specific", targeted, computer-generated guidelines detailing to front-line employees (Branch staff) not only the current status of each application but also some immediate next steps expected soon after the application has been processed (so as to facilitate critical-path activities) as well as long-term pending tasks to be completed prior to loan disbursement. And, although a specific case is presented, the methodology developed and employed is intuitively and fruitfully extended to other similar situations, hence providing a robust foundation for measuring the operational efficiency of knowledge- or information-dependent processes.

The remainder of this paper is organized as follows: Section 2 presents the relevant background and data to the case, while Section 3 develops the appropriate methodological framework and presents the results obtained. Finally, Section 4 summarizes and concludes.

BACKGROUND AND DATA

Mortgage loan applications – the specific context within which this study took place – involve quite complex verification, underwriting and administrative procedures and, although they are subject to a broadly defined sequence of high-level steps (or, rather, stages), each application typically demonstrates considerable peculiarities. To facilitate then the efficient handling of those applications between the front-line (Branch network) and the back-office (two underwriting units in Athens and Thessaloniki respectively), the Bank under study initiated a "Customer Service" department which acts as liaison and knowledge buffer between the two.

The vast majority of communication between Branches and Customer Service takes place via telephone and, hence, the number of calls answered promptly (i.e., within 30 seconds) is one of the primary Key Performance Indicators (KPIs) for the department. Of course, the department also tracks the total number of calls attempted by the Branches, hence intuitively documenting the following categorization:

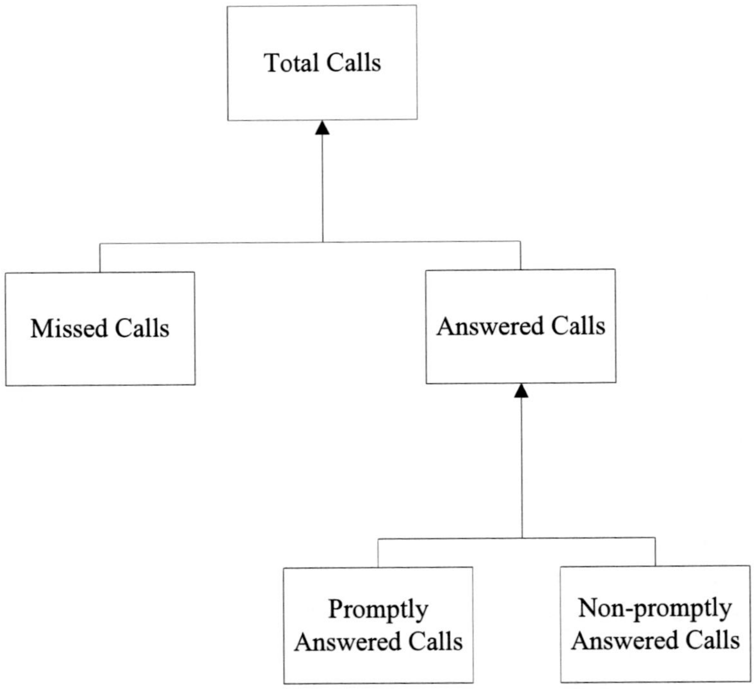

Figure 1.

The total number of calls for each category for twenty-four (24) months prior to and twelve (12) months after the introduction of computerized guidelines is presented in the following table, along with the number of applications received during each specific month[2]:

A few remarks concerning the mortgage loan application processing and loan disbursement process are worth here:

[2] Actual numbers have been scaled in order to protect the Bank's identity.

- Mortgage loans' applications typically underwent three major stages: (a) the 'financial approval' stage, (b) the 'collateral approval' stage and (c) the pre-notation and loan disbursement stage. Each stage (briefly) involves the following:
  - Financial approval: financial approval is the first of the three steps (typically) and, essentially, involves the assessment of the financial capacity of the applicant(s) to repay the loan. In addition, financial approval (assuming granted) also details certain important terms of the loan, such as pricing, tenor, etc.
  - Collateral approval: assuming financial approval has been granted and the client wishes to proceed further with the specific Bank (by that time, clients typically receive and evaluate numerous competing financial approvals from competing Banks), the Bank proceeds to a legal and technical appraisal of the property to be mortgaged against the loan using certified collaborators (lawyers and engineers). Assuming that the value of the property and all its relevant technical and legal properties are to the Bank's satisfaction, the Bank issues a final approval and drafts relevant contracts and supporting documents.
  - Pre-notation and loan disbursement: at this last stage, the client signs the loan contract and any other supporting documents, the property is mortgaged ("pre-noted" according to the Greek legal term) and, ultimately, the loan is disbursed.
- Mortgage loans' disbursement is – as already mentioned above – a time consuming process: the average application-to-disbursement time of course has been around forty-five (45) calendar days, although it did vary significantly either due to internal processing capacity available or due to external random shocks such as judicial system strikes preventing the pre-notation of properties.
- During the time window considered, customer service agent capacity (measured as agent 'Full Time Equivalent' units – FTE) has not changed significantly: minor FTE additions have taken place at time of peak demand but given Bank labor legislation and the highly correlated demand for additional manpower across all Bank activities (Branches, underwriting units, administrative units, etc.), customer service has not been considered a top priority. At times, this has led in deterioration of service levels.

In light of the above, the following Section develops an appropriate methodology for testing the effectiveness gains of the new computerized workflow guidelines system.

METHODOLOGY

In order to determine the effects from the introduction of the computerized workflow guidelines, an analysis of the beta coefficient of the linear regression model involving the generated total calls as dependent variable and the monthly volume of applications as independent variable. Under this model configuration, the beta coefficient (b) of the aforementioned linear regression model can be thought as naturally describing the marginal number of incoming calls generated by each additional "incoming"mortgage loan application (on average).

Table 1.

Month	*Applications*	*Total Calls*	*Missed*	*Answered*	*Answered Promptly*	*Answered Non-Promptly*
t-24	499	656	7	649	648	1
t-23	693	741	9	732	731	1
t-22	518	811	2	809	788	21
t-21	274	597	8	589	588	1
t-20	591	510	3	507	495	12
t-19	708	843	8	835	833	2
t-18	932	1.102	17	1.085	1.083	2
t-17	886	1.460	57	1.403	1.361	42
t-16	810	1.364	34	1.330	1.317	13
t-15	1.304	1.566	56	1.510	1.502	8
t-14	1.326	2.172	100	2.072	2.003	69
t-13	968	1.993	81	1.912	1.896	16
t-12	1.217	1.745	64	1.681	1.649	32
t-11	1.481	2.105	95	2.010	1.940	70
t-10	1.872	2.729	208	2.521	2.388	133
t-9	1.992	3.108	228	2.880	2.778	102
t-8	1.688	2.871	206	2.665	2.554	111
t-7	2.261	3.052	243	2.809	2.633	176
t-6	1.822	3.564	453	3.111	2.671	440
t-5	2.550	3.431	254	3.177	3.013	164
t-4	2.136	4.022	515	3.507	2.978	529
t-3	2.207	3.325	219	3.106	2.975	131
t-2	1.949	3.281	232	3.049	2.829	220
t-1	1.639	3.011	211	2.800	2.654	146
t	1.271	2.407	170	2.237	2.125	112
t+1	1.395	2.195	89	2.106	2.034	72
t+2	1.057	2.031	78	1.953	1.871	82
t+3	1.336	1.753	73	1.680	1.582	98
t+4	1.251	1.761	75	1.686	1.658	28
t+5	941	1.389	28	1.361	1.358	3
t+6	933	1.115	19	1.096	1.081	15
t+7	187	803	9	794	792	2
t+8	80	177	2	175	175	-
t+9	293	154	1	153	151	2
t+10	279	307	5	302	297	5
t+11	361	328	3	325	324	1
t+12	474	428	3	425	420	5

Once this model configuration has been formulated, a testing of the effectiveness gains from the introduction of the new computerized guidelines may be directly tested through a one-tail test for the (hypothesized) difference of the beta coefficient prior and after the implementation of the initiative as follows:

$$\begin{aligned} H_0 &: b_{before} \leq b_{after} \\ H_a &: b_{before} > b_{after} \end{aligned} \tag{1.1}$$

Under the null hypothesis then, each mortgage loan application prior to the implementation of the new computerized workflow guidelines generates equal or (even) less calls (i.e., the introduction of the new guidelines has not increased the efficiency of the system) while, under the alternative hypothesis, each mortgage loan application prior to the implementation of the new computerized workflow guidelines generates a strictly higher number of calls (hence, the introduction of the new guidelines has increased the overall efficiency of the system).

The standard test for testing the above hypothesis is the *t*-test for the difference of beta coefficients (Wuench, 2007), i.e., :

$$t = \frac{b_{after} - b_{before}}{\sqrt{s^2_{b_{after}} + s^2_{b_{before}}}} \tag{1.2}$$

where s_b^2 is the standard error of each beta coefficient and with $(N-4)$ degrees of freedom[3](Wuench, 2007).

The above then describes the high-level framework for the measurement of comparative effectiveness before and after the introduction of the computerized guidelines. Certain benefits of this approach are the following:

- The use of the beta coefficient of the linear regression model provides for a "natural", intuitive interpretation of the system (in)efficiency. The higher the slope of the regression line, the less efficient may be considered the system at any given point in time.
- The simple linear regression model itself provides for an intuitive understanding of the *raison d'être* of the customer service unit – it exists exactly because of the inefficiency of the other components of the system (Branch network, underwriting units) to handle the workflow of the numerous applications "travelling" through completion. The use of this particular model, though quite simplistic from a statistical perspective, exhibits some very interesting managerial properties (e.g., communication, intuition, etc.) which are – bottom line considered – more important than pure statistical eloquency.
- By definition, the line of best fit generated through simple linear regression provides a useful benchmark of the number of calls to be expected at any given month, given the forecasted or actual volume of incoming mortgage loan applications. This, in itself, provides us with at least two additional areas for value generation:
  - First, it enables management to focus its attention upon the root causes generating above- or below-average calls by providing a vivid benchmark of what is to be deemed "high" and "low" volume of calls *after* acknowledgement of the effects of incoming applications volumes. Such analysis then becomes pivotal for the establishment of TQM efforts (Evans, 2004).

[3] Please note that the test on betas utilized here uses a pooled error term. If the variance in the dependent variable is much greater in one group than in the other, there are alternative methods (KleinbaumandKupper, 1978).

– Second, it allows for more efficient management of the customer service unit itself, as – through the application of further statistical techniques as well as cost / service level optimization algorithms – an optimal number of FTEs may be assigned (per month), given the number of incoming applications expected.

While the above shape the overall framework for the analysis, at the operational level, our methodology employed presents some peculiarities as follows:

- Given that the mortgage loan application processing is a lengthy process (taking more than one month), it follows that it is rather unlikely that current month mortgage loan applications would have the highest influence on the generated calls. In fact, it is most likely (given that the average application-to-disbursement time is approximately forty-five (45) calendar days) that the previous month's applications generate the highest number of calls at each given month.
- The implementation of the new computerized guidelines system is highly unlikely to have been adopted by users (Branch networks) immediately, as is a well-known case with IT innovations (Lee and Xia, 2006). For our purposes, this might imply the existence of an "adoption" period, whereby the slope of the regression line would be gradually adjusting to its new equilibrium level (assuming of course that there is one). If this is the case, and assuming that there have been no other shocks in the system, it might be argued that the potential for noticeable differences might be lowered by the degree of prolongation and nature of behavior during the adoption period. To counter this effect, we have performed several regression models for the second ("after") period, each excluding additional observations lying close to the time of implementation of the new computerized guidelines (time '*t*'). The comparison of the slopes from those models (even without formal testing for differences) provides a first indication of adoption period effects.

The following Section then presents the obtained results from the application of the above methodology.

Table 2.

Model Metric	Concurrent model	Lagged t-1 model	Lagged t-2 model
No. of observations (N)	37	36	35
Adjusted R^2	0, 91	0, 95	0, 75
Model Metric	Concurrent model	Lagged t-1 model	Lagged t-2 model
Significance F	0, 00	0, 00	0, 00
Beta (slope)	1, 60	1, 64	1, 47
Beta p-value	0, 00	0, 00	0, 00
Alpha (intercept)	-69, 4	-109, 8	72, 1
Alpha (p-value)	0, 54	0, 21	0, 71
Autocorrelation	1, 00	0, 88	0, 83

ESTIMATING CUSTOMER SERVICE EFFECTIVENESS IMPROVEMENT

The primary step for determining the functional form of the model has been the choice of lagged variable. The following table presents the determination coefficients (adjusted R^2) as well as most metrics of statistical interest for the simple linear regression models involving the use of concurrent and lagged incoming mortgage loan applications as independent variables:

From the obtained results, it follows that while all models are significant ($F< 0, 00$), the Lagged t-1 model (highlighted in the above table) is to be preferred due to its highest R^2. Nonetheless, a number of additional remarks may be made:

- The impact of current as well as two-month earlier "vintages" of mortgage loan applications is evident and noteworthy (R^2values of 0, 91 and 0, 75 respectively). Nonetheless, the need to maintain the model's applicability as an intuitive efficiency measurement tool rather than as a precise statistical forecasting framework has refrained us from introducing those variables into the model. Even more, the mortgage loans application demonstrates a high level of autocorrelation (0, 88 and 0, 83 for t-1 and t-2 respectively), hence rendering the introduction of additional variables ineffective from a statistical perspective.
- Another key concern from both a managerial as well as statistical perspective would be the value and interpretation of the intercept (alpha coefficient). Any value significantly different than zero (0) would imply that calls are to be expected even if production of new applications is eliminated, an inherently difficult phenomenon to explain. However, from the statistical results obtained, the p-values for the intercept demonstrate that the values obtained might not be considered to be statistically different than zero (0), at any reasonable level of confidence.

Having determined the operational model, a comparison of the betas obtained from the simple linear regressions *before* and *after* the introduction of the computerized guidelines is as follows:

Table 3.

Regression Statistics: "Before" model	
Adjusted R Square	0, 96
Standard Error (model)	222, 85
Observations	24

Table 4.

"Before" model	*Coefficients*	*Standard Error*	*t Stat*	*P-value*	*Lower 95%*	*Upper 95%*
Intercept	5, 71	105, 48	0, 05	0, 96	(213, 05)	224, 47
Applications (t-1)	1, 60	0, 07	22, 62	0, 00	1, 45	1, 75

Table 5.

Regression Statistics: "After" model	
Adjusted R Square	0, 89
Standard Error (model)	259, 72
Observations	12

Table 6.

"After" model	*Coefficients*	*Standard Error*	*t Stat*	*P-value*	*Lower 95%*	*Upper 95%*
Intercept	(92, 61)	143, 00	(0, 64)	0, 53	(411, 25)	226, 03
Applications (t-1)	1, 44	0, 16	9, 27	0, 00	1, 10	1, 79

Performing then the standard hypothesis test identified in (1.2), the following value for the t-statistic is obtained:

$$\begin{aligned} t &= \frac{b_{after} - b_{before}}{\sqrt{s^2_{b_{after}} + s^2_{b_{before}}}} \\ &= \frac{1,44 - 1,60}{\sqrt{0,07^2 + 0,16^2}} \\ &= -5,25 \end{aligned} \tag{1.3}$$

which is significant at any reasonable level of significance (p-value < 0, 001), hence proving that the implementation of the new computerized workflow guidelines have indeed increased overall system effectiveness, significantly. A visual representation of the effects is shown below:

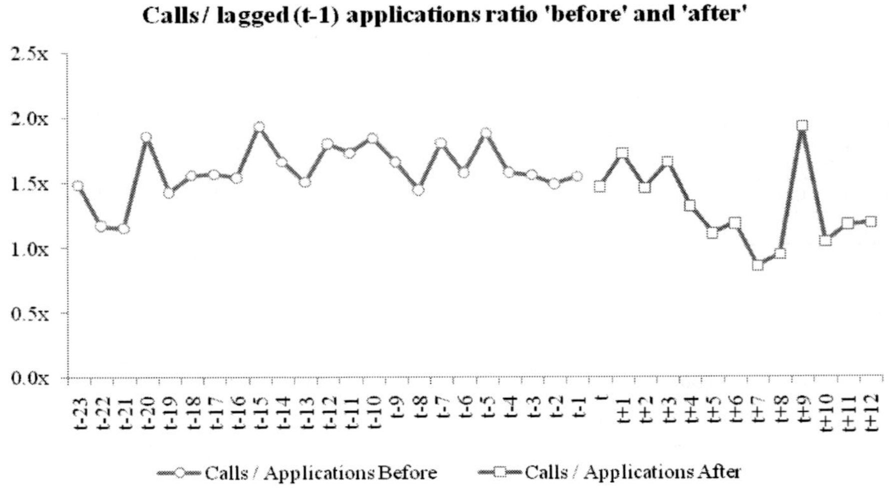

Figure 2.

In addition, the above figure demonstrates the existence of adoption period effects, as more recent observations exhibit lower calls / lagged (t-1) applications ratios, stabilizing in the 1:1, 10 to 1:1, 20 region. Indeed, by excluding the first four (4) observations (i.e., from time = t to time = t+3), the "post-adoption" effects ratio becomes:

Table 7.

Regression Statistics: "Post-adoption" model	
Adjusted R Square	0, 94
Standard Error (model)	137, 33
Observations	9

Table 8.

"Post-adoption" model	*Coefficients*	*Standard Error*	*t Stat*	*P-value*	*Lower 95%*	*Upper 95%*
Intercept	(19, 73)	77, 87	(0, 25)	0, 81	(203, 87)	164, 41
Applications (t-1)	1, 17	0, 10	11, 71	0, 00	0, 94	1, 41

Hence demonstrating that the long-run efficiency improvement might be considered to be even lower (beta of 1, 17 versus 1, 60 prior to the implementation of the new computerized guidelines). In that sense, it might be argued that the introduction of the computerized workflow guidelines has improved system efficiency by 26, 9%, a quite impressive factor.

REFERENCES

Attica Bank (2007). Press release of the 17th of May, 2007. Attica Bank.

Emporiki Bank (2009). Corporate strategy and restructuring presentation. Accessed online at http://www.combank.gr/files/GR/Investor_Presentations/Default%20Binder/07_10_plan/dff/presentation.pps , June 18, 2010.

Eurobank EFG (2006) *The Greek banking system in 2006: Comparative performance.* Research and Forecasting Division.

Eurobank EFG (2009) Risk management.Extract from annual financial statements report. Accessed online at http://www.investis.com/reports/efg_ar_2005_gr/pdf_cache/efg_ar_2005_gr_extract_38-41.pdf, June 18, 2010.

Evans, J. R. (2004) *Total Quality: Management, Organization and Strategy.* South-Western College Publishing.

Kleinbaum, D., G.andKupper, L., L. (1978). *Applied Regression Analysis and Other Multivariable Methods,* Boston: Duxbury.

Lee, G. and Xia, W. (2006). Organizational size and IT innovation adoption: a meta-analysis. *Information and Management*, 43 (8), pp. 975 - 985.

Wuench, K., L. (2007). *Comparing correlation coefficients, slopes and intercepts.* East Carolina University.Accessed online at http://core.ecu.edu/psyc/wuenschk/docs30/CompareCorrCoeff.doc, June 16, 2010.

In: Computational Techniques for Banking and Risk Management ISBN: 978-1-62618-522-7
Editors: C. Zopounidis and M. Doumpos

Chapter 9

A COMPARISON OF ALTERNATIVE METHODOLOGIES FOR CREDIT RISK EVALUATION

***Dimitrios Niklis*[1], *Michael Doumpos*[1*] *and Chrysovalantis Gaganis*[2]**
[1]Technical University of Crete, Department of Production Engineering and Management, Financial Engineering Laboratory, Greece
[2]University of Crete, Department of Economics, Greece

ABSTRACT

Credit risk refers to the likelihood that a firm or individual borrower will fail to meet a debt obligation. Credit risk evaluation is a very challenging and important problem in the domain of financial risk management. There are different methods and approaches for constructing credit risk assessment rating systems. The aim of this paper is to perform an empirical comparison of different popular techniques using a data set of Greek companies from the commercial sector. For this purpose three different methodologies are used, namely logistic regression, support vector machines, and the UTADIS (UTilités Additives DIScriminantes) multicriteria method. The results show that even with a considerable imbalanced data set with a small number of defaults, all methods provide good results. The UTADIS multicriteria method outperforms the two other techniques. Ensemble models are also tested, but are found to provide only marginal improvements.

Keywords: Credit risk evaluation, Multicriteria techniques, Logistic regression, Support vector machines, Ensemble models

1. INTRODUCTION

Credit risk assessment is a very challenging and important topic in the domain of financial risk management. The field of credit risk modeling has developed rapidly over the past decades to become a key component in the risk management systems at financial

[*] Author for correspondence: E-mail: mdoumpos@dpem.tuc.gr.

institutions (Lopez and Saidenberg, 2000). Credit risk can be defined as the potential risk that a bank borrower or counterparty will fail to meet its obligations in accordance with agreed terms (BIS, 2004). There are many factors that have increased the need for accurate credit risk measurement. Among others, these include: (i) a worldwide structural increase in the number of defaults, (ii) a trend towards disintermediation by the highest quality and largest borrowers, (iii) more competitive margins on loans, (iv) a declining value of real assets (and thus collateral) in many markets, and (v) a dramatic growth of off-balance sheet instruments with inherent default risk exposure (McKinsey, 1993), including credit risk derivatives (Altman and Saunders, 1998). Accounting-based credit scoring systems have been the most popular tools for credit risk assessment and rating.

Such systems combine key accounting variables, which are properly weighted to produce either a credit risk score or a probability of default. If the credit risk score, or probability, attains a value above a critical benchmark, a loan applicant is either rejected or subjected to increased scrutiny (Altman and Saunders, 1998). Altman et al. (1977) developed the commonly used ZETA discriminant model. Platt and Platt (1991) used logistic regression to test whether industry relative accounting ratios, are better predictors of corporate bankruptcy. Smith and Lawrence (1995) used a logit model to find the variables that offer the best prediction of a loan moving into a default state. Despite their good performance, multivariate accounting-based creditscoring systems developed using statistical methods have been subject to criticism. They are based on book value accounting data models which have the disadvantage to be static and thus often fail to follow the changes in the economic and business environment. Furthermore, most of these models are linear, thus failing to model the available information accurately, as linearity does not always exist among explanatory variables. Due to these limitations, non-parametric methods have become popular over the past couple of decades. Among others, one can mention techniques such as neural networks (Altman et al., 1994; Piramuthu, 1999; Atiya, 2001; Baesens et al., 2003; Westet al., 2005; Angelini et al., 2008), rough sets (Dimitras et al., 1999), support vector machines (Huang et. al, 2004; Stecking and Schebesch, 2003), multicriteria decision aid (Bugera et al., 2002; Doumpos et al., 2002; Kou et al., 2005; Hu, 2009; Doumpos and Zopounidis, 2011), and data envelopment analysis (Troutt et al., 1996; Cielen et al., 2004).

The aim of the study is the evaluation of different techniques and modeling settings in developing credit scoring models. In particular, three popular techniques are taken into consideration, namely logistic regression, support vector machines, and the UTADIS multicriteria method.

The analysis is based on a sample of Greek commercial firms, spanning the period 2006–2009. We examine the stability and robustness of the results using a bootstrap sampling approach, focusing on different settings with regard to the size of the model fitting (training) samples and their composition (number of default vs. non-default observations). The construction of ensemble models is also tested and their results are compared against the individual models developed on the basis of the full sample.

The rest of article is organized as below. Section 2 outlines the basic characteristics and features of the different methodologies used in the analysis. Section 3 discusses the data, while section 4 presents the empirical results. Finally, Section 5 concludes the article, summarizes the main findings of this research and proposes some future research directions.

2. Classification Methods

The development of credit risk assessment and rating systems is based on classification methods. The objective is to fit a model that discriminates default from non-default cases as accurately as possible. In this study three popular methods are used, including logistic regression, support vector machines, and the UTADIS multicriteria method. Logistic regression is the most commonly used approach in the domain of credit risk modeling. It leads to a linear classification model which is easy to construct and understand. Support vector machines (SVMs) have become a popular statistical learning approach with numerous applications in classification, regression, and clustering problems. SVMs provide a common theoretical basis for the development of both linear and non-linear model. Finally, the UTADIS multicriteria method uses linear programming to construct additive models, which are monotone with respect to the input variables. The following subsections provide a brief outline of the selected techniques.

2.1. Logistic Regression

Logistic regression (LR) is the most widely used statistical approach for building credit scoring and rating models. In LR, the probability of non-default for a firm i is modeled based on a set of independent variables through the logistic function:

$$P(\mathbf{x}_i) = \frac{1}{1+e^{-(\alpha+\beta_1 x_{i1}+\beta_2 x_{i2}+\ldots+\beta_m x_{im})}}$$

with $\mathbf{x}_i = (x_{i1},\ldots,x_{im})$ representing the input data vector for firm i on a set of m independent variables, α is the constant term and $\beta_1,\ldots,\beta_m$ are the regression coefficients of the independent variables. On the basis of the posterior probability estimates, each company is classified as default or non-default using an optimal probability cut-off point, which is specified so that the type I and type II errors[1] are minimized.

2.2. Support Vector Machines

Support vector machines (SVMs) have become an increasingly popular non-parametric methodology for developing classification models. In a dichotomous classification setting, and assuming a linear classification model, the objective is to construct a linear decision function $f(\mathbf{x}_i) = \alpha + \beta_1 x_{i1} + \beta_2 x_{i2} + \ldots + \beta_m x_{im}$ that distinguishes the two classes as best as possible. The decision function classifies observation i in the class of positive cases (i.e., the non-default group) if and only if $f(\mathbf{x}_i) > 0$. The analysis of the generalization performance of the decision function has shown that the optimal model f is the one that maximizes the margin induced in the separation of the classes, which is defined in terms of the vector of coefficients

[1] TypeIerrorreferstotheclassificationofadefault firmasanon-defaultone.On the other hand, type II error refers to the classification of a non-default firm as a default one.

$\boldsymbol{\beta} = (\beta_1, \beta_2, \ldots, \beta_m)$ as follows $2/\|\boldsymbol{\beta}\|$ (Vapnik, 1998). Therefore, given a training sample of *n* observations, the maximization of the margin can be performed through the solution of the following quadratic programming problem:

$$\begin{aligned} \text{minimize} \quad & \tfrac{1}{2}\boldsymbol{\beta}^\top\boldsymbol{\beta} + C\mathbf{e}^\top\mathbf{s} \\ \text{subject to:} \quad & \mathbf{Y}(\mathbf{X}\boldsymbol{\beta} + \alpha) + \mathbf{s} \geq \mathbf{e} \\ & \mathbf{s} \geq \mathbf{0},\ \boldsymbol{\beta}, \alpha \in \mathbb{R} \end{aligned}$$

where **Y** is a $n \times n$ diagonal matrix with the class labels in its diagonal (1 for the non-defaulted cases in -1 for the defaulted ones), **X** is a $n \times m$ matrix with the training data, **e** is a vector of ones, **s** is a vector of non-negative slack variables associated with the misclassification of the training objects when the classes are not linearly separable, and $C > 0$ is a parameter used to penalize the classification errors.

To generalize a linear SVM model to a non-linear one, the problem data are mapped to a higher dimensional space *H* (feature space) through a transformation of the form $\mathbf{x}_i\mathbf{x}_j^\top \rightarrow \phi(\mathbf{x}_i)\phi^\top(\mathbf{x}_j)$. The mapping function ϕ is implicitly defined through a symmetric kernel function $K(\mathbf{x}_i, \mathbf{x}_j) = \phi(\mathbf{x}_i)\phi^\top(\mathbf{x}_j)$. Popular choices for the kernel function include the polynomial kernel, the radial basis function (RBF) kernel, the sigmoid kernel, etc. (Schölkopf and Smola, 2002). The representation of the data using the kernel function enables the development of a linear model in the feature space *H*. Since *H* is a non-linear mapping of the original data, the developed model is non-linear in the original input space. The model is developed by applying the above linear analysis to the feature space *H*.

In this study we explore the development of both linear and non-linear SVM models with an RBF kernel. The width of the RBF kernel was selected through a cross-validation analysis to ensure the proper specification of this parameter. A similar analysis was also used to specify the trade-off constant *C*. All the data used during model development were normalized to zero mean and unit variance.

2.3. The UTADIS Multicriteria Method

The UTADIS method leads to the development of an additive value function that is used to score the firms and decide upon their classification. The developed additive value function has the following general form:

$$V(\mathbf{x}_i) = \sum_{j=1}^{m} w_j u_j(x_{ij}) \in [0,1]$$

where w_j is a non-negative trade-off constant for criterion *j* and $u_j(x_j)$ is the corresponding marginal value function normalized between 0 and 1. The marginal value functions provide a mechanism for decomposing the aggregate result (global value) in terms of individual assessments to the criteria level.

The value function provides an aggregate score $V(\mathbf{x}_i)$ for each firm i. To classify firms in their original groups (default or non-default), it is necessary to estimate a value threshold t, such that firms with global value at least equal to t are classified in the non-default group and all others are assigned in the default class.

The estimation of the additive value function and the cut-off threshold is performed through linear programming techniques. The objective of the method is to develop the additive model that minimizes the classification errors for the firms in the training sample. Detailed description of the mathematical programming formulation used in the UTADIS method can be found in the works of Zopounidis and Doumpos (1999) and Doumpos and Zopounidis (2002).

3. Data and Variables

3.1. Training and Testing Samples

The data were obtained from the financial database of ICAP[2]. The sample consists of 10, 468 non-defaulted firm-year observations and 248 defaulted cases. All the firms in the sample belong to the commercial sector. The time period of the analysis covers the years 2006–2009. There are two groups of companies (defaulted and non-defaulted). Table 1 presents the observations per year and category.

Table 1. Sample observations by year and category

Year	Non-defaulted	Defaulted	Total
2006	2748	52	2800
2007	2846	53	2899
2008	2731	99	2830
2009	2143	44	2187
Total	10468	248	10716

The available data was partitioned into two disjoint data sets, namely a training and a testing sample. The model is fitted on the training data and its classification performance is analyzed on the basis of the testing sample. Generally, one can adopt different approaches to implement a training-testing scheme for assessing the performance of credit rating models. Barnes (1990) points out that due to inflationary effects, technological changes and numerous other reasons (e.g., changing accounting policies), it is unreasonable to expect that the distributional cross-sectional parameters of the financial ratios will remain stable over time. Thus, a realistic validation approach would require the evaluation of the model in future period, since this approach more closely reflects a real world setting. As Espahbodi and Espahbodi (2003) mention that "*After all, the real test of a classification model and its practical usefulness is its ability to classify objects correctly in the future. While cross-*

[2] ICAP is the largest company in the Business Information and Consulting Services sector in Greece.

validation and bootstrapping techniques reduce the over-fitting bias, they do not indicate the usefulness of a model in the future."

Therefore, in this study, in order to consider the case of population drifting (i.e. change of population over time) and determine whether the models remain stable over different time periods, we split the sample in to two distinct datasets. The first consists of data from the period 2006–2007 and serves as a training sample. The second contains data from the subsequent two years (i.e. 2008 and 2009) and serves as a testing sample. Overall, the training data consist of 5, 699 observations including 5, 594 from the non-default group and 105 from the default class. The testing sample includes 4, 874 non-defaulted cases and 143 defaulted ones (overall 5, 017 firm-year observations). It should be noted that, due to the crisis that started to emerge in Greece during 2008, the default rate is higher in the testing sample compared to the training sample (2.9% in the testing sample vs 1.8% in the training sample).

3.2. Variable Selection

The use of financial ratios in order to evaluate business failures and also credit risk is very common. One of the first researchers who used financial ratios in order to predict the bankruptcy of companies was Beaver (1966). A drawback of his analysis was the use of each ratio per time and the creation of a cut off point for each one of them. Altman (1968) used a combination of six different ratios in order to classify the firms between healthy and distressed. Ohlson (1980) examined nine different ratios using logistic regression. Piramuthu (1999) used 18 different combinations of variables in order to classify a set of firms into those that would default and those that would not default. Atiya (2001) used 5 ratios in order to predict corporate bankruptcies.

The choice of the appropriate financial ratios is a challenging issue. First, there is a plethora of ratios that can be used as proxies for the same financial attributes (i.e., profitability, solvency, liquidity, etc.) and is often unclear which the best selections that can be made are. Second, using a large number of ratios increases the time and the cost of data collection and management. Third, a large set of ratios can lead to multicollinearity problems (Gaganis et al., 2007).

Hamer (1983) pointed out that the selected set of variables should be constructed on the basis of: (a) minimizing the cost of data selection, and (b) maximizing the applicability of the model. However, it is not easy to determine how many ratios a particular model should consider.

If a very small set of attributes is used, the model will not include all the relevant information, whereas the use of too many attributes could lead to two problems: (a) overfitting the training sample, and (b) time and effort spent to insert data (Kocagil et al., 2002).

Some studies start from a large list of potentially useful attributes, which are later reduced through a statistical selection process such as hypotheses testing or multivariate data analysis (Emel et al., 2003). However, Palepu (1986) criticizes such an approach and argues that "*this method of variable selection is arbitrary and leads to the statistical overfitting of the model to the sample at hand*". Therefore, to avoid such criticisms, and at the same time enhance the applicability of the model, we include ratios that cover all aspects of business cycle of a company together with ones that their contribution is found statistically significant in order to classify firms according to previous studies.

Overall, the analysis is based on a set of 11 indicators (7 financial and 4 non-financial ratios), which are shown in Table 2.

Table 2. Variable descriptions

Panel A: Financial Ratios			
Category	Variables	Relationship to default	Previous Studies
Management efficiency	Short-term liabilities*365 / Cost of Sales (STL/CS)	+	Lacher et al. (1995); Lee et al. (1996)
	Accounts receivable*365 / Sales (AR/S)	+	McKee (2003); Hamerle et al. (2006); Altman and Narayanan (1997)
	Inventories / Cost of sales (I/CS)	+	Ahn et al. (2000); Cielen et al. (2004); Karels and Prakash (1987)
Profitability	Profit before tax / Total assets (PBT/TA)	–	Bryant (1997); McKee (2003); Min and Lee (2005); Bonfim (2009)
	Financial expenses / Sales (FE/S)	+	Lee et al. (1996); Park and Han (2002); Shin and Lee (2002).
Solvency	Quick assets / Short-term liabilities (QA/STL)	–	Piramuthu et al. (1998); Dimitras et al. (1999); Cielen et al. (2004); Ko L.J, et al.(2007)
	Total liabilities/Total assets (TL/TA)	+	Kolari et al. (2002); Swicegood and Clark (2001); Tung et al. (2004); Greco et al. (1998)
Panel B: Non-financial indicators			
	Logarithm of employees (LOGE)	–	Leshno and Spector (1996); Tung et al. (2004)
	Exports indicator (EXP)	–	Becchetti and Sierra (2003); Yurdakul and Tansel (2004)
	Imports indicator (IMP)	–	
	Representations indicator (REPR)	–	

We have four categories of financial ratios (efficiency, profitability, liquidity and financial leverage) and four non-financial indicators that are crucial for commercial companies. In the next paragraph we will briefly discuss the relevance of the selected attributes in the context of credit risk evaluation.

Management efficiency ratios are typically used to analyze how well a company uses its assets and liabilities. Efficiency ratios are important because an improvement in the ratios usually translates to improved profitability. We have selected three ratios in this category, which are positive related to credit risk, in the sense that the higher their value, the higher is the probability of default.

The profitability indicators are used to assess ability of a firm to generate earnings as compared to its expenses and other relevant costs incurred during a specific period of time. The profitability ratios considered in this study include the return on assets ratio and ratio of financial expenses to sales. The first one is negative related to credit risk in contrast with the second one which is positively associated to the probability of default.

Finally, the category of solvency indicators includes two ratios related to the liquidity and the financial leverage of the firms. Liquidity determines a company's ability to pay off its short-term debt obligations. In this study the quick ratio (Current assets-Inventories/Short-term liabilities) is used which is negative related to credit risk. On the other hand, financial leverage provides an indication of the long-term solvency of a firm. Here the ratio of total liabilities to total assets is used which is positive related to credit risk.

Apart from financial indicators there should be a consideration of other factors that affect the operation of a firm. Here two factors are examined:

1. Logarithm of employees. This is an indicator of the size of a company, which has been shown in past studies to be negatively associated to the probability of default.
2. Activity indicator. For commercial companies it is important to take into consideration the type of their activities. In this study, in accordance with ICAP's modeling approach, the activities of the companies in the sample as characterized as exporting, importing, or as representative (i.e., companies that are local resellers of products of foreign companies). For each of these three classes of business activities, three binary indicators are used to describe the sample observations.

3.3. Univariate Analysis

Table 3 presents some descriptive statistics for the numerical variables (means and standard deviations for each group). The *p*-values from a *t*-test are also reported. As it is evident, all the variables are significant at 1% level of significance, except the ratio inventories/cost of sales. For the significance of the binary attributes regarding the business activity of the firms was tested with a χ^2 test and all three indicators were found significant at the 1% level.

Table 3. Descripted statistics for the numerical attributes (training sample)

	Non-defaulted		Defaulted		
Variables	Mean	SD	Mean	SD	*p*-value
STL/CS	424.012	365.509	618.821	460.722	0.000
AR/S	210.207	200.712	343.483	337.496	0.000
I/CS	168.433	243.625	224.000	334.918	0.148
PBT/TA	0.043	0.132	–0.037	0.156	0.000
FE/S	0.026	0.034	0.052	0.054	0.000
QA/STL	1.123	0.854	0.847	0.613	0.000
TL/TA	0.726	0.265	0.854	0.264	0.000
LOGE	1.009	0.559	0.492	0.495	0.000

The discriminating power of the selected predictor attributes is also tested with a non-parametric test, namely the area under the receiver operating characteristic curve (AUROC). The results presented in Table 4 confirm the aforementioned remarks on the discriminating power of the variables.

Table 4. Area under the receiver operating characteristic curve (AUROC)

Variables	AUROC	*p*-value
STL/CS	0.374	0.000
AR/S	0.398	0.000
I/CS	0.503	0.923
PBT/TA	0.718	0.000
FE / SAL	0.373	0.000
FE/S	0.634	0.000
QA/STL	0.351	0.000
TL/TA	0.748	0.000
EXP	0.586	0.002
IMP	0.660	0.000
REPR	0.586	0.002

4. RESULTS

4.1. Setting of the Empirical Analysis

The analysis is performed under three different settings. In particular, first a full sample analysis is undertaken, where the full training data are used to build classification models (general models) with the selected methods. The models are then compared on the basis of the training data.

Through the second setting, we analyze the impact of using training samples of varying size on the performance and stability of the models. This analysis is performed by constructing different sets of 100 bootstrap samples with different proportions of defaulted/non-defaulted observations (adjusted model). Given the major imbalance in the size of the two classes in the training sample, we construct different bootstrap samples for the two groups. The observations in the samples corresponding to the default group are selected at random with replacement from the default cases in the training sample.

These bootstrap samples have size equal to the number of default cases in the training sample (i.e., 105). On the other hand, we vary the size of the bootstrap samples corresponding to non-default group, beginning with n_D observations up to n_{ND} (i.e., with $2n_D$, $5n_D$ and $10n_D$ serving as the intermediate cases), where n_D and n_{ND} denote the number of default and non-default observations, respectively, in the full training sample (n_D=105, n_D=5594). Thus, we begin with small-size bootstrap samples in which the two classes are fully balanced (i.e., 105 observations from each group), and gradually increase the size of the bootstrap samples, holding the number of default observations fixed, but increasing the number of the non-default.

Finally, in the third setting considered in the analysis, we examine the aggregation of results developed in the previous setting through the bagging approach (Breiman, 1996) in order to test the usefulness and predictive power of ensemble models.

The assessment of the predictive performance of all models is done using two metrics. The first one involves the accuracy rates, which show the ability of the models to correctly classify the firms. In particular, we consider the accuracy rates for each group of firms, the mean accuracy (the mean of the accuracies for each group) and the overall accuracy (i.e., the ratio of the correct predictions to the total observations in the testing sample). Additionally, the area under the receiver operating characteristic curve is also used, which enables the analysis of the predictive performance of classification rules under different hypotheses with respect to the misclassification costs and the a priory class membership probabilities (Fawcett, 2006).

4.2. Classification Results

Tables 5–7 summarize the results of the analysis. In particular, Table 5 presents the accuracy rates for each group of firms. Panels A and B present the accuracy rates for the two groups of firms, obtained with the models developed through each method for different sizes of the bootstrap samples. The results obtained the models fitted on the full training sample are also reported in the last column. The accuracies range between 75–80% in most of the cases for the non-default group, whereas the accuracies for the default class are lower, with the exception of the models developed with the UTADIS method. Overall, the UTADIS method achieves the best balance between the two groups, followed by the non-linear SVM model with the RBF kernel. Furthermore, it is worth observing that increasing the size of the bootstrap samples leads to higher estimates for the accuracy rates for the non-default group, whereas the predictions for the default class are almost unaffected. Compared to the results of the models fitted on the full sample, the bootstrap results tend to overestimate the accuracy rates for the non-default group (as the size of the bootstrap samples increases), whereas the accuracy rates for the default group are consistently underestimated.

Panels C and D in Table 5 present the accuracy rates for the two groups of firms for the ensemble models. Compared to the full models, it is evident that the ensembles perform better for the non-default group (especially as the size of the bootstrap samples increases), but worse for the default class. However, the differences are generally small. In fact, even with the smaller bootstrap samples satisfactory results can be obtained.

Table 6 summarizes the results for the mean and overall accuracy of all models. The LR and linear SVM model perform best on the basis of their overall accuracy, but this is due to their much better performance for the non-default group (which is much larger compared to the default class). On the other hand, the more balanced performance of the UTADIS models leads to improved average accuracy which is much higher compared to the other methods. The performance of the individual models built with bootstrap samples of small size is lower compared to the models developed using the full sample, but the results improve as the size of the bootstrap samples increases. Nevertheless, using the bootstrap analysis results to build ensemble models leads to results which are comparable and in some cases slightly better compared to the models developed through the full sample, even for bootstrap sample of small size. It should be noted that even through in terms of their overall accuracy the ensemble models seem to outperform the models developed through the full training sample, the average accuracy suggests that the improvement is marginal at best (it is slightly higher when small bootstrap samples are used).

Table 5. Accuracies rates (in %) for each group of observations

	Bootstrap samples size					Full sample
	205	315	630	1, 155	5, 699	
Panel A: Non-default group - individual models						
LR	74.92	76.85	78.36	78.57	79.51	78.50
SVM	74.47	75.89	76.69	76.90	78.07	77.39
SVM RBF	74.38	75.96	76.94	77.30	78.49	76.77
UTADIS	72.60	74.48	75.22	75.50	76.28	75.61
Panel B: Default group - individual models						
LR	67.61	66.73	67.36	67.50	66.09	67.80
SVM	69.45	69.06	69.59	69.96	68.38	70.63
SVM RBF	68.95	68.38	69.11	69.29	67.74	72.03
UTADIS	74.21	73.85	74.29	74.24	74.09	78.32
Panel C: Non-default group - ensemble models						
LR	77.39	77.94	79.26	79.13	80.00	
SVM	76.53	77.39	77.60	77.80	78.83	
SVM RBF	76.49	77.45	77.76	77.86	79.01	
UTADIS	74.68	76.32	76.32	76.51	77.35	
Panel D: Default group- ensemble models						
LR	69.93	67.83	67.13	67.83	65.73	
SVM	73.43	70.63	72.03	70.63	69.23	
SVM RBF	72.73	70.63	71.33	70.63	69.23	
UTADIS	78.32	79.02	77.62	77.62	76.22	

Table 6. Mean and overall accuracies

	Bootstrap samples size					Full sample
	205	315	630	1155	5699	
Panel A: Mean accuracy of individual models						
LR	71.27	71.79	72.86	73.04	72.80	73.15
SVM	71.96	72.47	73.14	73.43	73.23	74.01
SVM RBF	71.67	72.17	73.02	73.30	73.11	74.40
UTADIS	73.41	74.16	74.75	74.87	75.18	76.96
Panel B: Overall accuracy of individual models						
LR	74.72	76.56	78.05	78.26	79.13	78.20
SVM	74.32	75.69	76.49	76.70	77.79	77.20
SVM RBF	74.23	75.74	76.71	77.08	78.18	76.64
UTADIS	72.65	74.46	75.19	75.46	76.21	75.68
Panel C: Mean accuracy of ensemble models						
LR	73.66	72.89	73.20	73.48	72.87	
SVM	74.98	74.01	74.81	74.21	74.03	
SVM RBF	74.61	74.04	74.54	74.25	74.12	
UTADIS	76.50	77.67	76.97	77.07	76.79	
Panel D: Overall accuracy of ensemble models						
LR	77.18	77.66	78.91	78.81	79.59	
SVM	76.44	77.20	77.44	77.60	78.55	
SVM RBF	76.38	77.26	77.58	77.66	78.73	
UTADIS	74.79	76.40	76.36	76.54	77.32	

The conclusions drawn from the above comparisons are further confirmed by the results shown in Table 7 on the AUROC. Again UTADIS provides the best results among the methods considered in the comparison and the ensemble models are only marginally better compared to the ones fitted on the full sample. Furthermore, the ensembles' results are not significantly affected by the size of the bootstrap samples and the associated imbalance in the size of the two classes.

Table 7. Area under the receiver operating characteristic curve

	Bootstrap samples size					Full sample
	205	315	630	1155	5699	
Panel A: Individual models						
LR	0.776	0.789	0.796	0.799	0.798	0.802
SVM	0.788	0.791	0.798	0.802	0.801	0.809
SVM RBF	0.783	0.788	0.797	0.802	0.801	0.812
UTADIS	0.800	0.807	0.813	0.814	0.816	0.824
Panel B: Ensemble models						
LR	0.807	0.799	0.809	0.810	0.806	
SVM	0.813	0.806	0.810	0.813	0.810	
SVM RBF	0.812	0.805	0.811	0.813	0.810	
UTADIS	0.824	0.826	0.828	0.829	0.828	

Conclusion and Future Perspectives

This study presented an empirical comparison of three popular techniques for constructing credit risk assessment models using a large sample of more than 10, 000 observations involving Greek firms from the commercial sector, over the period 2006–2009. The comparative analysis focused on different settings for the handling the training data in order to analyze the effect of the considerable class size imbalance on the predictive performance of the models. A bootstrap sampling approach was employed for this purpose and the construction of ensemble models through the bagging approach was tested.

Overall, the results showed that the UTADIS a multicriteria method performed better than logistic regression and support vector machines. Using training data of different size, it was observed that even with small samples good results can be obtained, which are improved as the sample size increases. On the other hand, an ensemble approach leads to results similar or slightly better compared to the full models, even with bootstrap samples of small size. This finding may have significant implications as far the computational aspects of the model development process is concerned, mainly for methods that do not scale well with the size of the training data.

Future research can be extended towards several directions. First, there should be a consideration of other methods (neural networks, multicriteria methods, rule-based models). Furthermore, other modeling approaches such as hazard models and survival analysis or option-pricing models could also be applied. Finally, it would be worthwhile considering additional predictors including among others economic conditions, stock market data and qualitative aspects (e.g., management's performance).

References

Ahn, B.A., Cho, S.S., and Kim, C.Y. (2000), "The integrated methodology of rough set theory and artificial neural network for business failure prediction", *Expert Systems with Applications* 18, 65–74.

Altman, E.I.(1968), "Financial ratios, discriminant analysis and the prediction of corporate bankruptcy", *Journal of Finance* 13, 589–609.

Altman, E.I., Haldeman, R., and Narayanan, P. (1977), "ZETA™ analysis: A new model to identify bankruptcy risk of corporations", *Journal of Banking and Finance*1(1), 29–54.

Altman, E.I., Marco, G., and Varetto, F. (1994), "Corporate distress diagnosis: Comparisons using linear discriminant analysis and neural networks (The Italian experience)", *Journal of Banking and Finance*18(3), 505–529.

Altman, E.I., and Narayanan, P.(1997), "An international survey of business failure classification models", *Financial Markets, Institutions and Instruments* 6(2), 1–57.

Altman, E.I. and Saunders A. (1998), "Credit risk measurement: Developments over the last 20 years", *Journal of Banking and Finance* 21(11–12), 1721–1742.

Angelini, E., Di Tollo, G., and Roli, A. (2008), "A neural network approach for credit risk evaluation", *The Quarterly Review of Economics and Finance* 48, 733–755.

Atiya, A. (2001), "Bankruptcy prediction for credit risk using neural networks: A survey and new results", *IEEE Transactions on Neural Networks* 12(4), 929–935.

Baesens, B., Setiono, R., Mues, C., and Vanthienen, J. (2003), "Using neural network rule extraction and decision tables for credit-risk evaluation", *Management Science* 79(3), 312–329.

Barnes, P. (1990), "The prediction of takeover targets in the UK by means of multiple discriminant analysis", *Journal of Business Finance and Accounting* 17(1), 73–84.

Beaver, R. (1966), "Financial ratios as predictors of failure", *Journal of Accounting Research* 4, 71–111.

Becchetti, L. and Sierra, J. (2003), "Bankruptcy risk and productive efficiency in manufacturing firms", *Journal of Banking and Finance* 27(11), 2099–2120.

BIS (2004), *International Convergence of Capital Measurement and Capital Standards: A Revised Framework*, Basel Committee of Banking Supervision, Bank for International Settlements.

Bonfim, D. (2009), "Credit risk drivers: Evaluating the contribution of firm level information and of macroeconomic dynamics", *Journal of Banking and Finance* 33(2), 281–299.

Breiman, L.(1996), "Bagging predictors", *Machine Learning* 24, 123–140.

Bryant, S.M. (1997), "A case-based reasoning approach to bankruptcy prediction modeling", *Intelligent Systems in Accounting, Finance and Management* 6, 195–214.

Bugera, V., Konno, H., and Uryasev, S. (2002), "Credit cards scoring with quadratic utility functions", *Journal of Multi-Criteria Decision Analysis* 11(4–5), 197–211.

Cielen, A., Peeters, L., and Vanhoof, K. (2004), "Bankruptcy prediction using a data envelopment analysis", *European Journal of Operational Research* 154(2), 526–532.

Dimitras, A.I., Slowinski, R., Susmaga, R., and Zopounidis, C., (1999), "Business failure prediction using rough sets", *European Journal of Operational Research* 114(2), 263–290.

Doumpos, M., Kosmidou, K., Baourakis, G., and Zopounidis, C. (2002), "Credit risk assessment using a multicriteria hierarchical discrimination approach: A comparative analysis", *European Journal of Operational Research* 138(2), 392–412.

Doumpos, M. and Zopoounidis.C. (2002), *Multicriteria Decision Aid Classification Methods*, Kluwer Academic Publishers, Dordecht.

Doumpos, M. and Zopounidis, C. (2011), "A multicriteria outranking modeling approach for credit rating", *Decision Sciences* 42(3), 721–742.

Emel, A.B., Oral, M., Reisman, A., and Yolalan, R. (2003), "A credit scoring approach for the commercial banking sector", *Socio-Economic Planning Sciences* 37, 103–123.

Espahbodi, H. and Espahbodi, P. (2003), "Binary choice models for corporate takeover", *Journal of Banking and Finance* 27, 549–574.

Fawcett, T. (2006), "An introduction to ROC analysis", *Pattern Recognition Letters*27(8), 861–874.

Gaganis.C., Pasiouras, F., Spathis, C., and Zopounidis, C. (2007), "A comparison of nearest neighbours, discriminant and logit models for auditing decisions", *Intelligent Systems in Accounting, Finance and Management* 15, 23–40.

Greco, S., Matarazzo, B., and Slowinski, R. (1998), "A new rough set approach to evaluation of bankruptcy risk", in: C. Zopounidis (ed.), *Operational Tools in the Management of Financial Risks*, Kluwer Academic Publishers, Dordrecht, 121–136.

Hamer, M.M. (1983), "Failure prediction: sensitivity of classification accuracy to alternative statistical methods and variable sets", *Journal of Accounting and Public Policy* 2, 289–307.

Hamerle, A.H., Liebig, T.L., and Scheule, H. (2006), "Forecasting credit event frequency - empirical evidence for West German firms", *Journal of Risk* 9(1), 75–98.

Hu, Y.-C.(2009), "Bankruptcy prediction using ELECTRE-based single-layer perceptron", *Neurocomputing* 72(13–15), 3150–3157.

Huang, Z., Chen, H.C., Hsu, C.J., Chen W.H., and Wu, S.S. (2004), "Credit rating analysis with support vector machines and neural networks: A market comparative study", *Decision Support Systems* 37(4), 543–558.

Karels, G.V. and Prakash, A.J. (1987), "Multivariate normality and forecasting of business bankruptcy", *Journal of Business Finance and Accounting* 14(4), 573–593.

Ko, L.J. Blocher E.J., and Lin, P.P. (2007), "Prediction of corporate financial distress: An application of the composite rule induction system", *The International Journal of Digital Accounting Research*1(1), 69–85.

Kocagil, A.E., Escott, Ph., Glormann, F., Malzkorn, W., and Scott, A.(2002), "Moody's RiskCalc for private companies: UK", Moody's Investors Service, Global Credit Research.

Kolari, J., Glennon, D., Shin, H., and Caputo, M. (2002), "Predicting large US commercial bank failures", *Journal of Economics and Business* 54(4), 361–387.

Kou, G., Peng, Y., Shi, Y., Wise, M., and Xu, W. (2005), "Discovering creditcard holders' behavior by multiple criteria linear programming", *Annals of Operations Research* 135(1), 261–274.

Lacher, R.C., Coats, P.K., Sharma, S.C., and Fantc, L.F. (1995), "A neural network for classifying the financial health of a firm", *European Journal of Operational Research* 85(1), 53–65.

Lee, K.C., Han, I., and Kwon, Y. (1996), "Hybrid neural network models for bankruptcy predictions", *Decision Support Systems* 18, 63–72.

Leshno, M. and Spector, Y. (1996), "Neural network prediction analysis: The bankruptcy case", *Neurocomputing* 10, 125–147.

Lopez, J.A. and Saidenberg, M.R. (2000), "Evaluating credit risk models", *Journal of Banking and Finance* 24(1), 151–165.

McKee, T.E. (2003), "Rough sets bankruptcy prediction models versus auditor signaling rates", *Journal of Forecasting* 22, 569–589.

McKinsey (1993), Special Report on the "New world of financial services", The McKinsey Quarterly, Number 2.

Min, J.H. and Lee, Y.-C. (2005), "Bankruptcy prediction using support vector machine (SVM) with optimal choice of kernel function parameters", *Expert Systems with Applications* 28, 603–614.

Ohlson, J.(1980), "Financial ratios and the probabilistic prediction of bankruptcy", *Journal of Accounting Research* 18, 109–131.

Palepu, K.G. (1986), "Predicting takeover targets: A methodological and empirical analysis", *Journal of Accounting and Economics*8, 3–35.

Park, C.-S. and Han, I. (2002), "A case-based reasoning with the feature weights derived by analytic hierarchy process for bankruptcy prediction", *Expert Systems with Applications* 23(3), 255–264.

Piramuthu, S., Ragavan, H., and Shaw, M.J. (1998), "Using feature construction to improve the performance of the neural networks", *Management Science* 44(3), 416–430.

Piramuthu, S. (1999), "Financial credit-risk evaluation with neural and neurofuzzy systems", *European Journal of Operational Research* 112(2), 310–321.

Platt, H.D. and Platt, M.B. (1991), "A note on the use of industry-relative ratios in bankruptcy prediction", *Journal of Banking and Finance*15, 1183–1194.

Schölkopf, B. and Smola, A.(2002), *Learning with Kernels: Support Vector Machines, Regularization, Optimization and Beyond*, MIT Press, Cambridge.

Shin, K.-S. and Lee, Y.-J. (2002), "A genetic algorithm application in bankruptcy prediction modeling", *Expert Systems with Applications* 23(3), 321–328.

Smith, L.D. and Lawrence, E. (1995), "Forecasting losses on a liquidating long-term loan portfolio", *Journal of Banking and Finance*19, 959–985.

Stecking, R. and Schebesch, K.B. (2003), "Support vector machines for credit scoring: Comparing to and combining with some traditional classification methods", in Schader, M., Gaul, W., and Vichy, M.(eds.), *Between Data Science and Applied Data Analysis*, Springer-Verlag, Berlin, 604–612.

Swicegood, P. and Clark, J.A. (2001), "Off-site monitoring for predicting bank under performance: A comparison of neural networks, discriminant analysis and professional human judgment", *International Journal of Intelligent Systems in Accounting, Finance and Management* 10, 169–186.

Troutt, M.D., Rai, A., and Zhang, A.(1996), "The potential use of DEA for credit applicant acceptance systems", *Computers and Operations Research* 23(4), 405–408.

Tung, W.L., Quek, C., and Cheng, P. (2004), "GenSo-EWS: A novel neural-fuzzy based early warning system for predicting bank failures", *Neural Networks* 17, 567–587.

Vapnik, V. (1998), *Statistical Learning Theory*, Wiley, New York.

West, D., Dellana, S., and Qian, J. (2005), "Neural network ensemble strategies for financial decision applications", *Computers and Operations Research* 32, 2543–2559.

Yurdakul, M. and Tansel, Y. (2004), "AHP approach in the credit evaluation of the manufacturing firms in Turkey", *International Journal of Production Economics* 88, 269–289.

Zopounidis, C. and Doumpos. M. (1999), "Business failure prediction using the UTADIS multicriteria analysis method", *Journal of Operational Research Society* 50(11), 1138–1148.

In: Computational Techniques for Banking and Risk Management ISBN: 978-1-62618-522-7
Editors: C. Zopounidis and M. Doumpos

Chapter 10

A SERVICE QUALITY EVALUATION METHOD IN THE TOURISM INDUSTRY BASED ON MULTICRITERIA ANALYSIS

Marianna Tsitsiloni[1*], Evangelos Grigoroudis[1] and Constantin Zopounidis[2]

[1]Technical University of Crete, Decision Support Systems Laboratory, University Campus, Kounoupidiana, Chania, Greece

[2]Technical University of Crete, Financial Engineering Laboratory, University Campus, Kounoupidiana, Chania, Greece

ABSTRACT

The quality evaluation of the provided tourism services constitutes the most important issue for the viability of this particular sector and the improvement of the total tourism product.

This paper presents the results of a tourist satisfaction survey that took place in an Aegean island during the period of May-September 2009. The final sample consists of 1026 questionnaires that were distributed to Greek and foreign tourists during their departure from the island (harbor and airport). The main objective of this paper is to evaluate tourists' satisfaction and identify the strong and the weak points of the tourism services offered.

These results may help the development of a strategic plan for the quality improvement of the overall tourism product. Besides descriptive statistical techniques, the analysis of the collected data is based on the multicriteria method MUSA. The method is able to combine satisfaction importance and performance results and provide a SWOT (Strengths-Weaknesses-Opportunities-Threats) analysis for the whole set of the tourist satisfaction criteria. The presented analytical results reveal that the main strong points of the offered tourist product refer to the fame and the natural beauties of the island, as well as the high level of expenses. On the other hand, the most important weak

[*] E-mail: mtsitsiloni@yahoo.gr.

points concern the small duration of stay, as well as the low level of satisfaction in specific service quality criteria (local transports, information, and environment).

Keywords: Tourist Satisfaction, MUSA Method, SWOT Analysis, Service Quality

INTRODUCTION

The tourism industry constitutes one of the most important sectors in many local economies in Greece, mainly because of its constant increasing contribution to the income of these regions, but also due to the opportunities offered for further growth (Karakitsiou et al., 2007). The importance of tourism sector is presented in the work of Naisbitt (1995), who emphasizes that the world economy in the current century will be dominated by three sectors: information technology, telecommunications, and tourism.

Modern business organizations consider service quality as the most reliable source of market information. Service quality is considered as the main determinant of customer satisfaction, which in turn influences purchase intentions (Spreng and Mckoy, 1996; De Ruyter et al., 1997). The importance of service quality evaluation through customer satisfaction measurement is reinforced by the necessity of adopting a "continuous improvement" philosophy and understanding customer perceptions (e.g., needs, expectations).

Generally, the main reasons for measuring customer satisfaction are summarized in the following (Grigoroudis and Siskos, 2010):

- Customer satisfaction constitutes the most reliable market information. This way, a business organization is able to evaluate its current position against competition, and design its future plans accordingly.
- A large number of customers avoid expressing their complaints or their dissatisfaction from the product or service provided, either due to a particular attitude or because they are not sure that the company will perform any corrective action.
- Customer satisfaction measurement is able to identify potential market opportunities.
- The main principles of continuous improvement require the development of a specific customer satisfaction measurement process. This way, any improvement action is based on standards that take into account customer expectations and needs.
- Customer satisfaction measurement may help business organizations to under-stand customer behavior, and particularly to identify and analyze customer expectations, needs, and desires.
- The application of a customer satisfaction measurement program may reveal potential differences in the service quality perceptions between the customer and the management of the business organization.

The necessity of customer satisfaction measurement in the tourism industry may be justified by the importance of the tourism sector for local economies and the intense competition among alternative tourism destinations that is evident in recent years. Furthermore, tourism sector is heavily influenced by significant external factors form the global economic environment, and thus it is necessary to improve the quality of the services offered in order to gain competitive advantages and increase tourist loyalty levels.

However, tourist satisfaction from a destination area is a general and ambiguous notion, since tourism goods and services should be treated as a subset of goods and services in general. For this reason, as noted by Yuksel (2001), a large number of researchers have studied components of experiences, which contribute to tourist satisfaction within different tourism and hospitality contexts (e.g., guest satisfaction with hotels and restaurant services, satisfaction with destination services, satisfaction with recreational services, satisfaction with tours or cruise travel). As suggested by Pizam et al. (1978), tourist satisfaction is the result of interaction between tourist's experience at the destination areas and the expectations she/he had about that destination. This confirmation/disconfirmation approach is rather common in tourist satisfaction research (Bowen and Clarke, 2002).

The HOLSAT model is a characteristic approach used to evaluate satisfaction from a particular destination (Tribe and Snaith, 1998). The model is based on the disconfirmatory paradigm outlined before and adopts the philosophy of the SERVQUAL model (Parasuraman et al., 1985; 1988; 1991). The main results of the HOLSAT model focus on the difference between "expectation" and "experience" scores for each attribute, which gives a quantitative measure of the level of satisfaction shown by the vacationers (Truong and Foster, 2006). Other research efforts in tourism management combine the disconfirmation paradigm with additional quality improvement tools, like QFD, Kano's model, etc. (Pawitra and Tan, 2003).

Despite the context and the multivariate nature of tourist satisfaction measurement, Multiple Criteria Decision Analysis (MCDA) has not been widely applied in evaluating service quality in the tourism industry. Rozman et al. (2009) apply the DEX method, which combines traditional MCDA approaches and elements of expert systems and machine learning, in order to assess tourist farm service quality. An AHP model, combined with fuzzy TOPSIS, is applied by Hsu et al. (2009) in a preference analysis for tourist choice of destination in Taiwan. The MUSA method has been also applied by Arabatzis and Grigoroudis (2010) in order to examine the level of visitors' satisfaction regarding the National Park of Dadia–Lefkimi–Souflionarea.

The main objective of this paper is to present an application of a MCDA approach in tourist satisfaction measurement from a destination area. Moreover, the presented study aims to demonstrate how a SWOT analysis approach may be applied in the context of tourism management. The paper is organized into 4 more sections. Section 2 briefly presents the adopted methodology, including the development of the MUSA method and the proposed gap analysis approach. The main results of the tourist satisfaction survey are presented in section 3, giving emphasis on the determination of the strong and weak point of the services offered. Finally, section 4 summarizes some concluding remarks.

METHODOLOGY

MUSA Method

The MUSA (MUlticriteria Satisfaction Analysis) method is a multicriteria preference disaggregation approach, which provides quantitative measures of customer satisfaction considering the qualitative form of customers' judgments (Siskos, et al. 1998; Grigoroudis and Siskos, 2002). The main objective of the MUSA method is the aggregation of individual judgments into a collective value function, assuming that client's global satisfaction depends on a set of n criteria or variables representing service characteristic dimensions. This set of criteria is denoted as $\mathbf{X}=(X_1,X_2,\ldots,X_n)$, where a particular criterion i is represented as a monotonic variable X_i .

The MUSA method infers an additive collective value function Y^* and a set of partial satisfaction functions X_i^* , given customer's global satisfaction Y and partial satisfaction X_i according to criterion *i* (ordinal scaling). The main objective of the method is to achieve the maximum consistency between the value function Y^* and the customers' judgments Y . Based on the modeling of preference disaggregation approach, the ordinal regression equation becomes as follows:

$$\tilde{Y}^* = \sum_{i=1}^{n} b_i X_i^* - \sigma^+ + \sigma^- \text{ with} \sum_{i=1}^{n} b_i = 1$$

where $\tilde{Y}^*$ is the estimation of Y^* , b_i is the weight of the *i*-th criterion, n is the number of criteria, and σ^+ , σ^- are the overestimation and the underestimation errors, respectively.

The most important results provided by the MUSA method are the estimated global and partial value functions, the criteria weights, and the average satisfaction, demanding, and improvement indices. In particular, regarding performance and importance results, the following should be noted:

- *Criteria weights*: they represent the relative importance of the assessed satisfaction dimensions; the decision whether a satisfaction dimension is considered important by the customers is also based on the number of assessed criteria; their properties are also determined in the context of multicriteria analysis (e.g., the weights are value trade-offs among the criteria).
- *Average satisfaction indices*: they show in a range of 0–100% the level of customers' satisfaction and they can be considered as the basic performance norms; the average satisfaction indices are basically the mean value of the global and partial value functions.
- *Average demanding indices*: these indices are calculated according to the shape of global and partial value functions, which indicate customers' demanding level; they represent the average deviation of the estimated value functions from a "normal" (linear) function; the average global and partial demanding indices, D and D_i , respectively, are normalized in the interval $[-1,+1]$ and the following possible cases hold:
  - Neutral customers (D or $D_i \in [-0.33,+0.33]$): the value function has more or less a linear form; the more satisfied these customers express they are, the higher the percentage of their fulfilled expectations is.

- Demanding customers (D or $D_i \in [+0.33, +1.00]$): this refers to a case of a convex value function; customers are not really satisfied, unless they receive the best quality level.
- Non-demanding customers (D or $D_i \in [-1.00, -0.33]$): this refers to a case of a concave value function; customers express that they are satisfied, although only a small portion of their expectations is fulfilled.
- These indices are used in customer behavior analysis, but they may also indicate the extent of company's improvement efforts: the higher the value of the demanding index, the more the satisfaction level should be improved in order to fulfill customers' expectations.
- *Average improvement indices*: they represent the improvement efforts and they depend on the importance of satisfaction criteria and their contribution to dissatisfaction as well; these indices are normalized in the interval $[0,1]$ and they can show the improvement margins on a specific criterion.

Detailed presentation of the mathematical development of the MUSA method may be found in Grigoroudis and Siskos (2002, 2010), and Siskos et al. (1998), while several applications to business organizations can be found in the literature (Siskos et al., 1998; Grigoroudis et al., 2000; Mihelis et al., 2001; Grigoroudis et al., 2002; Politis and Siskos, 2004; Grigoroudis and Siskos, 2004).

SWOT Analysis

SWOT analysis is widely used in management science to identify strengths, weaknesses, opportunities and threats when studying a particular product/service or an entire company/organization. In service quality literature, SWOT analysis appears either as gap analysis or as performance-importance comparison (Grigoroudis and Siskos, 2010). In both cases the main objective is to identify the quality gap of the service offered, i.e., identify the gap between what customers want and what customers get.

The MUSA method, using the previous results, provides additional diagrams that may help to determine improvement actions. In particular, the action diagrams are developed by combining weights and average satisfaction indices. These diagrams indicate the strong and the weak points of customer satisfaction, and define the required improvement efforts. Each of these maps is divided into quadrants, according to performance (high/low) and importance (high/low) that may be used to classify actions (Figure 1):

- *Status quo* (low performance and low importance): Generally, no action is required.
- *Leverage opportunity* (high performance/high importance): These areas can be used as advantage against competition.
- *Transfer resources* (high performance/low importance): Company's resources may be better used elsewhere.
- *Action opportunity* (low performance/high importance): These are the criteria that need attention.

These diagrams are similar to SWOT maps, since status quo quadrant refers to threats, leverage opportunity quadrant refers to strengths, transfer resources corresponds to opportunities, and action opportunity quadrant corresponds to weaknesses.

In addition, they appear in the service quality literature as importance-performance analysis (Dutka, 1995; Naumann and Giel, 1995) or gap analysis (Hill, 1996; Woodruff and Gardial, 1996; Vavra, 1997). Similar gap analysis tools have been widely used in tourism research, mainly for the evaluation of hotel and restaurant services and facilities (Oh, 2001; Karakitsiou et al., 2007) or the measurement of visitors' satisfaction (Wade and Eagles, 2003; Ryan and Cessford, 2003; Tonge and Moore, 2007; Hanim et al., 2010).

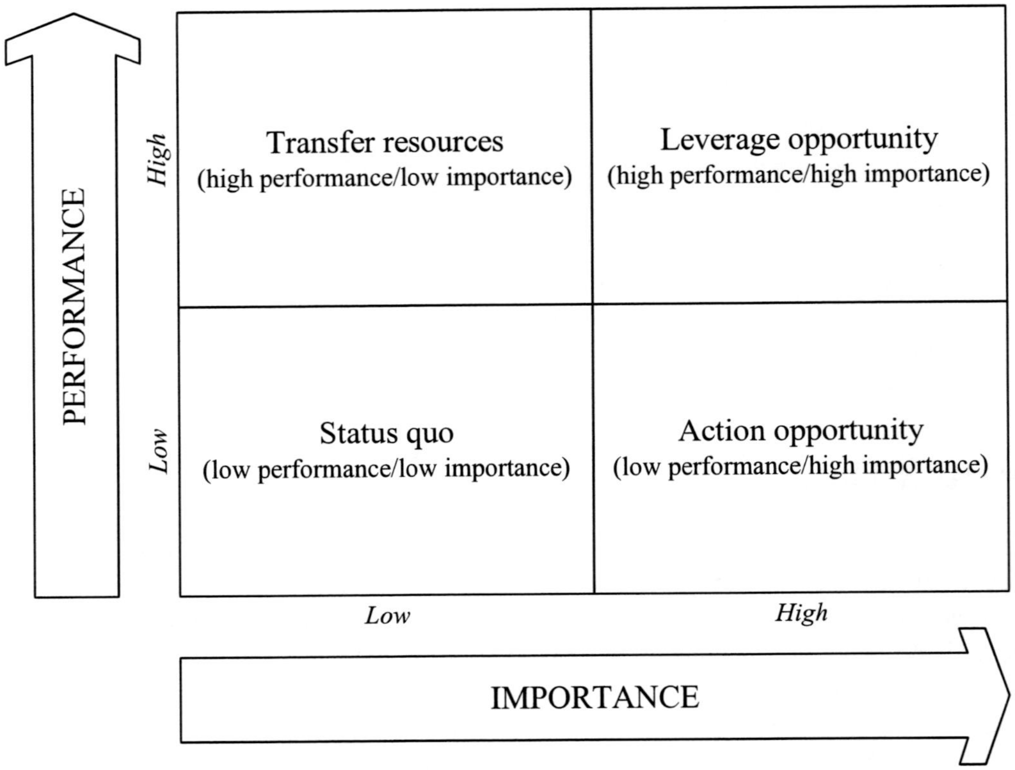

Figure 1. Action diagram (Grigoroudis and Siskos, 2010).

Another type of map provided by the MUSA method concerns the improvement diagram, which takes into account customers' demanding level and it is used in order to rank improvement priorities (Figure 2). Similarly to the previous maps, each of these diagrams is divided into quadrants according to demanding (high/low), and effectiveness (high/low). Thus, the first priority should be given to satisfaction criteria having large improvement margins and need small effort. On the other hand, the last priority should be given to satisfaction dimensions with low dissatisfaction level that need substantial effort to improve. Finally, the second priority quadrant includes satisfaction dimensions that have either a low demanding index or a high improvement index.

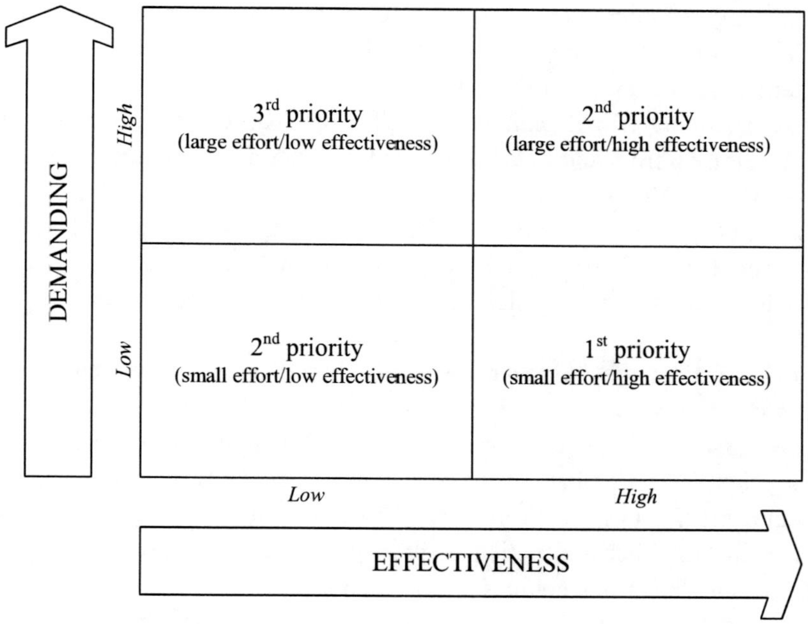

Figure 2. Improvement diagram (Grigoroudis and Siskos, 2010).

SURVEY AND RESULTS

Satisfaction Criteria and Questionnaire

The most important phase in the implementation of the MUSA model is the assessment of the set of satisfaction criteria and the definition of the value hierarchy. Based on previous applications of the MUSA method and customer satisfaction surveys in the tourism sector (Pizam et al., 1978; Yuksel, 2001; Karakitsiou et al., 2007; Arabatzis and Grigoroudis, 2010; Tsitsiloni, 2010), the set of satisfaction criteria used in the survey consists of:

1. *Accommodation*: all the characteristics of accommodation are included in this criterion, e.g., service offered, facilities, staff, prices.
2. *Food/Cuisine*: this particular criterion refers to the local cuisine and the food offered inside or outside the accommodation facilities and includes food quality, the variety of dishes, the environment (decoration, aesthetics), the provided services, the prices, etc.
3. *Natural environment*: this criterion refers mainly to the natural environment, the climate conditions, as well as the local architecture.
4. *Urban environment*: the criterion is related to the urban environment and the infrastructures of the island and includes the cleanliness of public spaces, the noise pollution, the roads and the traffic, the available parking, etc.
5. *Hospitality*: this characteristic is related with the hospitality, the behavior, and the friendliness of the locals.
6. *Information*: the information available to tourists though desks, kiosks, signs, and maps are included in this dimension.

7. *Entertainment/Recreation*: this criterion refers to the entertainment/recreation choice offered to tourists during their stay and includes the available choices, the service offered, the venues, the prices, etc.
8. *Transportation (from and to island)*: this particular dimension concerns the transportation from and to the island and includes all the characteristics of the service provided in island's port and airport.
9. *Local transportation means*: the criterion refers to the local transportation means, i.e. bus and taxi services, rented cars, etc. and includes all the characteristics of the provided services (availability, service from personnel, prices, etc.).

The final questionnaire has been developed based on the aforementioned satisfaction criteria, in which tourists were asked to express their satisfaction using a 5-point Likert type ordinal scale (dissatisfied, somehow dissatisfied, neither satisfied nor dissatisfied, somehow satisfied, satisfied). The first part of the questionnaire contains questions about the tourist's personal characteristics (sex, age, income, purpose of trip). The second part is devoted to travel information (number and period of previous visits, alternative destination examined, reasons of choosing the island, sources of information), while the third part includes questions about accommodation, length of stay, and expenses. The fourth part of the questionnaire refers to the satisfaction criteria, while the next part of the questionnaire contains loyalty-related questions.

Sample and Tourists' Profile

The final sample consists of 1026 questionnaires that were distributed to Greek and foreign tourists during their departure from the island (harbor and airport). The questionnaires were collected through personal interviews during summer 2009.

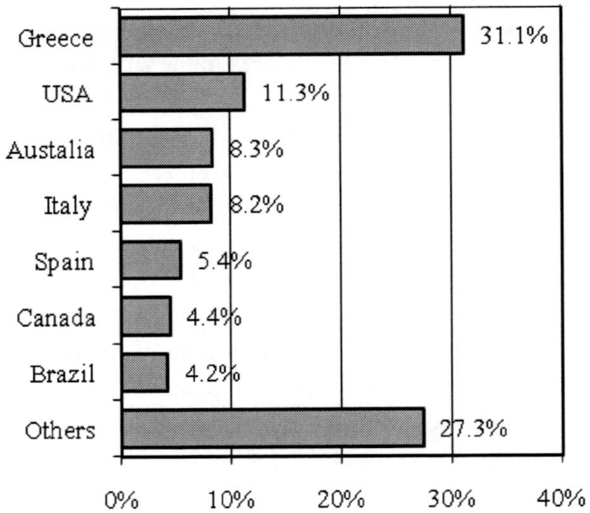

Figure 3. Nationality groups.

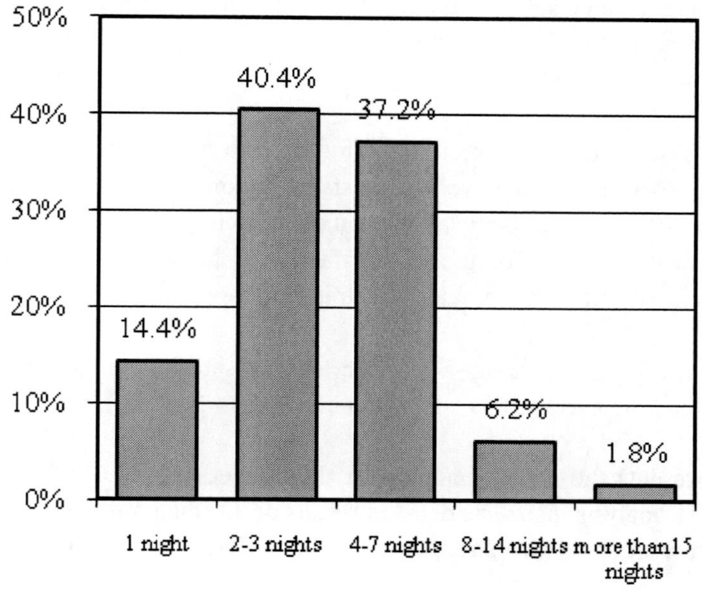

Figure 4. Length of stay (number of nights spent).

In order to formulate a customer profile, tourist's characteristics have been studied. The sample is almost equally distributed between males and females (male 46.5%, female 53.5%). Also, the majority of visitors are less than 40 years old (74.8%); while the group of older visitors is very small (less than 4% are older than 60 years).

Regarding nationality, it should be noted that the 31% of the sample refers to Greek tourists, while the rest 69% consists of foreign visitors. Figure 3 shows that the distribution of the sample in the different nationalities is relatively high, and the most important foreign tourist groups refer to visitors from the USA, Australia, Italy, Spain, Canada, and Brazil. Generally, there is no nationality group larger than 10% of the sample, while almost 50 different nationality groups have been identified in the final sample. Also, it seems that the length of stay is relatively low, since the majority of tourists spend 1-3 nights in the island (almost 55%). As shown in Figure 4, only 8% of the sample stays more than 1 week in the island. Additional analyses regarding other tourists' personal characteristics have been performed in order to develop a complete profile for the visitors (see more details in Tsitsiloni, 2010). In general, it seems that the most characteristic tourists' segments with distinguished preferences and behavior refer to the nationality (Greek and foreign visitors).

Satisfaction Analysis

The results of the MUSA method reveal that the tourists give particular importance in the criterion of entertainment/recreation (weight 18.53%), while the importance of urban environment and transportation criteria is relatively lower (less than 10%). Moreover, it seems that generally the visitors are relatively satisfied from their vacations in the island, since the estimated overall average satisfaction index is 86.40%. Although this overall satisfaction level is relatively high, it seems that there are significant improvement margins.

Regarding the detailed satisfaction criteria, as shown in Table 1, it appears that there are important differences regarding tourist satisfaction level. In particular, the results of Table 1 reveal the following:

- Tourists seem to be quite satisfied by the criteria of entertainment/recreation and natural environment (the average satisfaction indices are approximately 90%), which are also the most important satisfaction dimensions.
- In contrast, the level of tourist satisfaction is quite low regarding the criteria of environment, information, and local transportations (average satisfaction indices 70-78%).
- The rest of criteria present a medium level of satisfaction (80-83%), comparatively lower than the average total satisfaction index.

Figure 5 presents the action diagram for the whole sample, which is used in order to develop a SWOT analysis map. The detailed results of this diagram reveal that the criterion of entertainment/recreation is the strongest point of offered tourist product, since it is the characteristic that visitors consider very important, while at the same time they appear particularly satisfied by this. In addition, it seems that no satisfaction criteria appear in the action opportunity area (high importance and low satisfaction/performance). Thus, no critical characteristics exist that require direct improvement actions. The criteria of urban environment (cleanliness of public spaces, roads, noise pollution, parking, etc.) and the local transports are the main basic threats of the tourist product, since they present a relatively low satisfaction level. They are currently considered as a threat and not as a weak point because of their lower importance.

For the rest of the satisfaction criteria, the categorization is not easy, since they present a relatively medium satisfaction and importance level. However, it seems that the natural environment is a potential strong point, while the information criterion is a potentially critical characteristic.

In general, it seems that there is no "gap" regarding tourist satisfaction (i.e., what tourists want and what tourists get), since visitors seem to be more satisfied by those characteristics that they consider as important.

Table 1. Average satisfaction indices and criteria weights

Satisfaction Criteria	Weight (%)	Average satisfaction indices (%)
Accommodation	10.49	82.85
Food/Cuisine	10.90	80.87
Natural environment	11.11	89.11
Urban environment	9.13	72.61
Hospitality	10.12	80.19
Information	11.11	77.87
Entertainment/Recreation	18.53	90.49
Transportation (airport/harbor)	9.90	80.48
Local transportation means	8.70	68.55
Overall satisfaction		86.40

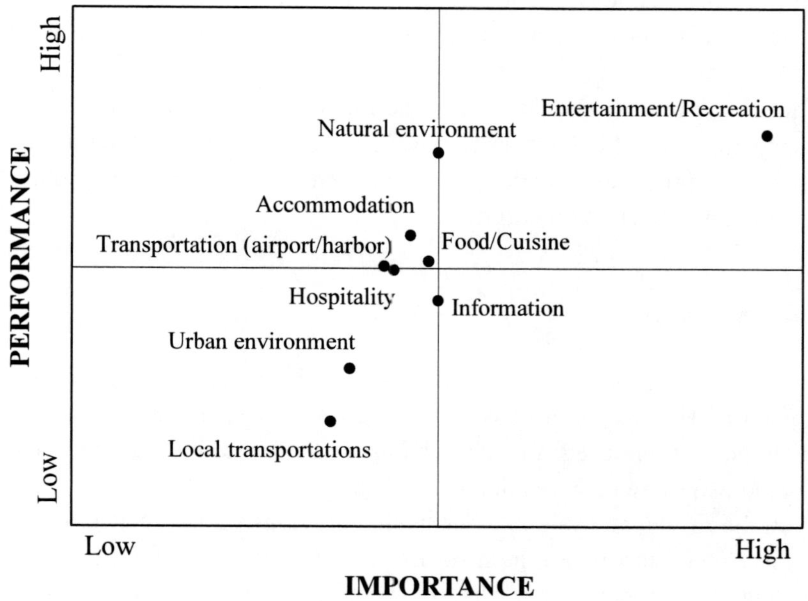

Figure 5. Action diagram for the tourist satisfaction criteria.

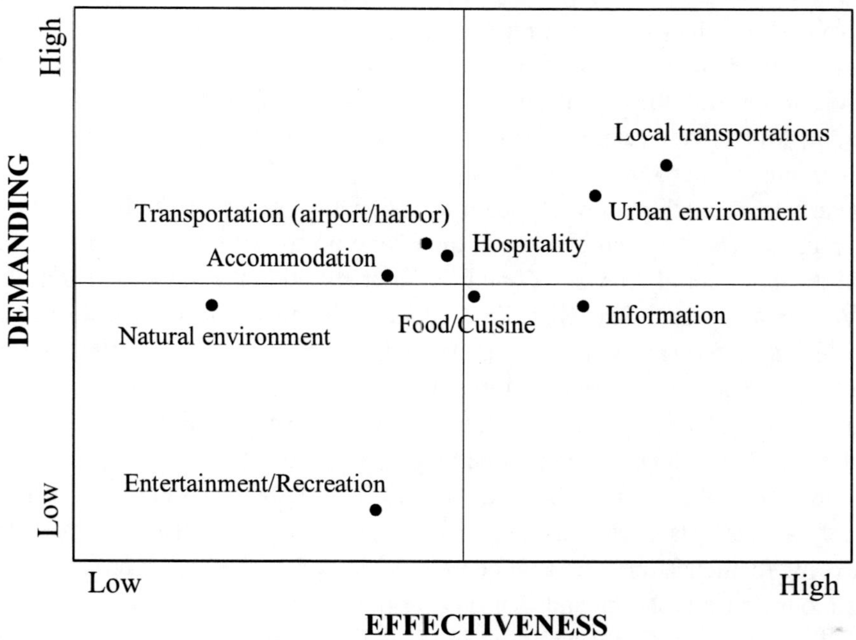

Figure 6. Improvement diagram for the tourist satisfaction criteria.

Similarly, Figure 6 shows the improvement diagram for the whole sample. This diagram takes into account the demanding level of tourists, as well as the effectiveness of potential improvement actions. The most important results of Figure 6 reveal the following:

- Improvement actions should be focused firstly to information and food/cuisine, which are the most important satisfaction criteria with the lowest performance (see also Figure 5).
- The second priority should refer to the improvement of urban environment and local transportations, which appear to have a relatively lower performance. Alternatively, further improvement action may concern the natural environment and the entertainment/recreation criteria.

Statistical Analyses

This section presents the results of additional statistical analyses in selected variables of the questionnaire. The results are based on a series of correlation analyses (i.e. chi-square tests), which have been used for identifying particular tourist clusters with distinctive preferences and expectations in relation to the total set.

Based on the results of Table 2, it seems that previous visit is related with nationality. In particular, the Greek tourists are the most loyal visitors, while there are many visitors from North and Central Europe, who had already visited the island. The 80-95% of the rest of the nationalities has visited the island for the first time.

Some nationalities appear more loyal regarding the examination of alternative destinations (Table 2). In particular, the Greeks and the Asians, in general, do not examine alternative destinations when deciding their holidays. Similarly, visitors over 60 years appear more loyal, since they do not examine other alternatives when choosing their holiday destination. In general, there is no strong relation between income and examining alternative destinations. Moreover, as expected, the tourists who have already visited the island are more loyal, regarding this particular characteristic.

Similarly, the length of stay is related to nationality (Table 2). Additional analyses show that the tourists who stay more days on the island are mostly Italians, Greeks and visitors from North and Central Europe. Contrarily, tourists with the smallest length of stay are mostly Asians and Australians-New Zealanders. Age and length of stay do not seem to be strongly related, although the older tourists (more than 40 years old) affect the overall low average length of stay of the whole sample. Furthermore, there seems to be no strong relation between income and length of stay. On the contrary, a previous visit to the island significantly affects the duration of stay, since repeated visitors stay more days.

As shown in Table 2, there is no significant relation between the level of expenses and the age of tourists. Also, nationality appears to affect the amount of expenses that tourists spent (except for tickets and accommodations), since the highest expenses are observed in European tourists (Italy, North and Central Europe). Contrarily, the amount of expenditures is related to the annual family income of visitors, while repeated visitors seem to spend more, as expected.

Finally, the chi-square tests between overall satisfaction and several tourist characteristics are presented in Table 2.

Table 2. Results of chi-square tests for tourist characteristics

Variables	Chi-square	df	p-level
Previous visit-Nationality	298.353	7	0.000
Previous visit-Income	12.458	3	0.006
Previous visit-Age	7.526	3	0.057
Alternative destinations-Nationality	41.497	7	0.000
Alternative destinations- Age	10.912	3	0.012
Alternative destinations-Income	5.173	3	0.160
Alternative destinations-Previous visit	14.378	1	0.000
Length of stay- Nationality	252.472	28	0.000
Length of stay- Age	24.185	12	0.019
Length of stay-Income	20.428	12	0.059
Length of stay- Previous visit	57.296	4	0.000
Expenses- Nationality	78.479	21	0.000
Expenses- Age	15.751	9	0.072
Expenses- Income	59.879	9	0.000
Expenses- Previous visit	26.485	3	0.000
Overall satisfaction-Age	17.473	12	0.133
Overall satisfaction-Income	24.458	12	0.018
Overall satisfaction-Previous visit	16.712	4	0.002
Overall satisfaction-Length of stay	33.228	16	0.009
Overall satisfaction-Expenses	19.218	12	0.083

As it can be observed, there is no strong relation between overall satisfaction and age or expenses. On the other hand, repeated tourists appear more satisfied, while a negative relation appears between overall satisfaction and income or length of stay. These results constitute a significant threat for the tourism services of the island.

Additional analyses, based on cross-tables, study the relation between nationality and reasons for choosing the island. The main reasons for Greeks and Italians refer to “service quality” and “entertainment-recreation”, while “climate-natural beauty”, “historical-archaeological monuments”, and “relaxation” do not seem to play an important role. On the other hand, Europeans seem to choose the island for its “climate-natural beauties”, “service quality”, and “historical-architectural monuments”, while “value for money” does not seem important. The reputation of the island seems to play an important role for groups originating from the outermost countries (North America, Australia, New Zealand, Asia, and Latin America). In general, it seems that there is no relation between age of income and reasons for choosing the island, although monuments and price/value appear important for the older and the younger tourists, respectively. Finally, repeated tourists give importance to service quality and entertainment, while first-time visitors give relatively greater emphasis on the historical-archaeological monuments and the fame of the island.

Regarding the sources of information, there is a clear grouping among Greek and foreign tourists: The Greek visitors prefer to collect information for the island either from past personal experience, or from other media (magazines, newspapers, TV), while they do not seem to prefer the Internet and the tourist offices (tour operators) as a source of information. Almost the opposite may be observed in the case of foreign tourists. In addition, younger tourists prefer the Internet of their friends/relatives, while older visitors prefer their personal experiences and the tourist offices in order to collect information for the island.

Table 3. Results of chi-square tests for loyalty measures

Variables	Chi-square	df	p-level
Revisit intention- Age	27.594	12	0.006
Revisit intention-Income	12.736	12	0.389
Revisit intention-Previous visit	39.220	4	0.000
Revisit intention-Length of stay	21.976	16	0.144
Revisit intention-Expenses	28.834	12	0.004
Revisit intention-Overall satisfaction	283.812	16	0.000
Recommendation - Age	30.407	12	0.002
Recommendation -Income	39.847	12	0.000
Recommendation -Previous visit	6.504	4	0.165
Recommendation -Length of stay	17.373	16	0.362
Recommendation -Expenses	27.042	12	0.008
Recommendation -Overall satisfaction	627.969	16	0.000
Confirmation of expectations-Age	23.809	12	0.022
Confirmation of expectations-Income	25.522	12	0.013
Confirmation of expectations-Previous visit	34.365	4	0.000
Confirmation of expectations-Length of stay	17.371	16	0.362
Confirmation of expectations-Expenses	19.139	12	0.085
Confirmation of expectations-Overall satisfaction	508.674	16	0.000

Table 3 presents the chi-square tests regarding several loyalty measures included in the questionnaire. As presented, the intention to repeat the visit is negatively related with age and previous visit and positively related with expenses.

Similarly, the intention to recommend the island to friends/relatives is strongly related with age, income, and expenses (Table 3). Contrarily, repeated visitors or tourists who stay longer do not appear more loyal according to this variable.

Table 3 shows that the confirmation of expectations is not related with the expenses or the length of stay, while repeated tourists in general think that their holidays were better or somehow better than expected.

In addition a weak relation may be observed between the confirmation of expectations and age or income.

Finally, it should be emphasized that overall satisfaction is strongly related to all three loyalty measures (revisit intention, recommendation, and confirmation of expectations), which is consistent with the relative literature (see for example Vavra, 1999 or Grigoroudis and Siskos, 2010).

Consequently, it seems that nationality is the major discriminant variable that assesses the distinguished tourist segments. This is confirmed by several other studies, which emphasize that tourist perceptions of a destination or hospitality businesses may vary according to countries of origin (see for example Kozak, 2001).

These results are justified by the different languages, food consumption, and other national cultural differences (including values, ideas, attitudes, or symbols), and they can be used in the decision-making process of destination management regarding destination positioning and market segmentation strategies.

CONCLUSION

This paper presents an application of the multicriteria method MUSA for the service quality evaluation in the tourism industry. The results are based on a tourist satisfaction survey that took place in an Aegean island and the main objective of the presented research is to evaluate tourists' satisfaction and identify the strong and the weak points of the tourism services offered.

Combining satisfaction importance and performance results and taking into account additional results (tourist profiling, potential tourist segments, etc.) it is possible to perform a SWOT analysis for the total tourism product offered. In this context, the SWOT analysis reveals the following:

- The strong points (competitive advantages) of the total tourism product are the fame and the natural environment (natural beauties, climate, local architecture) of the island. In addition, the visitors seem to be loyal (it is likely to visit the island again or suggest their friends/relatives to visit it), while their expenses during their vacations are relatively high.
- The short period of stay on the island is the most important weak point of the tourism product. Another weak point concerns the relatively low satisfaction that is observed in specific characteristics (e.g., urban environment, local transportations).
- On the other hand, the most important threats refer to the intense competition from other Greek islands, as well as the high level of expectations created by the fame of the island. Also, a potential threat is the lower satisfaction observed for the repeated visitors.
- The opportunities refer to the historical-archaeological monuments and the provided quality of services. These characteristics are not considered important by tourists, although they can be the competitive advantages of the island, due to their high performance.

The presented study may also reveal the advantages of MCDA approaches in tourist satisfaction evaluation problems. In particular, the results provided by the MUSA method are able to give a complete set of tourist/customer behavior information. These results may help destination management organizations to analyze the problem of tourist satisfaction evaluation and determine potential improvement actions. Moreover, it should be emphasized that the MUSA method fully respects the qualitative form of input information (i.e. tourists' judgments on the defined satisfaction criteria). This way, the ordinal variables are not arbitrary quantified (this quantification is rather an output of the method).

Consequently, the MUSA method provides an important alternative for studying service quality gaps and performing SWOT analysis. Following service quality literature, SWOT analysis in the MUSA method is performed using a series of action (performance–importance) diagrams, which are able to analyze tourist perceptions and determine the strong and weak points of a destination.

REFERENCES

Arabatzis, G. and E. Grigoroudis (2010). Visitors' satisfaction, perceptions and gap analysis: The case of Dadia–Lefkimi–Souflion National Park, *Forest Policy and Economics*, 12 (3), 163-172.

Bowen, D. and J. Clarke (2002). Reflections on tourist satisfaction research: Past, present and future, *Journal of Vacation Marketing*, 8 (4), 297-308.

De Ruyter, J.C., J.M.A. Bloemer, and P. Peters (1997). Merging service quality and service satisfaction: An empirical test of an integrative framework, *Journal of Economic Psychology*, 18 (4), 387-406.

Dutka, A. (1995). *AMA handbook of customer satisfaction: A complete guide to research, planning and implementation*, NTC Business Books, Illinois.

Grigoroudis, E. and Y. Siskos (2002). Preference disaggregation for measuring and analysingcustomer satisfaction: The MUSA method, *European Journal of Operational Research*, 143 (1), 148-170.

Grigoroudis, E. and Y. Siskos (2004). A survey of customer satisfaction barometers: Results from the transportation-communications sector, *European Journal of Operational Research*, 152 (2), 334-353.

Grigoroudis, E. and Y. Siskos (2010). *Customer satisfaction evaluation: Methods for measuring and implementing service quality*, Springer, New York.

Grigoroudis, E., Y. Politis, and Y. Siskos (2002). Satisfaction benchmarking and customer classification: An application to the branches of a banking organization, *International Transactions in Operational Research*, 9 (5), 599-618.

Grigoroudis, E., Y. Siskos, and O. Saurais(2000). TELOS: A customer satisfaction evaluation software, *Computers and Operations Research*, 27 (7-8), 799-817.

Hanim, N. M. Salleh, and R. Othman (2010). Importance-satisfaction analysis for Tioman Island Marine Park, MPRA paper, 22679, Munich University Library.

Hill, N. (1996). *Handbook of customer satisfaction measurement*, Gower Publishing, Hampshire.

Hsu, T.-K., Y.-F. Tsai, H.-H. Wu (2009). The preference analysis for tourist choice of destination: A case study of Taiwan, *Tourism Management*, 30 (2), 288-297.

Karakitsiou, A., A. Mavrommati, A. Migdalas, and K. Tsiakali, (2007). Customer satisfaction evaluation in the tourism industry: The case of Chania, *Foundations of Computing and Decision Sciences*, 32 (2), 111-124.

Kozak, M. (2001). Comparative assessment of tourist satisfaction with destinations across two nationalities, *Tourism Management*, 22 (4), 391-401.

Mihelis, G., E. Grigoroudis, Y. Siskos, Y. Politis, and Y. Malandrakis (2001). Customer satisfaction measurement in the private bank sector, *European Journal of Operational Research*, 130 (2), 347-360.

Naisbitt, J. (1995). *Global paradox*, Nicholas Brealey Publishing, London.

Naumann, E. and K. Giel (1995). *Customer satisfaction measurement and management*, Thomson Executive Press, Cincinnati.

Oh, H. (2001). Revisiting importance-performance analysis, *Tourism Management*, 22 (6), 617-627.

Parasuraman, A., V.A. Zeithaml, and L.L. Berry (1985).A conceptual model of service quality and its implications for future research, *Journal of Marketing*, 49 (4), 41-50.

Parasuraman, A., V.A. Zeithaml, and L.L. Berry (1988). SERVQUAL: A multiple item scale for measuring consumer perceptions of service quality, *Journal of Retailing*, 64 (1), 14-40.

Parasuraman, A., V.A. Zeithaml, and L.L. Berry (1991). Refinement and reassessment of the SERVQUAL scale, *Journal of Retailing*, 67 (4), 420-450.

Pawitra, T.A. and K.C. Tan (2003). Tourist satisfaction in Singapore: A perspective from Indonesian tourists, *Managing Service Quality*, 13 (5), 399-411.

Pizam, A., Y. Neumann, and A. Reichel (1978). Dimensions of tourist satisfaction with a destination area, *Annals of Tourism Research*, 5 (3), 314-322.

Politis, Y. and Y. Siskos (2004). Multicriteria methodology for the evaluation of a Greek engineering department, *European Journal of Operational Research*, 156 (1), 223 -240.

Rozman, C., M. Potočnik, K. Pažek, A. Borec, D. Majkovič, and M. Bohanec (2009).A multi-criteria assessment of tourist farm service quality, *Tourism Management*, 30 (5), 629-637.

Ryan, C. and G. Cessford (2003). Developing a visitor satisfaction monitoring methodology: Quality gaps, crowding and some results, *Current Issues in Tourism*, 6 (6), 457-507.

Siskos, Y., E. Grigoroudis, C. Zopounidis, and O. Saurais(1998). Measuring customer satisfaction using a collective preference disaggregation model, *Journal of Global Optimization*, 12 (2), 175-195.

Spreng, R.A. and R.D. McKoy (1996). An empirical examination of a model of perceived service quality and satisfaction, *Journal of Retailing*, 72 (2), 201-214.

Tonge, J. and S.A. Moore (2007). Importance-satisfaction analysis for marine park hinterlands: A western Australian case study, *Tourism Management*, 28 (1), 768-776.

Tribe, J. and T. Snaith (1998). From SERVQUAL to HOLSAT: Holiday satisfaction in Varadero, Cuba, *Tourism Management*, 19 (1), 25-34.

Truong, T.-H. and D. Foster (2006). Using HOLSAT to evaluate tourist satisfaction at destinations: The case of Australian holidaymakers in Vietnam, *Tourism Management*, 27 (5), 842-855.

Tsitsiloni, M. (2010). *Evaluating service quality and developing improvement plans in the tourism sector*, Diploma Thesis, Technical University of Crete, Chania.

Vavra, T.G. (1997). *Improving your measurement of customer satisfaction*, ASQC Quality Press, Milwaukee.

Wade, D.J. and P. Eagles (2003). The use of importance-performance analysis and market segmentation for tourism management in parks and protected areas: An application to Tasmania's National Parks, *Journal of Ecotourism*, 2 (3), 196-212.

Woodruff, R.B. and S.F.Gardial (1996). *Know your customer: New approaches to understanding customer value and satisfaction*, Blackwell Publishers, Oxford.

Yuksel, A. (2001). Managing customer satisfaction and retention: A case of tourist destinations, Turkey, *Journal of Vacation Marketing*, 7 (2), 153-168.

INDEX

D

G

H

I

J

L

S

T

U

V

W

Y